General Emory Upton
in the Civil War

General Emory Upton in the Civil War

The Formative Experiences of an American Military Visionary

ROBERT N. THOMPSON

McFarland & Company, Inc., Publishers
Jefferson, North Carolina

LIBRARY OF CONGRESS CATALOGUING-IN-PUBLICATION DATA

Names: Thompson, Robert N., 1953– author.
Title: General Emory Upton in the Civil War : the formative experiences of an American military visionary / Robert N. Thompson.
Description: Jefferson : McFarland & Company, Inc., Publishers, 2019 | Includes bibliographical references and index.
Identifiers: LCCN 2019025128 | ISBN 9781476678900 (paperback) ∞
Subjects: LCSH: Upton, Emory, 1839–1881. | United States. Army—Reorganization. | Generals—United States—Biography. | United States—History—Civil War, 1861–1865. | United States—Military policy.
Classification: LCC E467.1.U67 T47 2019 | DDC 355.0092 [B]—dc23
LC record available at https://lccn.loc.gov/2019025128

BRITISH LIBRARY CATALOGUING DATA ARE AVAILABLE

ISBN (print) 978-1-4766-7890-0
ISBN (ebook) 978-1-4766-3703-7

© 2019 Robert N. Thompson. All rights reserved

No part of this book may be reproduced or transmitted in any form or by any means, electronic or mechanical, including photocopying or recording, or by any information storage and retrieval system, without permission in writing from the publisher.

Front cover image: portrait of Major General Emory Upton, officer of the Federal Army (Library of Congress); *background* Battle of Spotsylvania Court House, L. Prang & Co., 1887 (Library of Congress)

Printed in the United States of America

*McFarland & Company, Inc., Publishers
Box 611, Jefferson, North Carolina 28640
www.mcfarlandpub.com*

For all the men and women
who have been part of the Long Gray Line
and those that will follow in their footsteps

So long as the Union has such soldiers as he to defend it, it will be perpetual.
General James Harrison Wilson

Table of Contents

PREFACE 1

1. Cadet Upton 5
2. Off to War 23
3. To the Artillery 34
4. Antietam 48
5. Upton's Regulars 60
6. Brigade Commander 83
7. Into the Wilderness 96
8. Hell Caldron 108
9. The Killing Ground 122
10. Winchester 132
11. To the Cavalry 142
12. The Final Battles 156
13. The Tragic Reformer 171

CHAPTER NOTES 179
BIBLIOGRAPHY 191
INDEX 195

Preface

While Emory Upton is probably not a familiar name to the casual Civil War history reader, some historians have argued that his influence on the modern U.S. Army equals that of Alfred Thayer Mahan on the U.S. Navy. While that may be something of an overstatement, there is no denying that the success of the U.S. Army in the 20th and 21st centuries is linked directly to Upton's late 19th-century proposals for army reform. Upton could see that a time was coming when the oceans would no longer protect the nation from a European adversary. Having observed the capabilities and organization of Europe's armies, he predicted disaster would befall the nation if the army continued to organize and operate based on a model designed in the early years of the nation's existence.

Upton had seen and experienced the horrors, disasters, and unnecessary loss of life that model produced during the Civil War, and what he saw filled him with outrage and anger. The Civil War was the seminal event in Emory Upton's life, and the ordeals and trials he lived through shaped his post-war campaign to not only revise the U.S. Army's tactics but also the culture and organization that were the army's foundation. He came to believe that the nation could no longer rely on a small Regular Army where inept officers were allowed to hold high positions based solely on seniority until they died or chose to retire, where state governments controlled the mobilization of untrained volunteer forces and filled them with officers unqualified to lead, where there was no professional post-graduate military education, and where the tactics used in battle reflected outdated weapons technology.

During the Civil War, Upton led units in every branch of the service—artillery, infantry, and cavalry—and witnessed the unnecessary slaughter of thousands upon thousands of American soldiers. He would not and could not ever forget what he saw at Spotsylvania, Cold Harbor, and many other battlefields. As a morally serious man of faith and a dedicated, consummate professional, he saw military reform as his duty, and as a debt owed to those who had served under his command during the war.

Given the importance of Upton's wartime experience, it is somewhat surprising that none of the books written about him have provided an in-depth examination of his Civil War service. To date, there have been three major works written about Emory Upton. The first was Peter Michie's *The Life and Letters of Emory Upton*, written in 1885, some four years after Upton's tragic and untimely death. While Michie spent three chapters and more than 130 pages discussing Upton's Civil War service, his flowery prose and romantic 19th-century approach tend to dilute the horrors Upton saw and mute the intense anger he felt toward the army's leadership.

The other two major works that have been written on Upton are Stephen Ambrose's

Upton and the Army and David Fitzpatrick's *Emory Upton: Misunderstood Reformer,* published in 1964 and 2017, respectively. Both books are excellent studies that focus primarily on the politics and controversies surrounding Upton's post-war reform campaign. As a result, however, while they both discuss Upton's service during the Civil War, they do not delve into his experiences in any real detail. This has created a vacuum in Upton's historiography that needed to be filled, as those events drove his passionate, almost single-minded effort to change the army for the better, hopefully saving lives and ensuring the nation's survival in the process.

This book seeks to remedy this oversight by focusing primarily on Emory Upton's service in the Civil War. In doing so, I chose to summarize his post-war life and efforts to reform the army while providing a more thorough examination of the ordeal he lived through during the war. My hope is that this book will provide both detail and substance for those seeking to understand the passion with which Upton pursued his reforms.

Moreover, I hope to provide a history of one man's unique experience during this national catastrophe. Upton was, after all, the only officer to serve in a significant command capacity in all three of the army's combat branches. Graduating from West Point only a few short weeks after the firing on Fort Sumter, he rose from the rank of Second Lieutenant in the Regular Army to become a Major General of Volunteers. While there were certainly other young officers who experienced a similar mercurial rise during the war, none of them could claim a record equal to Upton, who commanded at the battery, regiment, brigade, and division levels. Furthermore, he did so with unparalleled success, professionalism, and personal valor.

The latter is something that stands out about Upton's wartime experiences. He was an officer who always led from the front with his men during a fight, sharing the danger and demonstrating the brand of physical courage required of good officers during the Civil War. Moreover, he led in battle with uncommon skill, always cool under fire. Not surprisingly, his men truly believed in him, and their confidence in him is reflected in numerous wartime journals and letters, as well as memoirs written after the war. In many ways, Emory Upton was the sort of leader every military officer should aspire to be. He was a tough disciplinarian but not a martinet. He took care of his men, always seeing to their health and well-being and even fighting the army bureaucracy to ensure his soldiers had the material and organizational support they needed to fight, survive, and win.

One of the most remarkable experiences I had during my research was the opportunity to read hundreds of letters Emory Upton wrote to his family, friends, and colleagues. These have been preserved in a variety of collections and documented in Michie's book. Reading someone's personal correspondence can offer the chance to achieve a better understanding of who they really were, and that is certainly the case with Upton. His depth of feeling about the army and the war, as well as his unflinching dedication to his country and his God, are clearly reflected in his letters, providing an unequaled insight into his character. As a result, other historians and I owe a debt of gratitude to those in his family and the staff at the Holland Land Office Museum in Batavia, New York, who preserved his letters for posterity.

In developing my book, I felt that illustrations would help provide clarity and insight into Upton and this period in America's history. After all, this was the first American war to be both photographed and covered in detail by journalists. The result was thousands of photos and sketches of generals, soldiers, and scenes from the battlefield. These have been preserved and made available in digital form to historians like me by organizations such as the National

Archives and Records Administration, Library of Congress, and New York Public Library. Therefore, I also owe them my grateful thanks.

Finally, I would note that, in several places in the narrative, I have tried to provide additional explanation and amplification regarding Civil War army organization, weapons, and tactics. I did this deliberately to help those readers who are not familiar with this era or who are not typical readers of Civil War histories. I hope my efforts were successful and that they enhanced the reader's experience.

1

Cadet Upton

> I am passionately attached to West Point and would not give up my appointment here for a million dollars.
> —Emory Upton, February 25, 1857[1]

On June 3, 1856, Emory Upton arrived at West Point. Like many other aspiring cadets, he made the last leg of his journey on a Hudson River Railroad train. As the train groaned to a stop at the Cold Spring Station on the eastern banks of the Hudson River, he stood up from the hard seat he had endured since boarding in Rensselaer the night before and made his way to the rear of the car. It was a beautiful morning, warm, clear, and bright as the train had puffed its way along the river. The scenery along the way was lovely, almost breathtaking. Had he not been so deep in thought and so consumed by anticipation, Upton would have found it a most pleasant ride. But any young man as earnest, as focused, and as determined as Emory Upton would not have taken any notice of the natural beauty around him. He felt he was on the first leg of what he hoped would be a remarkable journey and one that was his destiny. Beauty would have to wait.

He stepped down from the passenger car onto the platform of the Cold Springs Station. At his side was one lone trunk containing everything he thought he might need for this next big step in his life. On the morning Upton arrived at the station, he was only 16 years old and would not turn 17 for another 12 weeks. At five feet, eleven inches tall, he was a solid, wiry young man. His sandy blond hair seemed to stand almost on end, and a broad wave of freckles covered his face. One friend described him as being always in a hurry, someone who "spoke like lightning" with a gift for quick perception. The latter often caused him to "cut a person off in the middle of a remark with his own reply, which was always to the point." His facial expression seemed to carry a look that betrayed a single-minded focus and a constant determination to overcome any obstacle laid before him.[2]

Today, the biggest obstacle of his young life lay across the Hudson River from the railroad station where he now stood. Like many others before him, he carried his trunk down to the river's edge, seeking a way to get across the Hudson. There was no ferryboat in those days, and only a single whaleboat awaited new cadets at the shore. The oarsman called out to him, knowing from long experience where a young man who is carrying a trunk on a warm June day needed to go. New cadets would hand the oarsman their trunk, climb in the boat, and begin their trip across the water. Some cadets recalled the smooth water as they pulled away from the shore, with the only sound made by the regular dip of the oars in the water and their clatter in the rowlocks. In just a few minutes, the boat would pass the head of Constitution Island. Through the groves of cedar on the far shore, you could now see the rocky slopes and the immense gray stone buildings atop the cliffs. For Upton, these buildings marked his objective, one he had sought since he first read stories of Napoleon and dreamed of becoming a soldier: The United States Military Academy at West Point.

Boyhood

Emory Upton was born on August 29, 1839, on his family's farm in Genesee County, New York, just a few miles southeast of the town of Batavia. He was the ninth child born to Electa and Daniel Upton, whose brood would eventually grow to total 13 children. The Upton family had come to America from Scotland in 1650, originally settling in Salem, Massachusetts. Emory Upton's father, Daniel, came to Batavia around 1820, purchased his farmland, cleared it, and built a cabin. Not long after arriving, he met 16-year-old Electa Randall, and they married on September 30, 1821.[3]

By the time Upton was born, his parents had expanded their farm to just over 276 acres and replaced the log cabin with a fine two-story wood frame house. The large house stood just off the road that ran north-south only about a half-mile from the New York Central Railroad line that connected Buffalo to Syracuse. A lovely row of tall poplar trees lined the country lane in front of the house, and the barn and a few small sheds were opposite the house on the far side of the lane. The rich farmland beyond the barn included two small streams that flowed north into Tonawanda Creek.

Like most children of his time, Upton's childhood included hard work on the farm, which commenced almost as soon as he could walk and became more arduous and demanding as he approached his teens. His parents believed in combining the classic Protestant work ethic with rigorous discipline for their children. At times, Daniel and Electa were, perhaps, too stern in the latter. Seeming to believe the world young Upton would grow into as a man had no

Emory Upton's parents, Daniel and Electa Upton (New York Public Library).

place for idle foolishness, his father inflicted punishments for what was often merely the normal frolicking of a child. Later in life, Upton forgave his father for "the many times he took advantage of my weakness to chastise me for acts which to a juvenile mind appeared perfectly proper."[4]

Daniel and Electa Upton were also strong believers in the value of education, and all their children attended the local public school in Batavia. Also, as each of the older children matriculated from their elementary education, they became responsible for supplementing the education of their younger brothers and sisters. John and James, the oldest boys in the family, were sent off to study at Oberlin College in Ohio in 1851 and both graduated in 1853.[5]

Perhaps the most influential element in Upton's upbringing was religious faith. His parents were prominent members of the local Methodist church and were almost zealous in their religious practices. They instilled a strong sense of love and respect for God in young Upton. But more than that, they taught him that, no matter what he chose to do with his life, he must strive to make the world a better place, to serve his fellow man, and do whatever his duty as a Christian called him to perform. Not surprisingly, Daniel and Electa were also ardent reformers who embraced the religious-based reform movements that swept upstate New York in the first half of the 19th century.[6]

The area around Batavia was on the outer fringes of what people referred to as the "Burned-over District," a name derived from the many evangelical revivals, Pentecostal beliefs, and reform movements prominent in the region. During Upton's formative years, these included Dorothea L. Dix, who advocated a more benevolent brand of treatment for the insane and William Miller, who convinced thousands that Christ would return on October 22, 1843. There were also Mother Ann Lee and Jemima Wilkinson, founders of the celibacy-based "Uni-

The Upton farm near Batavia, New York (New York Public Library).

versal Friend" communities, and Elizabeth C. Stanton and Lucretia Mott, who launched a female suffrage movement. But the most influential movement in the Burned-over District was abolitionism.[7]

By the time Upton entered his teens, his oldest brothers were prominent members of the Republican Party where they lived. James, in fact, was a militant Free-Soiler in Kansas, which meant that he campaigned against Kansas entering the Union as a slave state. Upton's parents also were strong abolitionists, and this influenced their choice of education for their sons. When Upton turned 15, his father obtained scholarships for he and his older brother, Henry, to follow in John and James footsteps by attending Oberlin College.[8]

The Oberlin College Years

Oberlin College had its origins in the early 1830s as a Utopian community dedicated to creating an institution of higher learning for Christians. Under the leadership of its president, Charles Grandison Finney, the school became a center for the education of reformers, evangelists, and abolitionists. By the time Upton arrived there, the college was both coeducational and integrated, with 5 percent of the student population being African American. Daniel Upton also appreciated the school's strict discipline and its manual labor system, which provided the students a means to pay for most of their expenses by working for local businesses, factories, and farms. Furthermore, Oberlin emphasized religion and required students to attend both church and numerous revivals.[9] However, as to the latter, Upton expressed some doubt about the usefulness of long prayer meetings, after which participants claimed to be converted. "[Y]oung and inconsiderate persons often catch the enthusiasm of an excited minister," he wrote to his sister Maria, "and believe they have found religion; but as soon as the meetings cease, their enthusiasm subsides, from the want of a thorough conviction, and they revert to their primitive state."[10]

From the moment Upton set foot on the Oberlin campus in the fall of 1854, his only goal was to establish an educational foundation that would serve him as a cadet at West Point. A year before Emory Upton's arrival at Oberlin, James had lent his younger brother a book on the life of Napoleon. The younger Upton devoured the text and, after finishing it, decided he would become a soldier. A short time later, the local member of the House of Representatives, Judge Benjamin Pringle, made a call at the Upton home to speak to Daniel Upton. Fourteen-year-old Emory seized the opportunity to tell Judge Pringle that he desired an appointment to West Point. The congressman was impressed by his eagerness but counseled him to wait to apply until he gained a stronger academic background.[11]

With a West Point position as his guiding star, Upton diligently focused on gaining what he saw as a practical education even though Oberlin's focus was on the liberal arts. Courses in literature and poetry held no fascination for him. At one point, a friend induced him to join a literary society, which Upton immediately quit, saying the group was nothing more than an "infidel affair."[12]

This same friend remembered Upton could write well but that he fell short in his oratory skills. Upton consoled himself on this deficiency saying that "a soldier did not need to be an orator, for that, if he ever had to speak, it would be to his men in the face of the enemy, and on such occasions an oration must be necessarily short, and he thought he would be able for that."[13] Upton also had no use for the sort of ornamental prose popular during the mid–19th century. He kept his writing concise and to the point and often rewrote anything he saw as being too flowery. He would review his compositions carefully and, if he saw too many adjectives and high-sounding words, he would stop, quietly mutter, "That sentence sounds poetical," and alter it to something more Spartan and straightforward.[14]

His intense desire to obtain an appointment from Congressman Pringle also drove his personal habits during his time at Oberlin. For instance, he would never sleep with a pillow and made sure his bed was perfectly level. He believed this practice would prevent him from getting "round shoulders." Further, since the Academy required that entering cadets have good teeth, Upton would never crack a nut with his teeth or place anything in his mouth that might injure them. He also worked hard both in and outside the classroom. He and his brother, Henry, both had after-school jobs at a local sash factory. Here, the two boys monitored the drying kiln, filling and emptying the poplar lumber used by the factory, all for eight cents a day.[15]

His behavior was also always of the highest order. He never participated in any of the typical student hijinks. Sunday provided the only time free for recreation, so Upton and his friends typically spent that time in the forest near the campus. But even here, he combined studies with pleasure, using the time to read his essays aloud or practice for the coming week's rhetorical exercises. One friend also recalled that Upton never used profanity. For him, "confound it" or "by Jiminy" was as colorful a language as his sensibilities would allow. He was also deeply respectful of women. "I never knew him to speak with the least levity of a woman," one fellow student at Oberlin recalled, "nor take any pleasure in jests or stories that inclined to anything disrespectful" of women.[16]

Upton's years at Oberlin were tumultuous ones in the nation, as arguments over the free status of Kansas broke out into open fighting between Northern and Southern sympathizers. While Upton harbored strong personal beliefs on the issue of slavery, he refused to take part in political demonstrations or engage in debates over the issue among his fellow students. In his mind, a soldier kept to himself on such matters. Moreover, he thought he could better spend his time at school doggedly pursuing his studies. "I am sick of such stuff," he said, referring to his fellow students who engaged vigorously in political activities. "Let those fellows learn their lessons now while at school," he added, "and by-and-by, if they have any brains, they may be able to do some good."[17]

But Upton was not a completely serious or humorless young man. At Christmas during his second year at Oberlin, he and Henry decided to go home to Batavia for the holidays. They found both work and passage on a steamer sailing from Cleveland to Buffalo. From there, they hitched a ride on a wagon heading east for Batavia. Before leaving, the two young men pooled their savings to buy a small supply of crackers and cheese. At a point where the wagon stopped briefly, they ate their somewhat austere meal. Emory, who sat on the wagon tongue idly swinging his long legs as he ate, turned to his brother, and said, "Say, Hen, if we ever become big men we will remember this as something funny."[18]

In early 1856, with three semesters of work to his credit at Oberlin, Upton wrote to Judge Pringle requesting consideration for an appointment to West Point. On March 12, 1856, the congressman replied by forwarding Upton's appointment from the Secretary of War to the United States Military Academy's Class of 1861. In his cover letter, Judge Pringle wrote, "I selected you for the place because, from representations made by your friends concerning you, and from my slight acquaintance with you, I believed that you possessed sufficient talent and ability, honesty and integrity, industry, energy, and perseverance to enable you to pass the ordeal at West Point creditably. Should you fail, it will be mortifying to me and to your other friends, but I trust there will be no failure."[19] Emory Upton would not disappoint him.

The New Cadet

As Upton made landfall on the western shore at the foot of the heights below the Academy, an omnibus[20] pulled up, and the driver climbed down, grabbed his trunk from the boat, and unceremoniously loaded it onto the wagon.[21] As the omnibus made its way up the steep winding road, Upton got his first close-up view of the Academy, a sight that many new cadets found intimidating. One young man later commented on his trip up the heights to West Point, noting "the freshness and fragrance of the well-kept slopes and shrubbery ... the enormous mortars and huge columbiads [large smoothbore cannon] with pyramids of balls and shells, such as I had seen in pictures. The moral effect of these symbols of war was a mixture of curiosity and dreadful appreciation."[22]

Once at the top of the hill, Upton could see the broad, smooth lawn of the parade grounds and the stately buildings beyond them. The latter included the massive gray stone barracks, complete with towers and sally port,[23] the academic building, the immense chapel, and the library, which had a tall pole flying the American flag atop its dome. If the view during the trip up the hill had been intimidating, seeing the Academy buildings was enough to shake the confidence of even the most self-assured new cadet.

The omnibus finally came to a stop opposite the path to the library, which was the location of the Superintendent's office. Here, the driver unloaded Upton's trunk, set it on the path, and told him he should report in at the office. As the omnibus moved off to await the next appointee's arrival, Upton carried his trunk down the quarter-mile walkway to the library. As he approached the entrance, he likely saw a young soldier walking back and forth under the shade of a nearby tree. The soldier wore a bright scarlet coat, tall hat with pompom and bright brass ornaments, white cross belts, a waist belt, and a sword. His attire was so soldierly and so impressive, Upton may have thought him to be the Superintendent, as did more than one new cadet. The soldier quickly moved to the entrance doorway, opened it, and politely motioned him to enter.[24]

After he was ushered inside, Upton found himself facing a small table where an officer in a blue frock coat with a single row of gilt metal buttons and straps on the shoulders was waiting. The officer identified himself as the Adjutant Lieutenant and asked if Upton was a new cadet. After telling him that he was, indeed, a new appointee, Upton stated his name. The officer then checked a list in front of him and, finding Upton's name; he asked a few questions related to his home location, the name of his appointing member of Congress, and his date of birth. As Upton provided the answers, the officer quickly marked off items on the list and then shouted, "Orderly!" At this, the red-coated soldier returned, and the officer directed him to escort Upton to the nearest cadet barracks.[25]

The orderly then guided Upton down a path to one of the massive cadet barrack buildings and took him inside. There, the soldier turned him over to an upperclassman who acted as Cadet Lieutenant. The older cadet was wearing his gray uniform and looked to Upton as every bit a soldier as the orderly. The cadet asked Upton to register his name in a log, after which he escorted Upton upstairs, down a long hallway, and into a room. Once Upton was inside, the cadet officer closed the door behind him, and Upton found himself in a room that seemed the living embodiment of the word Spartan.

Cadet quarters were functional and nothing more. The room, which was about 14 feet by 22 feet, had one large window, a fireplace with an iron mantel, and two alcoves at the inner end separated by a partition that had hooks on either side for hanging up clothing. While the room was spotless, there was not a single piece of furniture, which gave the space a cold, forbidding feel. Eventually, there would be metal bed frames and mattresses, but the staff removed these in the summer for renovation. Besides, new appointees such as Upton and his classmates would soon be living outside in tents on the grounds for their first summer encampment. Therefore, even though they would spend their first few nights in the barracks, the Academy saw no need for them to have beds in their quarters until the encampment was over.[26]

Before long, other new appointees joined Upton in the room, a collection of young men varying in both ages, social class, and geographic origin. They introduced themselves to one another, chatted, and discussed what might be coming next. Almost immediately, Upton's classmates noticed his quiet and unassuming behavior. A few made the mistake of believing that his natural reticence was a sign of an underlying lack of courage and conviction. Several of these would later painfully learn they had underestimated his character.[27]

The other thing that quickly became apparent was the de facto segregation between cadets from the North and those from the South. Almost immediately, the cadets from the South banded together and formed a "junta," as one cadet later described it.[28] This process was the product of several factors. First, the young men of the South were primarily from the region's upper class, and many were familiar with one another via family connections. Further, as members of what they saw as an aristocracy, the Southerners looked down on the Northerners, many of whom, like Emory Upton, were merely the sons of farmers and shopkeepers. Of course, the increasing sectional tensions also contributed to their desire to remain aloof from their Northern comrades. But as time went on, these groups became steadily more hostile to one another, and even the alignment in the cadet barracks reflected this. The Northern cadets eventually came to live in the east wing, while the Southerners occupied the west and south wings, separated by the sally port in the middle.[29]

After about an hour, the arrival of a Cadet Corporal cut the young cadet candidates' conversation short. He burst into the room shouting, "Attention!" To Upton and the others, this young man exhibited the most extreme military attitude and behavior. He shouted at them to stand and then forcibly demonstrated on one cadet what the position of "Attention" required. Another new cadet candidate later wrote that he found this initial step in the process of learning how to behave, how to stand, and how to walk as "confusing humiliation."[30]

The Cadet Corporal hurried the group downstairs and into the courtyard constantly shouting one angry epithet after another in what the Academy referred to as being "turned out." Upton and his comrades now marched down to the military storekeeper, Tim O'Makers, to collect their initial supply of clothing and equipment, what cadets referred to as their "kit." But marched might be too polite a term. New cadet candidates always tried to march the half-mile to the store but ended up stumbling over one another in the process as they vainly attempted to walk in lockstep. All in all, it was what one cadet later recalled as a "most amusing spectacle," and one that presented itself every summer at West Point. "A column of gawky boys of all sizes, from five to six feet tall," he wrote, "clad in all sorts of particolored raiment; our eyes fixed, yes, glued, on the coat collar of the boy in front of us, a grim dismalness hanging in every face; all of us trying mechanically to point our toes and to comply with the fierce orders."[31]

Once they reached the store, the cadet candidates lined up in the order of their arrival at the Superintendent's Office and marched into the library building to receive their kit, which consisted of two heavy gray blankets, a bucket, broom, washbasin, pillow, a ladle made from a coconut shell, candlestick, one pound of candles, a box of matches, a cake of soap, and a small mirror. Loaded down with their first collection of government property, the Cadet Corporal then marched them back to the barracks. Like many others before them, Upton's group looked like "a band of immigrants leaving Castle Garden" as they moved along, with the Cadet Corporal telling them in a very loud voice how their slovenly, unmilitary appearance was a disgrace to the dignity of West Point.[32]

Not long after Upton had stacked his kit in the room, the Cadet Corporal turned them out for a march to the dining hall and their first meal at West Point. As they ate, the upperclassmen ignored them, refusing to take notice of these lowly new arrivals. So, they ate their meal in relative comfort, sharing conversation, and getting better acquainted. Of course, this would be their last relaxed meal for some months to come. Once accepted as "conditional cadets," they would eat every meal seated at attention, eyes straight forward while upperclassmen barraged them with questions, many of them designed to elicit required but silly, nonsensical responses.

After dinner, Upton and the other new arrivals enjoyed an hour or so of free time until a bugle called "to quarters," at which he and his comrades had to rush back to their room. After a while, they heard the call for "tattoo" and hustled downstairs where the Cadet Corporal once more placed them into ranks. He quickly took the roll and gave them 15 minutes to return to their room, spread their blankets on the floor, and prepare for "Taps" when the cadets extinguished all lights for the night.[33]

Early the next morning, reveille awakened Upton and his comrades. Reveille, in this case, involved a dozen drums and fifes played by members of the cadet band. The Cadet Corporal burst through the door, rousted them, and sent them on a wild run down into the broad courtyard at the rear of the barracks. There, the new cadet candidates saw the band, which continued to play, marching at the quick step back and forth across the quadrangle as Orderly Sergeants and other cadet officers from the four upper-class companies took positions in front of the barracks building. Soon, other uniformed upper-class cadets began to appear, taking their positions in a series of perfectly straight lines. Precisely ten minutes after the reveille had begun, the band came to a halt, and the last drumbeat sounded, as the cadets stood "motionless as a gray wall."[34] Cadet Sergeants took the rolls, crisply saluted their cadet officers, and reported that all cadets were present. The officers dismissed the formation, and the day's work commenced.

For the new arrivals, their first full day at West Point consisted of periods of drill and academic recitations conducted by the upper-class cadets. The recitations were all in preparation for their first step in formal admission, the preliminary examination conducted by the Academic Board. The recitations continued until June 20, 1856, when all new cadet candidates were required to have reported for duty. On that day, Upton and his fellow appointees marched to the Academic Building to take the examination. Once inside, they took their seats on benches in the hallway outside the examination room. Shortly after that, an orderly appeared from the room and called out one of their names. One by one, each young man marched inside to take his turn.

When the orderly shouted out their name, the cadet candidate whose name had been called rose and marched into the room in as military a manner as he could manage. He walked around a line of large blackboards mounted on easels and stood in the center of the room facing 25 members of the Academy's academic staff. The staff all sat at small desks arranged in a crescent shape at the head of the room opposite the blackboards, which were behind them. Twenty-five pairs of eyes bore down on the nervous cadet as he appraised the men across from him, as well. Among the staff were men Upton would come to know well over the next five years: Doctor Albert Church, Professor of Mathematics; Doctor Dennis Mahan, Professor of Military and Civil Engineering; Doctor William Bartlett, Professor of Natural and Experimental Philosophy; the Reverend John French, Chaplain, and Professor of Ethics and English Studies; Doctor Henry Kendrick, Professor of Chemistry, Mineralogy, and Geology; Doctor Hyacinth Agnel, Professor of the French and Spanish Languages; and Robert Weir, Professor of Drawing.[35] In the center of the crescent was the chairman of the Academic Board, Major Richard Delafield, U.S. Army Corps of Engineers, who was also the Superintendent and Commandant of West Point. He was heavyset with sandy eyebrows, grayish sandy hair, and a pronounced nose. He wore glasses and "had the air of an officer and a man of cultivation, invested, furthermore, with the honor of a wide and well-earned distinction."[36]

To Delafield's immediate left sat a most formidable looking officer, resplendent in his full-dress uniform and epaulets. This man was Lieutenant Colonel William J. Hardee, 2nd U.S. Cavalry, the Commandant of Cadets. Colonel Hardee was tall with large, gray eyes, a low forehead, heavy, grizzled mustache and "imperial, and soldierly in bearing."[37] His eyes seemed to look right through the new cadets, and one wrote he was "mortally afraid" of Hardee.[38] Hardee was a close friend and associate of the Secretary of War, Jefferson Davis, which allowed him to exercise a great influence on the army. At Secretary Davis' direction, Hardee had recently published the first new tactics manual in almost 30 years, *Hardee's Rifle and Light Infantry Tactics, for the Instruction, Exercise, and Maneuvers of Riflemen and Light Infantry Including School of the Soldier and School of the Company*.

The first of the members to speak asked the cadet candidate to pick up a book from the table in front of him and read it aloud. Then they asked him to write from dictation on one of the blackboards, followed by a series of basic mathematics problems. The board designed all these to test to a common level of education standards. While the examination was thorough, it was relatively easy, especially for Upton who had two years of college to his credit.

Once the academic exam was complete, one of the orderlies ushered the cadet candidate down the hallway to another room where the Academy's two surgeons, Doctor Samuel Moore and Doctor John Campbell, waited. They proceeded to poke, prod and tap every major organ and joint, as well as peer into every orifice, much as military physicians do for every enlistee to this day.[39]

That evening, the new appointees gathered together as the Adjutant read the list of those who had passed the examination. Upton's name was among them, and he was now a "conditional cadet" of the Fifth Class or, as they are still known to this day, a plebe. His class totaled 59 cadets, all of whom now moved on to the next challenge, the summer encampment.[40]

Every summer at West Point, the cadet barracks emptied, and the Corps of Cadets moved to a tent city on the plain near old Fort Clinton. Here, the cadets erected their tents in predefined rows for each respective class company. There were even street names for the paths that crisscrossed through the tents such as McCook, Williams, Hartsuff, and Saxton. Along with the cadets, Colonel Hardee and several junior members of the Academy military staff joined the cadets in the encampment, with the latter serving as tactical instructors. At the time Upton and his fellow plebes arrived at their first encampment, the junior staff members included First Lieutenant John Gibbon, who would go on to be one of the North's best field commanders in the Army of the Potomac, and First Lieutenant John Pegram, who commanded artillery in the Confederate Army of Northern Virginia until his death at the Battle of Five Forks only a few days before the war ended.[41]

For the plebes, each day of the encampment consisted of seemingly endless hours of drill and parade. In the encampment, reveille awoke Upton at 5:00 a.m., when he and his fellow plebes policed the grounds until 5:30 a.m. Morning drill followed until 6:30 a.m., before preparation for inspection, with breakfast at 7:00 a.m. Morning parade began promptly at 8:00 a.m., followed by artillery drill at 9:00 a.m. Plebes then policed the encampment grounds again before lunch. Since the army expected military officers to have a grounding in the social graces, Upton attended dancing class from 3:00 p.m. to 4:00 p.m., before once more policing the grounds. Infantry drill then commenced at 5:30 p.m., with evening parade and inspection at 7:00 p.m., supper at 8:00 p.m., and bed with lights out at 9:30 p.m.[42]

In the evening, there was time for relaxation, but even then, upper-class cadets were con-

West Point cadets during summer encampment, 1860s (New York Public Library).

stantly on hand to haze the plebes and make their lives miserable. One plebe remembered lighting a small candle in his tent so he could write a letter. This act apparently offended one senior cadet who proceeded to thrust back the tent flap with a broom handle, dowsing the candle and spilling the plebe's ink all over his letter and the floor of the tent. As it was not yet time for lights out, the plebe relit the candle to assess the damage. But, no sooner than he got the candle lit, the broomstick flew back through the tent flap, putting out the candle once more. At this, the plebe decided the best thing to do was to just sit quietly in the darkness.[43]

Plebes also got their first taste of military duties during the encampment, such as assignment to perform night guard tours. The upper-class cadet sergeants and officers issued them their instructions with an awful seriousness, including the dreadful consequences should they fall asleep while on duty or violate procedures in any way.

General Morris Schaff, who was two years behind Emory Upton at West Point, vividly remembered his first tour as a sentinel during a "very murky, black night." The Cadet Sergeant issued Schaaf's orders in hushed tones and whispered the countersign he should use if someone unknown approached. The latter proved to cause young Schaaf some problems.[44] The Cadet Sergeant told him quickly and in a very low voice that the countersign was "Quatre Bras," the name of the battle between Lord Wellington and Napoleon two days before Waterloo. At that time, Schaaf spoke no French, and he had never heard of the battle. So, he asked the sergeant to please spell the phrase out. The sergeant quickly rattled it off and walked away as Schaaf struggled to process the spelling he had heard. "In my ear," he later recalled, "it did not at all spell the words he had pronounced."[45]

Schaaf then faithfully walked back and forth, still wondering what the word for the countersign might be. After a few hours, the evening's sergeant of the guard, Cadet John Wilson, appeared. Wilson was known for having an air that was "fiercely military" whether he was on or off duty. Schaaf demanded the countersign, which Wilson provided in perfect French. Still unsure of what the countersign was supposed to be, Schaaf did as ordered, lowering his rifle to the "charge bayonet" position and fiercely challenging Wilson. He demanded that the upperclassman spell the word. "He took that as almost an affront," Schaaf remembered, "and I am surprised that it did not bring on a fatal attack of military vertigo." Instead, Wilson angrily complied with the request before approaching to ask for Schaaf's orders "with overpowering importance, as if it depended on him and me whether the earth was to continue in its orbit that night."[46]

Despite the long days of arduous hours of drill and nights spent marching guard tours, most plebes seem to look back on their first encampment as an almost idyllic time. Their recollections focused on the beauty of the sunset gun and lowering the flag, swimming in the river, and the "soft illumination of the tent-lighted camp from which breathed forth the music of the violin and guitar, banjo, and flute."[47] But the best description of these memories of the first cadet encampment comes from Morris Schaaf:

> Every cadet will remember the night boat from New York; it passed about half-past nine, and with its numerous lights gleaming far down below was a gay and very pretty sight. He will remember also the large tows, with little, feeble, twinkling lights on the low canal boats; the dull splash of leaping sturgeon when all was still in the dead of night; and the propellers chugging on their way to New York, carrying livestock, from which from time to time would come a long, deep low, or a calf's bleating anguish; and the frail quivering voice of the screech owl that was said to nest in the ruins of old Fort Putnam.
>
> To every feature in the solemn progress of the night and the brightness of the coming day, the sentinel walking his post is a witness: the moonlight lying wan on the steps of the chapel; the clock in the tower strik-

ing the deep hours; the flushing of the dawn; the fog that has lain on the river lifting and moving off; and finally the note of the reveille at the soldiers' barracks, and the appearance of the soldiers at the morning gun, the corporal standing with the colors in his hand till the sun clears the east, when the gun fires, and the colors ascend lovingly to the head of the mast.[48]

Cadet Life

As camp ended in late August, Upton and his plebe company marched into the cadet barracks to begin their first academic year. The staff first broke the plebes into sections of about a dozen cadets each based on alphabetical order. After the first month, the staff reassigned them based on class standing, which the instructors calculated using a combination of academic performance and accumulated demerits for disciplinary infractions. The latter included demerits assigned for everything from tardiness or improper uniform wear to sitting on the window sill in their room. This process continued at the end of every month and plebes shuffled up and down the rankings. But by January, the transfers between sections significantly lessened as cadets seem to find their place, for better or worse.[49]

When Upton arrived at West Point, the Academy employed a five-year course of instruction for cadets, rather than the four-year program used previously. This program began in 1854 after a 24-year period during which the annual boards of visitors that oversaw West Point's curriculum complained about a perceived weakness in military training and an overemphasis on mathematics, science, and engineering. The boards felt this emphasis detracted from a study of the humanities. The new five-year program of instruction specified that none of the additional classroom time would be allocated to courses such as natural and experimental philosophy, mathematics, French, drawing, chemistry, mineralogy, and geology, or civil engineering. Rather, the additional academic hours were allocated to new courses in Spanish, history, geography, and military law plus augmentations to the current courses in English and professional military subjects.[50]

After reveille, Upton studied from 6:00 a.m. to 7:00 a.m. before attending classes. As a fifth-year cadet, his daily schedule of study started with Mathematics from 8:00 a.m. to 11:00 a.m. taught by Professor Church and Lieutenants Slemmer, Perry, and Blunt. The staff instructed mathematics every day except Sunday using Charles Davies' Descriptive Geometry plus his translation from French of Bourdon's Algebra and Legendre's Geometry. Lieutenant Slemmer, a slender officer who was "solemn, hollow-eyed" and wore glasses, led the daily recitations. His manner was always mild, almost meditative. He stood before Upton's class watching them recite "as if he were studying and trying to interpret an omen."[51]

Professor Church, meanwhile, was another matter entirely. Church graduated first in his class at West Point in 1828, later returning as a civilian to be an assistant professor and then the head of the mathematics department.[52] Those who knew Church described him as being a short, stocky man with brown eyes, a broad face, and "complaining voice." Church was almost bald and walked about with his head bowed, and his hands clasped firmly behind him under the tails of his dark blue dress coat. He intimidated the plebes, one of who said, "there never was a colder eye or manner than Professor Church's," describing him as an "old mathematical cinder, bereft of all natural feeling."[53]

English Studies and Literature followed mathematics from Monday through Friday beginning at noon and lasting until 4:00 p.m., with a one-hour break at 1:00 p.m. the Reverend

French led this course area with Lieutenants Silvey, Sill, and Greble assisting. They used Bullion's Principles of English Grammar, Morse's Geography Made Easy, Lossing's History of the United States, and Sargent's Elocution and Composition. Both French and Greble seem to have been popular members of the academic staff. French was described lovingly as "a small, plump man, with sparkling blue eyes, short and snappy in speech," while Grebel, who was the Reverend French's son-in-law, was remembered as "a very gentle and refined man of medium height. His forehead, defined by dark, silky hair, was the conspicuous feature of his face, in which nature had written plainly her autograph of gentleman."[54]

Upton wrote letters and read in the library from 4:00 p.m. until 7:00 p.m., then studied until lights out.[55] The library was an especially memorable place for Upton and other plebes, many of whom had never seen a library until their arrival at West Point. The Academy library contained about 20,000 volumes, all stored in 30-foot-high shelves against the walls. The staff librarian was an old retired soldier named Fries, who had "flaming red cheeks, a little brown silky hair trained from his temples up over his well-crowned head, and a voice and a manner that was sweetness and modesty itself."[56]

Many cadets liked to study at one of the seats in the library's windows. This was particularly true for plebes like Upton, who were under constant hazing assaults by the upperclassmen. It was a place of calm reflection amidst the frantic energy of the Academy grounds. Here, the light was soft, and the quiet seemed very deep, "broken only now and then by the mellow notes of a bugle, or at intervals by a vireo's limpid, short warble in the trees outside."[57]

Upton's grades were solid, if not outstanding here and there. "So long as I can keep up to these marks," he wrote Maria, "I am not in danger of being found deficient."[58] As the months went by, he earned the reputation of being a "reliable but not a brilliant" student. Upton was the sort of scholar who made up for any lack of natural intellect with hard work. Whatever he learned, he retained, always maintaining what seemed a plethora of "illustrative facts to fix theoretical principles in his mind." He especially embraced mathematics because it taught him the necessity to prove everything and take nothing for granted, using "consecutive logical processes, to the inevitable result."[59]

Upton and his fellow plebes remained on probationary status until January 1857, when the academy required them to take their first formal comprehensive examination. The Academic Board conducted these examinations in a large carpeted hall above the library. Glass cabinets containing a variety of scientific instruments lined one side of the room. In front of these, was a line of blackboards on easels, set up much as they had been for the initial entrance examination the previous summer. On the opposite side of the room, there was a raised platform where Major Delafield, Colonel Hardee, and the rest of the academic staff sat behind a large, ornate table. Unlike the summer examination, the plebes now performed their testing in groups of four.[60]

The Adjutant called out four names, and these plebes went to the blackboards where each was assigned an individual set of mathematics problems. One might be doing general theory while the plebe next to him worked on logarithms. Meanwhile, another group of plebes was called forward to face the Academic Board and answer questions put to them regarding history, literature, and geography. This test was much more demanding than the entrance examination, and more than one cadet was known to pass out from the stress. When this occurred, an orderly was summoned, and he would drag the unconscious plebe from the room until the young man could be revived, at which time he returned to continue his testing.[61] Some classes saw as many as 20 percent of their members fail the January examination. But only one of Upton's classmates, George Talbot of Missouri, failed to pass the examination due to a deficiency in English Studies.[62]

Following completion of the January examination, Upton and the rest of his class were removed from probation, which allowed them to receive warrants for their eventual commissions as officers. This act required each plebe to take the oath of allegiance and, in early February, the class marched into the library to do so. For the occasion, the plebes wore their full-dress uniforms, complete with side arms and dress caps. The Academic Board took their seats, and the ceremony was called to order. The Adjutant rose to read a letter from the Secretary of War, Jefferson Davis, explaining the nature and obligations of the oath. After that, the plebes came forward, six at a time. They first sat at a table where the Adjutant placed the full form of the oath in front of each young man. After reading and signing the oath, they went to stand before a large, open bible. As they laid their hands on the book, the Academy magistrate read the oath aloud and, once each plebe finished, they bent over to kiss the Bible. The final step in this very dignified and solemn process was to receive a copy of their warrant from Major Delafield. They were now official members of the Corps of Cadets.[63]

By the end of the academic year on June 6, 1857, two more plebes were eliminated, one for disciplinary reasons and another for medical issues. That left a total of 56 cadets in Upton's class and, based on a combination of academic and military performance; he was ranked 23rd at the end of the year. The records show that he was also 23rd in both Mathematics and English Studies, with a total of 65 demerits, 48 of which he accumulated in the final semester. His total demerits were quite good as compared to the rest of his class. Judson Kilpatrick held the best score for demerits with not a single black mark recorded against him while Leonard Martin came in last with a whopping 172 demerits.[64]

Upton's demerits became an item of debate in letters between himself and his sister, Maria. She apparently referred to his demerits as having been "bad marks," to which Upton took great offense. "*Bad* [italics in original] signifies to you, evil, wrong, immoral, and wicked, which placed before *marks* [italics in original] signifies that I have been doing something wrong or immoral, something which conscience disapproves," he wrote in response. "That is wrong, not only in the sight of a military man, but of God," he continued. He argued, "what moral wrong is there in 'laughing in ranks,' in being 'late at roll-call,' 'not stepping off at command,' and 'not having coat buttoned throughout,' and kindred reports?" He assured his sister that he had never received an "immoral report" such as a demerit for using profanity.[65]

This letter to Maria also indicates one constant for Upton during his years at West Point: his faith. Seemingly every letter referenced his religious beliefs in some manner or form. In one letter, Maria inquired if Upton sincerely believed in God. He replied to this question by writing:

"I can say yes. I also believe in the religion inculcated by the ministers of God. Few men now disbelieve religion, and those are mostly ignorant men. Voltaire, the greatest modern infidel, shrank from death; and why? Because of his unbelief. He was afraid to enter eternity. I hope that you will never desert the good cause you have espoused, and that you will do much good in your life. As for myself, I take the Bible as the standard of morality, and try to read two chapters in it daily."[66]

But at the same time, Upton did not approach his faith as did those who fervently sought to "find God." For him, his faith was part of the bedrock he stood upon as a human being. When he received a letter from his sister, Louisa, saying that she had "experienced religion" at an evangelist's revival, Upton wrote Maria that, while he hoped Louisa "may have the strength to defend and exemplify" her new-found faith, he tended to be dubious of these sorts of religious epiphanies. For himself, he wrote, "My reason for not seeking religion can only be ascribed to a queer kind of apathy."[67] But events were looming over the horizon that would test Upton's faith, events that would turn that faith from a solid foundation to a slippery rock in the middle of a raging river, and one that he would cling to desperately.

The years that followed at West Point saw Upton's confidence increase and, with that, his class standing rose steadily as each academic year passed. At the end of his fourth-class year, he had moved up from 23rd to 17th and, the next year, he climbed to 14th. By graduation, he had ascended all the way to eighth in his class.[68]

The Gathering Storm

Upton's years at West Point were tumultuous times for the nation and the Academy. Sectional conflict over slavery and the spread of that institution to the new western territories was splitting the nation apart, and the deepening rifts within the Corps of Cadets reflected this tension. This process of division among the cadets from North and South accelerated in the fall of 1859 after the radical abolitionist, John Brown, seized the federal arsenal at Harpers Ferry, Virginia, on October 16. Brown, who hoped his act would foment a violent slave revolt across the South, was arrested after a successful assault on the arsenal by U.S. Marines dispatched from Washington, D.C. He was charged with treason, tried, found guilty, and hanged on December 2. While Upton opposed acts like Brown's, he still became a target for the anger of Southern cadets.

Not long after Brown's trial began, one of the Southerners, Wade Hampton Gibbes of South Carolina, decided to openly criticize Upton. Gibbes knew Upton had attended Oberlin College and, like most of the Southern cadets, Gibbes hated the school because it was known as a hotbed of abolitionism. Worst of all to the Southerners, however, Oberlin had an integrated student population. So Gibbes made public comments regarding Upton's "intimate association with Negros."[69]

Hearing about Gibbes comments, Upton confronted Gibbes one evening just as the corps dismissed following supper and "demanded an explanation," which meant the two cadets would fight. He and Gibbes went upstairs to a private room while a large crowd of cadets gathered on the first floor of the First Division barracks to follow the coming battle. A plebe sentinel tried to stop the fight, but the crowd swept past him as he helplessly called out for the corporal of the guard.[70]

Soon, those cadets from the crowd who ventured up the stairs heard angry voices, the scuffling of feet, and the dull sounds of the two cadets striking blows. Before long, the room upstairs became quiet. Then, Upton and Gibbes came out, both with cuts and bruises, but neither claiming outright victory. While the Northern cadets cheered for Upton, several Southerners shouted profanities at him. Hearing these, John Rodgers, Upton's roommate from Pennsylvania and his second in the fight, came to the head of the stairs and with eyes bright with anger, he called out, "If there are any more of you down there who want anything, come right up." No one responded to the challenge, and no West Point cadet ever trifled with Emory Upton again.[71]

Not surprisingly, Upton's letters to Maria reflected his strong feelings on the issues confronting the nation. On January 20, 1860, he wrote, "We are living in perilous times. Government, society, everything seems to be on the verge of revolution." Clearly seeing the prospect of war increasing, he added, "If we are to have war, I shall have no conscientious scruples as to engaging in it, for I believe I shall be on the side of right. I am ambitious; but I shall strive to limit it to doing good."[72] Less than a month later, Upton wrote one of his sisters again, expressing his thoughts on the coming conflict and his choice to serve in the profession of arms. "Our profession differs from all others," he wrote. "It is a profession of fate and a fatal profession. A long war would make many of us, and prove the grave of as many; but you know it matters not how we meet death, provided we are prepared for it. We must leave all to the dispensation of an all-wise Providence."[73]

The following December, as South Carolina moved steadily towards secession, Upton's belief that any coming war would be long and arduous became more certain. "Truly troubling times have come upon us," he wrote Maria. "We are at sea with no chart to guide us. What the end will be our wisest statesmen can't foresee. The south is gone, & the question is whether the government will coerce her back. The attempt I think must be made, but we cannot tell what will be the result yet. Southern men are brave & will fight well, but their means for prosecuting a long war are wanting."[74]

When South Carolina seceded a few weeks later. Upton's response to the news was predictable. "Today's papers inform us that South Carolina has seceded," he wrote his sister on December 21, 1860. "The veil behind which Webster [Daniel Webster, Congressman from New Hampshire and famous Unionist] sought not to penetrate has been 'rent in twain,' and secession, with its evils, is now a reality. Let her go. She has been a pest, an eye-sore, an abomination ever since she entered the Union." Then he added, prophetically, "War, I believe, must speedily follow, and by her act."[75]

On January 9, 1861, cadets from South Carolina's state military academy, The Citadel, fired a cannon on the Star of the West, a commercial ship hired by the U.S. Navy to run supplies past Southern guns to the besieged federal garrison at Fort Sumter. To Upton, the war had now begun. Southern cadets began to resign one after another, going home to their respective states as more and more of them seceded. "The crisis has come," Upton wrote

Cadet Emory Upton in his final year at West Point (National Archives).

his sister on February 2. He wondered aloud in his letter how the nation might meet this challenge. His answer was that the people must preserve the nation, even if it meant years of civil war. "What do you think of compromise," he asked his sister. "I am opposed to it, as a dangerous precedent. If the Union could be preserved without compromise, even at the expense of a war, I think it would be preferable to a compromise, since it would demonstrate that a republican government is adequate to any emergency."[76]

On April 12, guns from the forces of the newly founded Confederate States of America fired on Fort Sumter, and the garrison surrendered the next day. To this news, Upton replied, "The attack on Fort Sumter has sealed the traitor's doom."[77] Within days, Upton and his fellow members of the First Class heard rumors that they might graduate early and go directly into active service. Upton was particularly enthusiastic about this prospect, saying he had no desire for the traditional post-graduation furlough "when such exciting scenes are being daily enacted."[78]

But his reasons for this position were also grounded in professional considerations. With President Lincoln's call for 75,000 volunteers to put down the Southern insurrection, the War Department might fill existing command vacancies in the army with civilian appointments. The longer the cadets waited for their commissions, the more desirable positions would be filled by what Upton and his fellow cadets saw as unqualified amateurs.

The situation was further complicated by the complex system of officer assignments and designations in place at the time the war began. West Point cadets received commissions as Second Lieutenants in the Regular Army upon graduation. They requested what branch of the service they desired and received assignments based upon class standing. The choices consisted of the Corps of Engineers, which was traditionally the most prestigious branch, followed by the cavalry, infantry, and artillery. The engineers, while prestigious, offered the slowest advancement; while the artillery promised fast promotion; the cavalry guaranteed excitement; and the infantry, who would see the most action, offered the best opportunity for heroism.[79] Heroism, in turn, offered the chance for what was called a brevet promotion. Commanders in the field could grant these promotions for acts of bravery or any conspicuous service. However, they were temporary and, once the war was over, any officers granted these promotions would revert to their permanent rank in the Regular Army.

There was also the possibility of serving as an officer in one of the hundreds of state volunteer regiments rapidly forming across the North to meet the president's call for volunteers. This required the application to and approval by a state governor with acceptance for the assignment by the War Department. The governors were short of experienced officers, and many eagerly sought home state West Point graduates to command their regiments. In addition, these assignments came with the immediate rank of Colonel of U.S. Volunteers. But as a mere farmer's son, Upton lacked the needed political influence in Albany to gain such an assignment to a New York regiment, a problem that would plague him in the war years that followed.

In mid–April, upon hearing that midshipmen at the U.S. Naval Academy were going to graduate early, Upton and 29 of his fellow fifth-year cadets sent a petition to the Secretary of War, Simon Cameron, requesting that they be immediately graduated, commissioned, and assigned to duty. Not surprisingly, 18 of his classmates from the South refused to sign. About these 18 cadets, Upton wrote, "The Government will know who are loyal and who are traitors."[80] Congress soon heard of the petition and authorized Secretary Cameron to graduate the Class of 1861 as soon as final examinations were complete. By May 4, Emory Upton's class finished their examinations, and he graduated two days later.[81]

Given his class ranking, Upton had his choice of service branches. He chose the artillery and, on May 6, 1861, was commissioned as a Second Lieutenant in the 4th U.S. Artillery Regiment. On May 13, he officially accepted his commission via a letter to Secretary Cameron.[82] Only eight days later, he was transferred to the 5th U.S. Artillery due to an opening in its ranks and was immediately promoted to First Lieutenant.[83] Meanwhile, the entire graduating class received orders to proceed immediately to Washington, D.C., for duty.

Emory Upton's journey to war had begun.

2

Off to War

> ... an opportunity will soon present itself for me to be under fire, and I would not miss it for all the world.
>
> Emory Upton, July 9, 1861[1]

To Washington

Upton and most of his graduating class departed West Point by train a few hours after their commencement ceremonies. They took the train from Cold Springs Station for New York City, where they waited to board a 6:00 p.m. train the next evening for Philadelphia. The newly minted second lieutenants were an interesting looking lot. Some had managed to get their hands on the standard blue uniform of the U.S. Army. Most, however, still wore their gray cadet uniforms. All of them were armed, carrying their swords and revolvers in their baggage.[2]

Everything went well until they got off the train in Philadelphia. As soon as they stepped on the station platform, a swarm of Philadelphia police surrounded them, taking the young officers and their baggage into custody. It seems the mayor of Jersey City had telegraphed the authorities in Philadelphia telling them that a group of 40 Southern cadets was on the train from New York carrying small arms for Confederate forces. The police escorted Upton and the other young officers to the "Rogues Gallery" where the new officers surrendered their swords and pistols and awaited the arrival of an army official. Once an army officer arrived from Washington, the suspected Confederate conspirators showed him their official orders from the War Department, and the police released them from custody. Since they had now missed their connecting train for Washington, Upton and the rest of his classmates spent the night in the luxurious Continental Hotel, all at city expense.[3]

Upton arrived in Washington the next day, May 8, 1861, and found the capital city in turmoil. The streets were packed with people, and every hotel was filled to capacity. New volunteer regiments were pouring into the city from across the Northern states along with thousands of reporters and opportunists of every sort, eager to profit from the coming war. At the same time, Southerners and their sympathizers fled the city, crossing the Potomac River into Alexandria before traveling further south to perceived safety. Almost overnight, the army established defensive strongpoints at the Capitol, City Hall, and the White House. Each was stocked with provisions and guarded by local militia troops while the Treasury Building was sandbagged and stocked with food and ammunition as the point for a last stand defense should the city be overwhelmed by Confederate forces.[4] It all made for a city of startling contrasts, described by one young volunteer soldier who wrote, "what a city! Mud, pigs, geese, Negroes, palaces, shanties everywhere."[5]

Upton went directly from the train station to the War Department, located on West 17th Street near the White House. There, he and the other West Point graduates reported to General Lorenzo Thomas, the Adjutant General of the Army. General Thomas told them to present themselves to General Mansfield, who commanded the troops in the area surrounding Washington, D.C.[6] At that moment, Mansfield's most pressing need was for officers who could help train the roughly 50,000 inexperienced volunteers now camped about the city.[7] So, he temporarily assigned all the new lieutenants from West Point to volunteer regiments, directing them to make soldiers of the raw recruits as quickly as possible. As for Upton, Mansfield ordered him to report to Colonel Daniel Butterfield of the newly formed 12th New York Infantry Regiment for duties as a training officer.[8]

As he prepared for his first active duty assignment, Upton also had the chance to experience his initial forays into the capital's social scene. William Seward, Lincoln's Secretary of State, invited Upton and some other officers to attend a party at his home. "We shall go in full dress," Upton wrote his sister. "It will be my debut in W[ashingto]n [sic] society. I am very desirous of making some lady acquaintances."[9] His comment is not surprising. From the time he arrived at Oberlin College, Upton worked too hard to have time for social or romantic activities, and West Point provided little opportunity for spending time in the company of the opposite sex. Further, if he eventually got the field assignment he sought, Upton's social prospects would be almost non-existent for the near future. However, once he reported to Butterfield and the 12th New York, his social activities quickly came to an end.

When Upton arrived in

1st Lieutenant Emory Upton, probably after his arrival in Washington, D.C. (National Archives).

the camps of the nation's new army, his reaction was less than enthusiastic. What he saw left an indelible impression on him, and it was not a good one. He wrote later that the marshaling of volunteer regiments at the outset of the Civil War "presented to the world the spectacle of a great nation nearly destitute of military force."[10] On the day Fort Sumter was fired upon, the Regular Army consisted of just over 16,000 men, and 92 percent of them were stationed far from Washington along the western frontier. As a result, mobilizing state militia units and the recruiting of new volunteer regiments was the government's only recourse to meet the threat posed by the Southern rebellion. The militia units should have at least had some military training, but even this was often not the case. "So destitute were they of instruction and training," Upton later wrote, "that—a few regiments in the large cities excepted—they did not merit the name of a military force."[11] Naturally, the newly recruited volunteer regiments were in far worse shape than the militia and were only slightly better than semi-organized mobs.

Furthermore, the entire structure and culture of the Regular Army rendered it virtually impotent to meet the challenge of organizing and leading a force as large as was now gathered around Washington, much less command and direct what would soon become a major war fought from the Atlantic coast to the Rocky Mountains. There was no general staff, and old men who should have retired years before ran the War Department's bureaus. General Winfield Scott, the army's general-in-chief and a hero of the Mexican War, resisted the very logical suggestion that he assign Regular Army officers such as Upton directly to service with volunteer units where they might do the most good.

Among the army's leadership, there was also the issue of the sheer size of this endeavor. At the time the war began, no officer North or South, including General Scott, had ever commanded more than 25,000 men. Now, this new army had twice that many just around Washington, D.C., with more units reporting to new army organizations west of the Appalachians. Within a year, one corps of one Federal army would number close to 25,000 men and, eventually, the individual Northern armies would have as many as 100,000 soldiers each.[12] The army's leaders simply had no idea how to clothe, feed, arm, and supply that many soldiers, much less train them to fight and then wield this huge force effectively in battle. So, they would have to make it up as they went along, and young officers like Emory Upton were an important part of that process.

Volunteers, Tactics and Training

The 12th New York Infantry Upton had been assigned to train had only recently arrived in Washington from the area around Syracuse, New York. The new regiment formed on May 8, 1861, and, while a few of its soldiers had belonged to a county militia regiment, the remainder were raw volunteers.[13] Each of the regiment's ten companies numbered between 65 and 100 men, typically recruited in different towns within the same county, in this case, Onondaga County, New York. So, like most Civil War regiments, many of the men knew one other and, within a company, one often found members of the same family.[14]

Like most volunteer recruits, these New Yorkers were brimming with confidence and patriotism. They were ready to fight and end the war as soon as possible. Their home states had equipped them with uniforms and enough supplies to allow them to at least look like soldiers. One New Hampshire volunteer wrote, "We are warriors now in full feathers and trappings."

He went on to list the equipment he and his comrades had been issued, which included a rifle, 80 rounds of ball cartridge, and one pound of powder, plus a knapsack, haversack, canteen, rubber blanket, woolen blanket, shelter tent, uniform, tin cup, tin plate, knife, fork, spoon, and a three-day supply of rations. As a result, the young volunteer joked, "We are a baggage train, freight train, ammunition train, commissary train, gravel train, and train-band, all in one."[15] But as with new soldiers in so many wars before and since, Upton would find that, while these men might look like soldiers, they were far from actually being soldiers.

To be able to fight, the regiment had to be able to execute the army's prescribed infantry tactics and do so smoothly and efficiently while under fire from the enemy. Preparing these volunteers to do that and accomplishing it in a very short period would be Emory Upton's first job as an army officer. The infantry tactics of the day were based on the use of the smoothbore musket and bayonet as dictated by General Scott's three-volume work, *Infantry-Tactics*, plus the later book written by Upton's former commandant of cadets, Colonel Hardee. While Hardee's book added a faster pace of march for infantry attacks, Scott's basic tactics were little changed from when he first wrote his manual in 1838.[16]

Scott based his approach on the French army's tactics during the Napoleonic era when the standard infantry weapon was the highly inaccurate smoothbore musket. Most of these weapons could not accurately hit a target beyond 100 yards. General Ulysses Grant later wrote that, when firing these weapons even from the distance of only a few hundred yards, "a man might fire at you all day without your finding it out."[17] Therefore, Scott's tactics sought to keep infantrymen in close-ordered lines to concentrate their firepower. When attacking, men were compressed together and marched in ranks two or three deep only 13 inches apart. The men in these ranks maintained a tight elbow-to-elbow spacing as they advanced at a steady, regulated pace to a point where they could unleash a volley of musket fire, followed by a bayonet charge.[18]

Colonel Hardee's newer manual allowed for a quick-step advance of 140 steps per minute rather than Scott's 110 per minute pace and added a "double quick-step" of 180 steps per minute. The only other significant changes from Scott's manual to Hardee's was that Hardee incorporated a system to allow troops to deploy quickly from the column formation they used when marching into the line formation needed in battle.[19]

The 12th New York Infantry Regiment during their initial training outside Washington (Library of Congress).

Hardee intended all his revisions to account for the changes demanded by the advent of the rifle. Unlike the old smoothbore musket, the new rifles had grooves inside the barrel, which caused their minié ball ammunition to spin. This meant the rifles were far more accurate than the musket, and infantrymen could not only hit targets at 300 yards, but also, when their minié balls struck an enemy soldier, they could inflict far more damage on the human body than the old musket rounds. While Hardee had meant to compensate for these capabilities, his changes made little difference from the tactics Scott had developed for weapons of another time. Emory Upton would eventually see first-hand what this meant, and it would make a deep, life-changing impression on him.

These tactics also complicated Upton's task for training his volunteer soldiers. The formations required by Scott's tactics were complex to learn, as well as to teach. One Civil War general complained that the tactics in Scott's book were "smothered by details." Furthermore, the general wrote, mastering them required "a student with a positive aptitude," a description that hardly described the volunteer soldiers Upton and other officers were now being asked to train.[20]

Moreover, the officers in command of the new volunteer units were just as inexperienced as their men, which made these companies and regiments ill-prepared for camp life, much less the rigors of battle. After observing one volunteer regiment, the 17th New York Infantry, Upton wrote his sister that the regiment was in "a miserable condition." To his mind the reasons were obvious. "The Col. [sic]," he wrote, "is not a military man, the commissary knows nothing of his business; the consequences is there is no discipline."[21] Therefore, when he arrived at the 12th New York and found a very similar situation, his only recourse was to drill both the officers and enlisted men from dawn to dark.

The training was grueling, and Upton wrote, "I worked really hard last week, but do not complain, when I think how much harder the poor privates have to work."[22] The drills Upton used were simple compared to those employed in later wars. This was because many Civil War era volunteers were not mentally prepared for anything too complex. For instance, some of these men did not know their left foot from their right. The answer to this problem was to attach a wisp of hay to their left shoe and a length of straw to their right. When they began to march, the men would look down at their feet and follow Upton's chants of "Hayfoot, Strawfoot, Hayfoot, Strawfoot!" Of course, Upton also had to see that the volunteer officers were properly trained and could execute basic drill movements. The soldiers of the regiment had often elected these officers to their positions, or the officers obtained an appointment from the governor based on political connections. Therefore, they knew as little about being a soldier as the men they would command. As one historian stated, "drill was akin to the ignorant leading the uneducated."[23]

The men drilled four-abreast in column formation and had to learn the intricate process of shifting quickly for battle from those columns to two closely aligned parallel lines. In this process, inexperienced officers tried to remember the right command, and untrained soldiers then attempted to follow their orders while maintaining tight spacing, proper cadence, and straight lines, which was unnerving for all involved. Soon, however, the army would expect them to execute these drills in the field while under fire and while loading and firing their weapons.

But the training in weapons also posed a challenge for drillmasters like Upton. First, many of the volunteers in his charge had never fired a weapon of any kind, and those that had were only familiar with weapons like shotguns. Most of them had never seen much less handled a rifle. This inexperience increased the likelihood that someone would be injured or killed during training and, tragically, that was too often the case. As a result, officers like Upton were hesitant to conduct live firing practice. Still, if they were to fight, these new volunteers had to learn to use their rifle.

The first task in using the rifle was to learn to load and fire the weapon. Units like the 12th New York were lucky in that the state issued them the latest in U.S. Army equipment, the .577 Springfield rifle. While more accurate and powerful than other models, it was still a muzzle-loaded weapon that required a multistep process to prepare for firing, just like the older muskets. First, the soldier reached into his cartridge box, which he slung over his shoulder and hung at his right hip. He extracted a cartridge from the box that consisted of a minié ball and powder charge, all wrapped in paper. He then tore open the cartridge with his teeth, emptied the powder down the rifle's barrel, and inserted the ball with the pointed end up. Next, the soldier grabbed the ramrod, which hung just below the rifle's barrel. He then used this long thin metal rod to tamp down the ball and powder in the barrel. Now, he half-cocked the hammer and placed the percussion cap that would ignite the powder for firing on the small protrusion at the back end of the barrel. Raising the rifle to his shoulder, he fully cocked the hammer, aimed, and pulled the trigger.[24] At best, the most experienced rifleman could perform this process and then make an aimed shot only three times in a minute.

Moreover, given that these rifles weighed about ten pounds, the process of loading, raising the gun to fire, loading, and then firing over and over again was exhausting. After an hour or so of shooting, soldiers' arms and shoulders "would ache as though a team of horses had been tugging at them."[25]

What may have been worse, however, was actually firing the rifle. Many new soldiers cringed as they squeezed the trigger and closed their eyes, fearing the blast of fire and smoke that would come from the muzzle of the barrel. This was followed by the tremendous kickback as the rifle fired its charge of powder and minié ball. This not only made one's aching shoulder hurt worse, but it also knocked some volunteers over right onto their backsides.

After two weeks working with the 12th New York, Upton received word to move to the camp of the 2nd Connecticut Infantry and begin their instruction.[26] At this point, Upton began to wonder if he would be training volunteers for the entire war and miss any opportunity for action. While he continued to believe the war would be a long one, many in the nation, both North and South, thought the war would be brief. Most people believed that one major battle and one victory would be enough to make the losing side reconsider their position and seek peace and reconciliation. In May 1861, no one could see the national nightmare that was coming.

On May 24, Upton applied for assignment to a battery of light artillery but was told there were no openings. However, just as he arrived at the 2nd Connecticut's camp, he received orders to report to General Daniel Tyler for duties as the general's aide-de-camp. Tyler was 62 years old and an 1839 graduate of West Point. He had recently returned to the army from a successful career in the railroad business to take command of the First Division of the army's newly created Department of Northeastern Virginia. Upton was quite thrilled with this assignment, writing his sister that he deemed the position "admirable."[27] It might not be field duty, but it was the next best thing.

Upton reported to Tyler, who assigned him a good horse and had him share the general's quarters. Soon after Upton's arrival, Tyler received orders to begin moving his division across the Potomac into Virginia at midnight on June 1. The division included four brigades composed of 15 volunteer infantry regiments from Connecticut, Maine, Massachusetts,

Michigan, New York, Ohio, and Wisconsin, plus four batteries of artillery from the Regular Army.[28] Tyler told Upton that his job would include everything from carrying messages to unit commanders to conducting reconnaissance.

The division crossed the river as ordered and marched three miles southeast to a spot known as Roach's Mill (located near the current intersection of South Glebe and West Glebe Roads, in Alexandria, Virginia). Upton rode ahead of the division, arriving there early on the morning of June 2. He began surveying the best spot for their camps, which took until around noon when he was able to catch a quick one-hour nap. A few days later, he noted the misplacement of a line of sentinels from one regiment and took it upon himself to adjust their position. Not wanting to seem too eager or even arrogant, he made sure to find the volunteers' commander, a young, inexperienced major, and explain why his men needed the repositioning. When he told General Tyler what he had done, Upton received his first compliment from the general, who emphatically stated, "That is right; you will do hereafter to go out on your own hook."[29] Upton was justifiably pleased by the old general's confidence in his abilities.

Bull Run

With the initial Federal advance into northern Virginia in early June, Confederate forces under the command of General Pierre Beauregard withdrew to positions along a creek called Bull Run near Manassas, Virginia, about 30 miles southeast of Washington. As June passed into July, pressure increased for Federal forces to act against the Confederate army. The glaring headlines of the June 25, 1861, edition of Horace Greeley's *New York Tribune* were typical of this pressure. Greeley, an aggressive and highly influential publisher, wrote, "FORWARD TO RICHMOND! The Rebel Congress Must Not Be Allowed to Meet There on the 20th of July. By That Date the Place Must Be Held by the National Army!"[30] Meanwhile, President Lincoln asked the Congress to approve additional funding for the army, as well as authorize the enlistment of 400,000 more men. He got both.[31]

Even though General Scott favored an extended strategy that sought to blockade and strangle the South economically, President Lincoln was convinced his government needed to take immediate action. Like Greeley, he hoped that seizing the new Confederate capital in Richmond might quickly end the conflict. Scott assigned General Irvin McDowell to command the Union forces in the Department of Northeastern Virginia, and McDowell soon found himself under siege to execute an offensive plan against the Confederates. McDowell set up his headquarters in Robert E. Lee's mansion at Arlington from where he surveyed his army. Rather than the 100,000 men trumpeted in the press, he only had about 30,000 men who were equipped and had received even minimal training. Worse, as McDowell told William Russell, a correspondent for the London Times, on July 8, he had no decent maps, no knowledge of the roads leading to Manassas, and no cavalry available to scout them.[32]

At this time, despite the confusion and disorder Upton had seen in the volunteer camps, he remained optimistic. On July 1, he wrote his sister, saying that the army hoped "to celebrate the Fourth of July at Fairfax Court House," adding, "Whether the move will involve battle I know not but I hope it will…. I think we shall have fighting soon beyond a doubt. I have been where I expected a fight but have not been satisfied as yet."[33] His sister soon replied, telling her brother that she wanted to visit him in Washington. Upton replied, saying, "I should like to accompany you at any other time than this; but you know an opportunity will soon present itself for me to be under fire, & I would not miss it for all the world."[34]

When McDowell met with President Lincoln and General Scott, he begged for more time to prepare. McDowell told the president, "There was not one in the army; I did not believe there was one in the whole country; at least, I knew there was no one there who had ever handled 30,000 troops. I had seen them handled abroad in reviews and marches, but I had never handled that number, and no one here had."[35] But the president's answer to his plea for additional time was "You are green, it is true; but they are green, also; you are all green alike."[36] McDowell had no choice—he would have to move his amateur army out to meet the enemy and do so sooner rather than later.

McDowell developed a plan that called for the Union army to take advantage of a split in Confederate forces. While Beauregard sat at Manassas with about 22,000 men, another Confederate force of approximately 10,000 men under General Joe Johnston was positioned at Winchester, Virginia in the Shenandoah Valley, some 50 miles to the northwest.[37] If he could prevent Johnston from coming to Beauregard's aid, McDowell would greatly outnumber his opponent. So, McDowell developed a plan to dispatch a force under the command of General Robert Patterson to block Johnston's path to Manassas while McDowell swung the main Federal force around Beauregard's left flank and defeated the Southern army.

McDowell ordered General Tyler to move his division to Centreville, Virginia, on July 18, which placed them about five miles from Beauregard's army. When the division arrived, they found the Confederate forces occupying the town had withdrawn. One enemy division had retreated southwest towards Gainesville, but the larger of the two divisions under General James Longstreet fell back to Blackburn's Ford on Bull Run, about two miles south of Centreville. With Upton at his side, General Tyler took a small cavalry detachment and two companies of infantry from General Richardson's brigade to scout Longstreet's position on the far side of the ford.[38]

Once there, Tyler and Upton could see a Confederate battery through the trees on the opposite bank, but no large numbers of enemy infantry. Suspecting that Longstreet might have a strong force defending the position, Tyler sent Upton to bring forward a battery of artillery and the remainder of Richardson's infantry, which included five regiments. When these reinforcements arrived at the ford, Tyler directed Upton to take the artillery up to the crest of a nearby hill about a mile from the single enemy battery on the opposite side of the creek. Once there, he was to open fire on the Confederate guns. Excited by this opportunity, Upton galloped up the hill, as the horse-drawn guns followed close behind. When they reached the top of the hill, Upton pointed to the spot he wanted the guns set up. The artillerymen quickly unlimbered the guns and soon had them in place, ready for action. Rather than leaving the task of sighting the guns to the battery section commander, Upton did it himself and then fired the first of about a dozen shells lobbed at the opposing battery.[39]

The Confederate guns fired back, and Tyler sent three infantry regiments forward to the creek to see if he could determine the strength of Longstreet's position. As soon as the Union infantry appeared at their front, the Confederates opened fire, revealing considerable numbers of Southern troops. While the Federal regiment commanders wanted to go forward and cross Bull Run, Tyler held them back, and they retreated to a position above the ford. It had been a minor skirmish, but Upton had seen his first action of the war.[40]

With the information from Tyler's reconnaissance, McDowell could see that most of Beauregard's army was firmly in place along Bull Run south of the Warrenton Pike at a place where the road crossed the creek at the Stone Bridge. McDowell decided to deploy most of his army several miles north upstream, so they could cross and strike the Confederate left flank and rear on July 21. As part of the attack, he ordered Tyler to take his division and advance down the Warrenton Pike to the Stone Bridge where his presence would draw Beauregard's attention and hopefully hold the Confederate army in place. Once his division arrived at the bridge, Tyler was to fire one cannon as a signal that he was in position. Then, while General Robert Schenk's brigade remained on the east side of Bull Run at the bridge, General William T. Sherman's brigade would cross the creek about a half-mile north of the bridge at Farm Ford with General Erasmus Keyes' brigade following later.[41]

General Tyler and his troops arrived at the Stone Bridge at 6:00 a.m. on the morning of July 21 and promptly fired the cannon shot to signal they were in position. Tyler told Upton to accompany Sherman's brigade across the creek, and his young aide rode off to the north, fording Bull Run with the troops from the 69th New York Infantry. As the New Yorkers moved up the opposite bank and through a small ravine before emerging on open ground, Upton rode a few yards ahead of the infantry. He went only a short distance when he saw troops to his front. Given the wide variety of uniforms and flags carried by both sides at this early stage of the war, Upton could not tell if they were friend or foe. So, he did what seemed logical and called out to them, asking which side they were on. The move was logical, perhaps, but did not demonstrate much common sense. The troops shouted back that they were Confederates. At this moment, Upton realized he was in a precarious position, sitting atop his horse between two opposing lines of infantry that were about to begin shooting at one another. He spurred his horse and galloped to get out of the line of fire.[42]

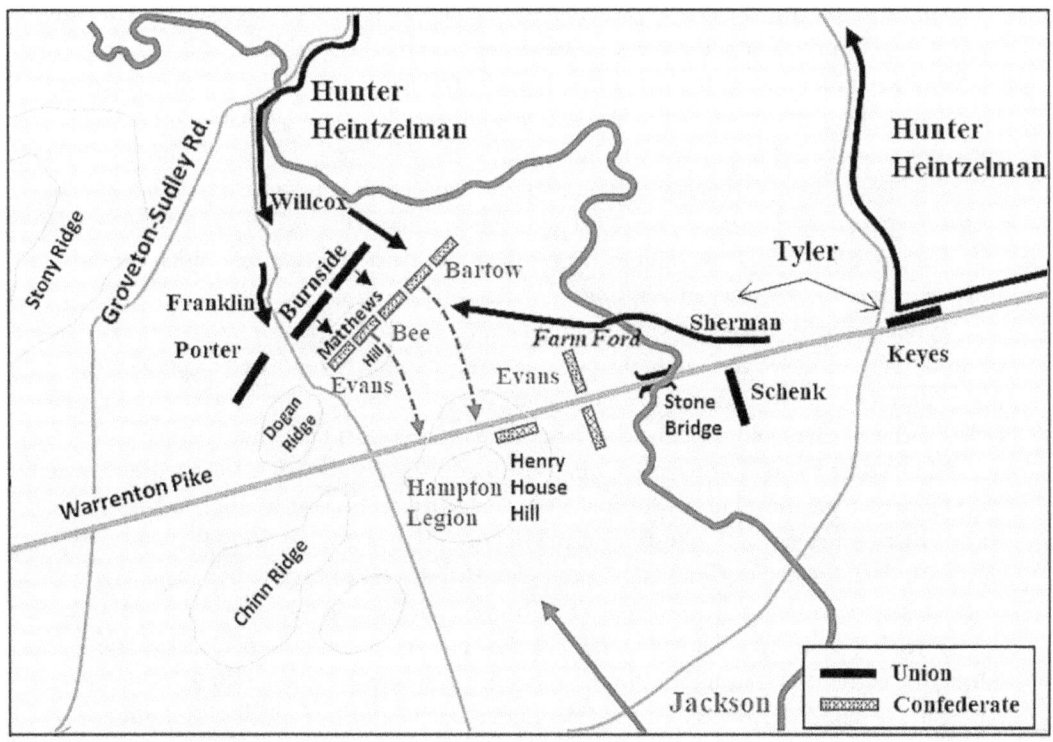

The Battle of First Manassas, July 21, 1862 (drawn by the author).

Just as Upton got out of the way, the opposing infantry opened fire on one another with a loud crash. Upton turned his horse around and rode back to a position just behind the line of the 69th New York's lead company. The firing between the Union and Confederate soldiers was continuous now, and bullets whistled all around him. Suddenly, his horse whinnied loudly in pain as an enemy bullet hit the animal. The mortally wounded horse started to collapse, and Upton leaped off to prevent being trapped underneath it. With his mount down, he began to walk up the sloping ground behind the New York volunteers as the rest of Sherman's brigade arrived and advanced south towards the main Confederate line.[43]

Sherman's brigade soon pushed the Confederates back and, as the rest of McDowell's army arrived on the enemy flank, the Southerners retreated to new positions south of the Warrenton Pike on Henry House Hill. At that point, Upton decided to turn around to go back to his horse so he could remove his saddle. As he did so, he noticed an intense burning in his left arm just underneath a very damp uniform sleeve. He examined his arm and found a bullet had hit him at the same time his horse fell. Luckily, the enemy minié ball had not hit bone, passing right through the flesh without doing much real damage. He did not seem to be bleeding too badly, so he decided to press on. He took his saddle off the horse and, with the saddle in his arms, he walked toward a small house where a field hospital was set up. There, he inquired about the possibility of finding another horse. He quickly located a rather old farm horse and commandeered it for the day from its civilian owner.[44] Once he saddled his borrowed horse, Upton rode off to locate General Tyler, and, soon, he found the general riding with Keyes' brigade, which was now crossing Bull Run to join Sherman in pursuing the enemy towards Henry House Hill.

Upton rode with the general as Tyler tried to bring Schenk's brigade across the Stone Bridge to join in the battle. However, as the afternoon progressed, things took a bad turn for McDowell and his army. As the army advanced against Henry House Hill, his men discovered that General Patterson had failed to bottle up Joe Johnston's force at Winchester. Even though Patterson thought the enemy was still there, Johnston had actually moved around the Union forces and joined with Beauregard at Manassas. The Confederates now had just as many troops on the field as did McDowell. About 4:00 p.m., the Southerners launched a massive counterattack that sent McDowell's raw volunteers running for the rear in total panic, and most did not stop running until they reached Washington.

When General Tyler saw what was happening, he ordered Upton to ride as fast as he could to General Keyes and tell him to get his brigade to safety on the east side of Bull Run before they were cut off by the Confederate counterattack. Upton galloped off to give Keyes his orders and tell him to join the retreating army once he got across Bull Run.[45]

The battered Union army arrived in Washington that night resembling a disorganized herd more than an army. Luckily for them, the Confederates became so disorganized by their success that Beauregard and Johnston elected to only advance close to the capital and take positions on the far side of the Potomac. Upton wrote his sister the next day, but all he said was "I regret to say we are defeated. Our troops fought well, but were badly managed."[46] For now, he did not tell her about his wounded arm, that he had been weak from loss of blood all afternoon during the battle, and that his arm hurt badly during the retreat to the capital. In his official report to General McDowell, General Tyler noted Upton's "gallant conduct and prompt and valuable assistance."[47]

Upton had now experienced war, and while casualties were relatively light as compared to the battles yet to come, it made an impression on him. His comment to his sister that Union troops had fought well was somewhat overstated. Certainly, they had fought well for volunteers with only a few weeks of training, but they had a long way to go. As one veteran wrote later of his fellow volunteers, "Only a short time was needed to teach them what war was. It took a longer time to make them soldiers."[48]

Most telling, perhaps, was Upton's feelings about the army's leadership during the battle. As he told his sister, the troops were badly managed at almost every level of command and, as General Tyler's aide, he had seen that first-hand. Tyler himself was slow and clumsy in commanding his division and, of his brigade commanders, only General Sherman demonstrated any real competence. The situation was similar throughout McDowell's army. Here and there, a professional soldier demonstrated some skill while everyone else struggled to maintain even a basic level of military aptitude. But none of this was surprising. Almost all the company and regiment commanders were volunteers, and the brigade and division commanders were a mix of either former professionals or politically appointed amateurs. Even the former soldiers and Regular Army officers, including McDowell himself, had never commanded units of these sizes in the field before.

It had been a recipe for disaster, and that is precisely what they got.

3

To the Artillery

> Of Upton's battery.... I cannot speak too highly. The officers and men ... have on all occasions manifested that coolness and bravery so necessary to this branch of the service.
>
> Brigadier General H. W. Slocum, Commander,
> First Division, XI Corps, July 10, 1862[1]

In the weeks following Bull Run, Upton rested and nursed his wounded arm as the army tried to sort out the debacle of its first major battle. Despite the wound, Upton had lost none of his apparent enthusiasm for seeking action. Furthermore, his strong belief in the righteousness of the Union cause had not wavered. When family members wrote expressing fears that Upton might be killed in battle, his response was filled with patriotic fervor. "If I am to be killed in battle no earthly power can avert it. My fate I know not. Whatever it may be I am ready & willing to meet it. I am fighting for right, & trust in God to defend me. If it be his will I desire no more happy or glorious death than on the battlefield in the defense of our flag. I owe all to the Government, and, in return, the Gov't shall have all."[2]

Upton's desires regarding his role in the army also remained unchanged, and he actively pursued a transfer from his staff position to a posting with a field unit. On August 14, 1861, he got his wish when he received orders to duty with Battery D of the 2nd U.S. Artillery Regiment.[3] Battery D was assigned to one of the forts in the defenses of Washington near Bailey's Crossroads (present-day Falls Church, Virginia). The unit was part of the Regular Army and had fought at Bull Run, where it fired more than 400 rounds. It also received severe counter-battery fire from the Confederates, losing two men killed, five wounded, and three missing, as well as 15 to 20 horses, killed.[4]

At the time Upton received his assignment, each Union artillery battery consisted of six guns with supporting equipment, men, and horses. In the case of Battery D, the guns were six smoothbore Model 1857 Napoleon cannons, which were the most common piece of artillery in both the Union and Confederate armies. The name Napoleon came from the fact that French designers originally developed the gun for the army of Napoleon III. The army also referred to it as a 12-pound cannon because that was the weight of the solid shot rounds it could fire. With a bronze barrel, each gun weighed 2,600 pounds and came with a caisson, which was a two-wheeled cart designed to carry ammunition, and a limber, which was a two-wheeled cart that supported the trail of an artillery piece. Given the combined weight of the gun, its ammunition, the caisson, and the limber, each cannon required six horses to pull it.[5]

The army organized each battery into three sections of two guns each. A crew of six men usually manned each piece, and Upton now commanded a total strength of 100 soldiers. Commanding a battery in battle required officers like Upton to employ a complex mix of art and science. They had to accurately calculate ranges, what type of ammunition to use, and how to fire them with the most effect. Further, the entire process of setting up and taking a battery into action required a disciplined ballet. Upon arriving in position, the men unlimbered the guns and placed them into line for firing while other soldiers moved horses and caissons to the rear. Upton would then have the soldiers align each gun by hand, load it, and fire. When fired, the gun recoiled a distance of a few feet up to a dozen yards, depending on the size of the powder charge and amount of ammunition used.[6]

After firing, gunners rolled the gun back into position by hand and quickly re-aligned it. As the gun moved back into place, they swabbed the barrel with a wet sponge mounted on the end of a long rod, which cooled the barrel and extinguished any lingering sparks that might inadvertently set off the next powder charge as the gunners inserted it. A gun crew that could efficiently dance this ballet could load, aim, and fire twice in one minute. In fact, when under heavy infantry attack, well-trained gun crews sometimes fired as many as four shots in less than a minute.[7]

Upton's next few months consisted primarily of typical garrison duties such as drilling. But his duties also included daily training in executing the process of setting up the battery and bringing the guns into action. His men were well-trained Regular Army soldiers, and his battery quickly became a highly efficient unit. In late September, the battery moved a few miles west to Munson's Hill where scouts reported the presence of Confederate guns. When the battery arrived, Upton found that the enemy had abandoned the fort and the reported heavy guns turned out to be fakes made of wood. The battery returned to Bailey's Crossroads where Upton heard about property destruction conducted by some nearby Union troops. "The conduct of our troops was disgraceful beyond expression," he wrote his sister. "They burned buildings, destroyed furniture, stole dishes, chairs, etc., killed chickens, pigs, calves, and everything they could eat…. Talk about the barbarity of the rebels! I believe them to be Christians compared to

Twelve-pound Napoleon cannon like those deployed in Upton's battery (Library of Congress).

our thieves."[8] This comment shows that, like most soldiers on both sides, Upton still saw war as something to be conducted in a civilized manner where certain rules of behavior applied.

At the same time, Upton still held onto his core beliefs about the war. He wrote his sister telling her, "I am opposed to Southern slavery in every form, viewed in any light political, social, or moral. I have taken an oath 'to bear true allegiance to the United States,' and I hope to observe that oath. Slavery is the cause of the rebellion, and I believe it is God's providence that it shall be overthrown. It will be the consequence, not the effect, of the war.... The rebels wish to establish a monarchy, and are fighting for that object. We are fighting for the Government, and against that object."[9]

When Upton took command of his battery, he also experienced his first encounter with a difficult commanding officer. He wrote his sister describing his relationship with Captain Edward Platt as "miserable." Apparently, the two men disagreed on virtually everything, and Upton wrote his sister saying, "I am bound to leave his company.... I will not serve with him.... I would resign before I would serve with Platt during the war." He made numerous efforts to transfer to a different command, even feeling that another staff job would be preferable to serving under Platt.[10] But no assignment came through, and Upton suffered until Platt was eventually promoted to be the division's chief of artillery, so much so that he even requested a transfer to a new volunteer battery from Connecticut. His superior officers approved the request but stipulated he could not leave his current command until the Connecticut battery was ready for service, which would not be for several months.[11]

In November 1861, the army experienced some great changes. General Scott retired, and President Lincoln named General George B. McClellan as general-in-chief of the army. McClellan was an 1842 graduate of West Point who had left active service to pursue a career with the Illinois Central Railroad. He returned to the Regular Army at the outbreak of the war, and President Lincoln appointed him as a Major General. McClellan achieved a few small successes in Kentucky and northwestern Virginia in the early months of the war, and since the Union was badly in need of someone successful at the helm of the army, McClellan succeeded General Scott.

In many ways, McClellan was the sort of commanding officer the army needed in the fall of 1861. He had incredible energy and focus with an innate ability to organize and train an army like no other. He reorganized the forces around Washington into a new 0rganization, the Army of the Potomac, and placed them under his personal command. Under his leadership, the ragtag volunteers began to look and act like real soldiers. Morale improved, and McClellan's soldiers soon came to love him, calling him "Little Mac."

Typical Civil War era limber and caisson like those used in Upton's artillery battery (Library of Congress).

Unfortunately, McClellan also had severe deficiencies. He was an imperious, obstinate, arrogant, pseudo-intellectual patrician who saw almost everyone as his inferior. He trusted no one, could not delegate authority, and had a massive ego. McClellan also possessed a messianic complex that caused him to see himself as the only person qualified to be the savior of the republic. Moreover, he was a class-conscious prig, who considered Abraham Lincoln, his commander-in-chief, as his inferior, both socially and intellectually, and a man clearly unqualified for any national leadership role. Maybe worst of all, McClellan identified with the Southern aristocracy that led the rebellion. As a result, he wanted a war that was limited in nature, respected property, and sought merely to restore the Union without emancipating the slaves, an act that he considered equal to inciting servile insurrection.

McClellan was also slow and deliberate in the extreme. Perhaps worse, he was more than a little paranoid. He always saw extreme danger everywhere, constantly believing the enemy had superior numbers when that was almost never the case. This habit caused him to resist any suggestions that he should take offensive action. McClellan responded to pressure from President Lincoln to attack the enemy with arguments that the Army of the Potomac was undersupplied, had too few men, or was simply not ready to fight. As the spring of 1862 arrived, Lincoln reduced McClellan's responsibilities by removing him from the position of general-in-chief and leaving him in command of only the Army of the Potomac. For whatever reason, this demotion spurred McClellan into action at last.

McClellan finally produced a grand strategic plan that mirrored the other plans created at the war's start in that its objective was the capture of the Confederate capital at Richmond. But rather than marching his army via the most direct route by advancing south 100 miles from Washington, he proposed to transport his entire force by

Major General George B. McClellan, the imperious, arrogant General-in-Chief and commander of the Army of the Potomac (Library of Congress).

ship, landing them along the Virginia Peninsula between the York and James Rivers. Then he would march only 70 miles northwest to Richmond and capture the city, which he believed would cause the South to sue for peace.

The Peninsula

Upton's battery was reassigned to the First Division of the XI Corps under General William Franklin, and his battery arrived on the peninsula at Yorktown on April 22, 1862. They waited there for about two weeks before boarding ship again on May 4, sailing 40 miles up the York River, and landing at West Point, Virginia on May 6. By dawn the next morning, Upton had his guns offloaded from the ship and ready to move into action.[12] General Franklin professed his "ignorance of the topography of the place of landing," which was understandable. One of the problems with the location McClellan chose for his great campaign was that the army had no reliable maps of the area. Furthermore, since most of the terrain was heavily wooded and swampy with only a few decent roads, advancing a large army was extremely difficult. Scouts reported enemy cavalry and infantry in the vicinity, so Franklin immediately set up a defensive perimeter around the landing site and sent out reconnaissance parties "in all directions to obtain as accurate a knowledge of the country as possible."[13]

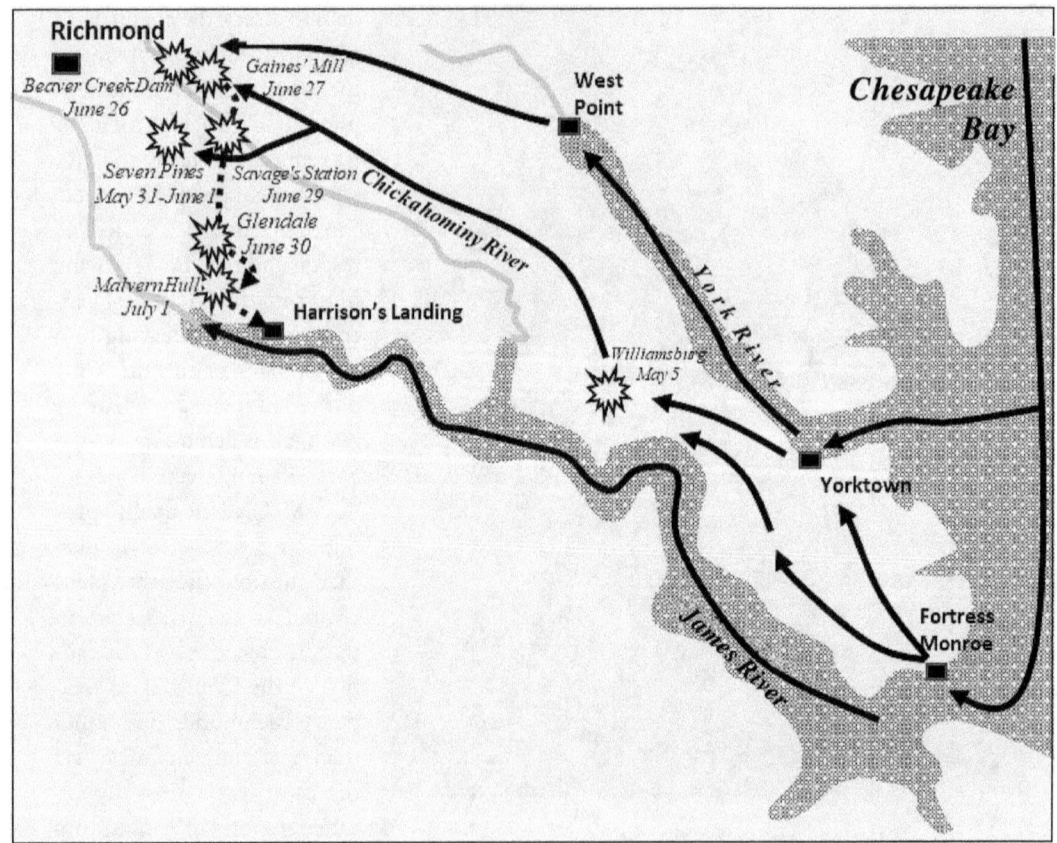

The Peninsula Campaign (drawn by the author).

Around 9:00 a.m., Upton heard rifle fire off to his left and, within minutes, Captain Platt sent orders to move the battery towards the sound of the shooting. Once on the left flank of the division, Upton and his men remained in reserve until noon, when they moved forward into a large open field and set up for action. His gun crews unlimbered the cannons from their caissons and set them in place with the men ready to service them. The Napoleons were about 1,400 yards from a forest where Confederate infantry had deployed among the trees, and Captain Platt ordered shells fired into the woods to see if they could get a reaction from the enemy.[14]

The explosive shells of the time required fuses that were cut to match the estimated flight time to the intended target. In this case, Upton calculated that five-second fuse lengths were required and ordered his men to prepare them. When fired, the first shell burst right on the edge of the woods, but the next four exploded nearly 500 yards short of the woods and very near another Union battery. Upton realized this meant the fuses were defective, and he immediately ordered a change to nonexplosive solid shot rounds. As these cannonballs went crashing into the woods, Platt ordered Upton to move the battery forward and to the right, only about 600 yards from the edge of the woods. Once deployed on this new line, his battery fired five rounds of spherical case shot into the trees. These rounds were anti-personnel explosive projectiles containing small iron balls wrapped around a powder charge. As soon as these shells landed in the woods, the enemy infantry retreated, and the skirmishing ended. Captain Richard Arnold, Franklin's Chief of Artillery, commended Upton's actions, stating that "the accurate firing of shell from the battery commanded by Lieutenant Upton ... contributed greatly to the repulse of the enemy, and gave all our troops on this flank increased confidence."[15]

The Seven Days Battles

As the month of May progressed, McClellan slowly moved his army forward in what had come to be called the Peninsula Campaign. In response to the Federal advance, General Joe Johnston, the Confederate commander, steadily gave way and retreated with his outnumbered army back towards Richmond. By May 15, the lead elements of the Army of the Potomac crossed the Chickahominy River, the final natural obstacle between them and Richmond. All

Alfred Waud's sketch of the Battle of Gaines' Mill (Library of Congress).

McClellan needed to do was get the rest of the army over the river and bring his large siege guns into range to shell the Confederate capital.

But the Federal advance soon slowed as a fortnight of heavy rain filled the Chickahominy, making it difficult for the army to cross the river and transforming the few decent roads into muddy bogs. Despite these challenges, most of the Army of the Potomac managed to cross the river at Bottom's Bridge on May 20, placing the entire army, less General Porter's V Corp, a mere 15 miles from Richmond. However, now, with success so close, McClellan's lingering fears got the better of him, as they would repeatedly do during his wartime service. Insisting that the enemy outnumbered his army, he halted his men and requested reinforcements.

With part of McClellan's army north of the Chickahominy and the rest to the south, Johnston decided to attack the divided Union forces. He advanced and assaulted the two Union corps south of the river on May 31, near the town of Seven Pines. While the Confederates managed to inflict some damage, McClellan's men held, causing the Rebels to fall back to Richmond's defenses. But the battle still proved critical to the outcome of the campaign and even the course of the war itself. During the fighting, Johnston was badly wounded, and Jefferson Davis ordered his personal military advisor, General Robert E. Lee, to assume command of the Confederacy's Army of Northern Virginia.

During the initial fighting, Upton and his battery had not participated in the battle. But that would soon change. Weeks passed, and McClellan eventually managed to shift two additional corps south of the Chickahominy. By late June, his army still sat in place and remained divided by the river, with one isolated corps on the far side of the Chickahominy. Here, Lee first demonstrated his desire to always seek the initiative. The new Southern commander decided to use the same geographic advantage that Joe Johnston observed a month before. If he could attack the isolated Union V Corps under General Porter north of the river, he might force McClellan back, and make sure those heavy siege guns did not come within range of Richmond.

On the morning of June 27, Upton's battery was camped south of the Chickahominy with the rest of XI Corps, anchoring the right flank of the army on that side of the river. Two miles to their right on the north side of the river, Porter had positioned his V Corps to protect the bridges across the river. He placed his men in a good defensive position near a grist mill called Gaines' Mill. He aligned men on top of a plateau facing northwest in a semicircle, with the swampy ground around a small creek to their front.

Everything was quiet, and the morning "broke hot and sultry."[16] About mid-morning, Porter could see Lee's army approaching from the north. "The dust from the immense columns of the enemy could be seen for miles," he later wrote, "and soon our scouts and pickets warned us that they were extending over our whole front."[17]

About 2:00 p.m., Confederate skirmishers from General A.P. Hill's corps began to move forward, engaging their Union counterparts. Thirty minutes later, Confederate artillery opened up with a "warm fire," and Hill's infantry attacked across the left and center of Porter's defensive line. The terrain was difficult for the attacking Confederates to cross and by 3:30 p.m., Hill's troops fell back to regroup. As the attackers withdrew, Porter could see two additional enemy corps under General Richard Ewell and General D.H. Hill coming into position opposite the center and right of his line. Realizing he was about to become badly outnumbered, Porter sent an urgent dispatch to McClellan requesting reinforcement by "all available troops."[18]

When Porter's request arrived at the army's headquarters, McClellan already had men moving to Porter's assistance. Around 2:00 p.m., he ordered General Franklin to send the First

Division of the XI Corps, now under the command of General Henry Slocum, across the river immediately. Slocum quickly had General Newton's brigade moving to cross via Alexander's Bridge, which was about two miles to the rear of Porter's line, and he ordered Upton to move his battery across the river in support of Newton's infantry.[19]

By 3:00 p.m., Slocum's entire division was north of the river and moving up to support Porter. Slocum rode to meet with Porter, who began to divide Slocum's forces and send them to various positions along his line. As for Upton, he was told to move his battery to a position about a quarter of a mile behind the center of the Union line and prepare for action. Once there, he could see that he had an almost perfect vantage point. From his position, Upton could make out the entire Union main line to his front as well as the 11th Pennsylvania Reserve Infantry Regiment, which was in position about 100 yards to his left-center. Looking to his right, he saw two batteries of the 3rd U.S. Artillery under Captain John Edwards approximately one-quarter mile away, while the 10th Pennsylvania Reserve Infantry Regiment waited in reserve along a road 50 yards to Upton's rear.[20]

After an hour or more of relative quiet, Lee began a second attack on Porter, and Upton watched it begin through his field glasses. Whatever the assault lacked in sophistication, it

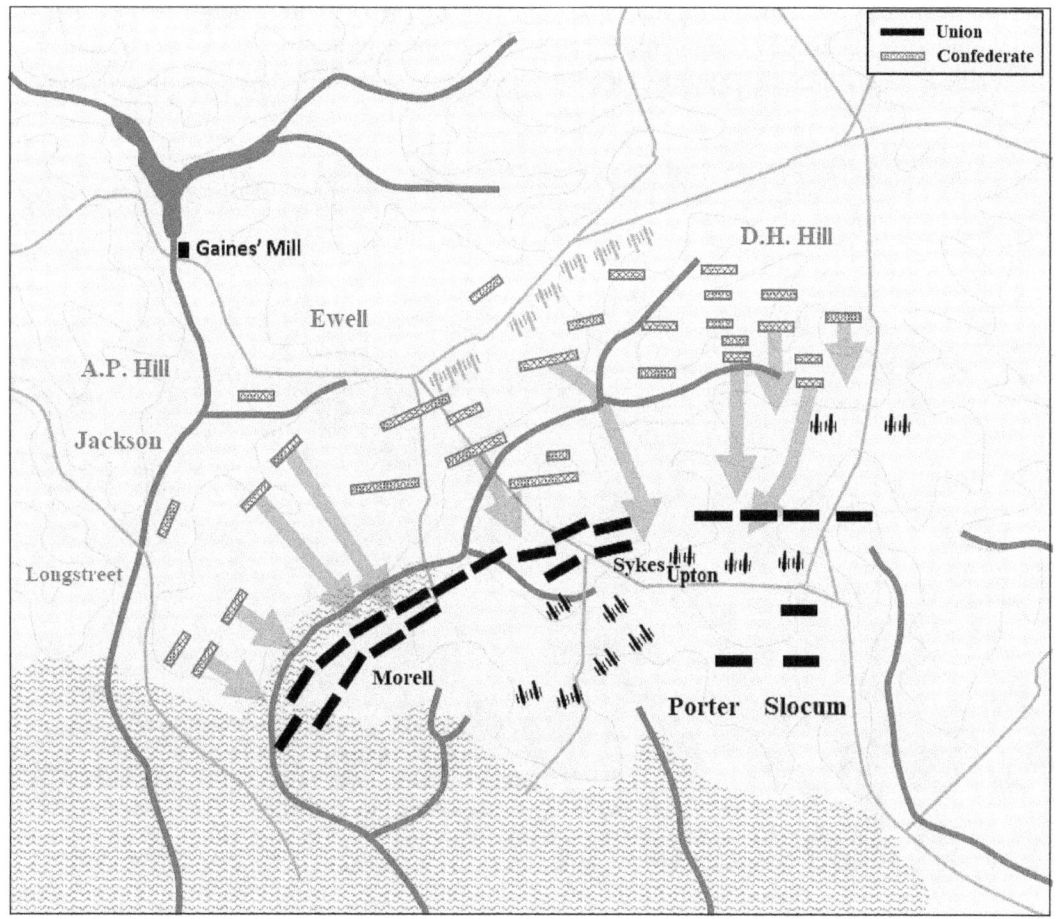

The Battle of Gaines' Mill, June 27, 1862 (drawn by the author).

made up for in brute force. One soldier described the attack, saying, "The shot and shell now began to fly in rather dangerous proximity, and the rushing sound they made was anything but agreeable music."[21] As Ewell's men advanced toward the center of the Union line and Federal artillery batteries began to respond, Upton ordered his men to open fire with spherical case shot. Despite an increasing shroud of smoke over the battlefield, Upton could see the appalling carnage his guns were causing on Ewell's advancing infantry. His battery kept up a steady fire until 4:30 p.m. when this latest Confederate assault lost steam.

However, around 6:00 p.m., when all three enemy corps pressed forward together in yet another attack, the Union line began to break. Upton barked out orders and moved from gun to gun urging his battery to increase the pace of its fire. As the Union troops began to fall back steadily, some of the rounds passed just over their heads, and the "shrieks of the balls through the air were continuous."[22] As the advancing Confederate troops closed in, Upton switched to canister rounds. These shells consisted of metal cans packed with iron balls that exploded outward from the can upon firing. They essentially turned Upton's 12-pound Napoleon cannons into massive shotguns, and their effect on infantry was often devastating.

However, nothing it seemed was going to stop the Confederate attack. At this point, all Upton and his battery could do was to slow down the tidal wave of the enemy advance. The Union infantry pulled out of the line rapidly and retreated towards the bridges over the Chickahominy. As the battery's ammunition began to run out, Upton ordered his men to limber up the guns, and he quickly moved his battery towards the rear with the rest of the retreating

Alfred Waud's sketch of the Union army burning its supplies before retreating to the James River (Library of Congress).

troops. As they fell back, the scene he saw was one typical of every retreat as a dense mass of stragglers and the wounded moved continually to the rear towards the bridges and safety.[23]

Once across the river, Upton took count and found he had five men wounded and one missing in his battery.[24] Other batteries had fared much worse, and more than one had been lost entirely during the battle with the Confederates capturing a total of 22 Federal guns.[25] As he took stock of his men's condition and obtained a new supply of ammunition, Upton learned the army would not be holding its position on the outskirts of Richmond.

Even though his men had fought well at Gaines' Mill, and he outnumbered Lee's army by more than 40,000 men, McClellan persisted in believing he faced a larger enemy force. As a result, he saw nothing but disaster looming ahead. In McClellan's mind, the only sensible option was to begin a retreat all the way back to the banks of the James River, where Federal gunboats could protect the army. On June 28, the Army of the Potomac began falling back to Harrison's Landing, some 20 miles to the south. When Upton and the rest of the soldiers in the army learned they were to retreat from the doorsteps of Richmond, most were dismayed.

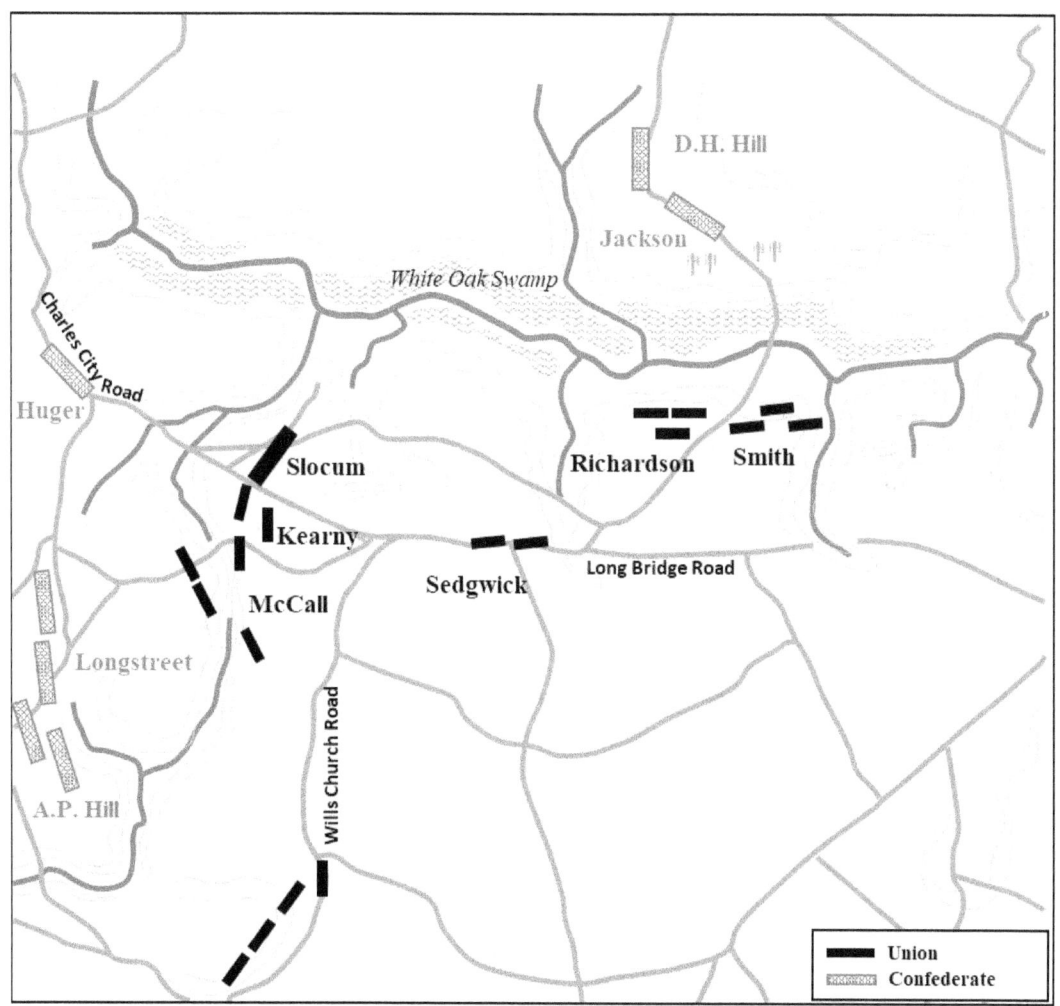

The Battle of Glendale, June 30, 1862 (drawn by the author).

They did not feel they had been defeated. As one veteran later recalled, "It was a time of humiliation and sorrow."[26]

At 11:00 p.m. that night, Upton's battery began moving southeast down the road towards Savage Station. McClellan's orders were to abandon everything that could not be carried. So as the battery moved off, it passed through a scene of utter desolation. Food and supplies littered the ground; stores burned in great bonfires; and tents were piled in heaps, having been cut to pieces first. Rather than appearing like an orderly withdrawal, it looked more like "a retreat under most disastrous circumstances."[27]

All night, Upton observed a seemingly endless stream of wagons, artillery, ambulances, and columns of men moving in parallel across the fields and down the roads away from the Chickahominy. Here and there, the soldiers mixed in with thousands of cattle driven through the woods next to the roads. When Upton and his men reached Savage Station around 5:00 a.m. on June 29, they found complete confusion. Supply trains and troops crowded together, and officers issued orders for the destruction of even more supplies before moving on. Worse, someone had decided that the wounded were slowing the army down. The medical staff collected all the sick and wounded unable to walk or ride in a field next to the road where they were left for the enemy's care. Men could be seen making sad farewells to their wounded friends before moving on to the south towards White Oak Swamp and the town of Glendale.[28]

The XI Corps split up, using two roughly parallel roads out of Savage Station. Upton's battery and Slocum's division made their way down the western road as a small rear guard remained behind to fight off the Confederates pursuing the army. The road was packed with wagons, ambulances, and artillery, all mixed in with cavalry and infantry. Everyone moved as fast as possible, and the sounds of enemy gunfire to the rear spurred them along. The resulting pace was brutal as the army marched throughout the day. The ground surrounding the roadway was nothing but impenetrable marshland, which added to the misery. One officer later called it "a terribly dreary pilgrimage," adding, "The heat was almost insupportable; there was not a breath of air, and we suffered intensely for the want of water, of which none could be had but the black, stagnant water of the swamp through which we were wading."[29]

At 2:00 p.m., Upton's battery and the remainder of Slocum's division crossed White Oak Swamp and took up positions along the Charles City Road northeast of Glendale near the farm of the Frazier family. The next morning, June 30, General Slocum received word that D.H. Hill's corps was advancing towards the division's position. He formed his command into the line of battle and deployed Upton's Battery D in support along with two volunteer batteries. With infantry posted on either flank of the three batteries, Upton and his men waited for the Confederate attack.[30]

Just before 11:00 a.m., Upton heard sporadic rifle fire to the division's immediate front. Within a few minutes, Union skirmishers emerged from a tree line on the far side of the large open field to the division's front and ran back towards the main Union defensive line. No sooner had the skirmishers arrived within Slocum's lines than a solid wall of Confederate infantry appeared behind them, advancing steadily across the field. Then the loud bark of Confederate artillery was heard, and their shells came screaming toward Upton and the other Union troops. As the first rounds exploded, Upton quickly estimated the range to the enemy batteries and ordered his gunners to return fire. Upton's men kept up a steady rate of fire, causing the enemy infantry to veer off to the left towards the positions defended by Generals Kearny and McCall.

For the rest of the afternoon, Upton's battery dueled with the Confederate guns at long range, but few casualties resulted on either side.[31]

About 7:00 p.m. that evening, Slocum ordered Upton to move his battery forward along with Colonel Bartlett's infantry brigade to take possession of the field in front of the division. Upton mounted his horse and told his men to limber up the guns and move forward quickly. As soon as his battery and Bartlett's infantry began advancing, a strong line of enemy infantry appeared from the trees and took up a position along a creek that divided the field. Seeing this, Upton ordered his men to drive their caissons forward and set up between the Union and Confederate infantry. His men whipped their horses and followed their commander, who galloped ahead to indicate where he wanted the battery placed. Within minutes, his men passed the lines of Union infantry, unlimbered their guns, and set up for action. Upton shouted at the gun crews to load canister rounds and, at his command; they unleashed a deadly fusillade on the line of gray- and butternut-clad Southern infantry. As the iron balls blasted into the enemy, their men fell in dozens, with huge gaps opening in their line. Only a few minutes had passed before what had been "well-formed" lines of infantry broke up and disappeared as the Confederate soldiers fled to safety.[32]

Upton's quick thinking and initiative had saved the lives of many of Bartlett's infantry. General Slocum wrote in his report to General Franklin, "Of Upton's battery.... I cannot speak

Cartoon lampooning McClellan's shipboard command during the Battle of Malvern Hill (Library of Congress).

too highly," adding that his actions and those of his men "manifested that coolness and bravery so necessary to this branch of the service."[33]

Union forces managed to hold off attacks by both D.H. Hill and Longstreet at Glendale before continuing their retreat south towards the James River. At dawn on July 1, Upton saw the broad, majestic river ahead, and he likely experienced a sense of relief, as did many soldiers in the XI Corps. George Stevens, a VI Corps surgeon, remembered that, upon seeing the James ahead, "every man took a long breath, as though relieved of a heavy load of anxiety."[34] Upton's battery pulled off the road as the corps filed into a broad field of clover for a rest. His men watered and fed the horses and found time to lie down briefly in the grass to nap. But the rest was short-lived. Dispatch riders arrived around mid-morning with orders to move south and form into a new line of battle.

As the lead elements of the Army of the Potomac had arrived at the James River, they took positions on a plateau called Malvern Hill, which stood about 150 feet above the plains to the north. The ground sloped gently away from the hilltop to the north and east, but deep ravines filled the approach. The only way an attacking force could assault the hill was by following the roads that crossed the ravines. The terrain and roads would essentially funnel any attacking force down narrow corridors where Union defenders could sweep them with fire, and that is what the Federals prepared to do.

They lined the crest of Malvern Hill with more than 300 pieces of artillery, supplemented by thousands of Union infantry arrayed just below them, hidden from view amid wheat and corn fields. The IV Corps and V Corps held the line on the left and center of Malvern Hill, respectively, with the III Corps to their immediate right. Upton and the rest of XI Corps moved through the woods, crossed a stream, and formed up in a wheat field on the far right of the line.[35]

At 2:30 p.m., Lee's entire army launched their attack, focusing on the positions of IV and V Corps. Some elements of the Confederate army moved around to the Union right opposite Upton's position, but the fighting there consisted mainly of brief skirmishes in which Upton's guns traded shots with distant enemy batteries. To the left, however, things were very different. Lee sent wave after wave of his men up Malvern Hill into the face of Union artillery as well as barrages from long range guns on Union vessels in the James River. In describing the resulting slaughter of Lee's troops, one soldier wrote in his diary, "O, the horrors of this day's work," adding, "The battle of today is beyond description."[36]

The fighting lasted until sundown when the firing died away at last. As the sounds of cannon fire and explosions faded, Upton heard cheering erupt as Union soldiers watched Lee's army fall back in complete disorder. As for McClellan, he spent the entire battle aboard a navy warship in the James River, communicating his orders by signal flags from safety. Once the battle ended, he came ashore and rode his horse along the line, so his men could cheer him. This command style, in which some generals led from the safety of the rear, was one Upton would often see in the years ahead, and it was a practice that drew his increasing ire.[37]

The army remained in position at Malvern Hill the next day before marching off for the final leg of the retreat to Harrison's Landing on the James. When they arrived, McClellan directed each corps to a separate camp area along the river, which was filled with gunboats and transport ships of all shapes and sizes. Upton's battery made camp and placed their guns in defensive positions along the perimeter, awaiting an enemy attack that never came. Despite the resounding victory at Malvern Hill, McClellan refused to resume the offensive. Instead, his army languished by the river into August, with disease spread by bad water and mosquitoes taking a heavy toll among his troops.

Upton was among those struck down by illness. In late July, he contracted typhoid fever, and his condition became so serious, that the regimental surgeon sent him home to Batavia to convalesce. The doctor gave him a leave of 20 days but, when the time approached for his return to duty, the family physician in Batavia told Upton he was too weak to do so. The doctor wrote out a certificate requesting an additional 20 days of leave, which Upton forwarded to the Adjutant General in Washington.[38]

Lee, meanwhile, moved most of his army to the northeast and began moving towards Washington in late August. McClellan finally ordered his army to embark aboard ship and return to the capital and, on August 23, 1862, the XI Corps arrived at the docks in Alexandria.[39] A week later, Lee soundly defeated another major Union army under the command of General John Pope at the Battle of Second Manassas, and Pope's troops fled back to the defenses of Washington. Many in the Lincoln administration accused McClellan of purposely delaying his army's arrival in Washington so that it could not support Pope, ensuring a second humiliating defeat at Manassas. As a result, Lincoln removed McClellan from his position as commander of the Army of the Potomac.

Meanwhile, Upton recovered faster than his doctor predicted, and he returned to his battery in Alexandria on September 5. However, when he arrived, he discovered that, while he was in Batavia, the army had issued an order prohibiting the extension of sick leaves. Technically, he had been absent without leave for 11 days. Hoping to avoid any disciplinary action, Upton decided to write a letter to President Lincoln explaining his absence, stating that he returned to duty as quickly as his health allowed. It must have worked because the entire issue was quickly forgotten.[40]

As it turned out, McClellan's absence from the Army of the Potomac was brief. On September 5, 1862, Lee moved his army across the Potomac and into Maryland, launching his first invasion of the North. Lincoln ordered McClellan to resume command of the army and move immediately to stop Lee.

At the same time, Upton also received a change of assignment and undertook his first major command responsibility.

4

Antietam

> I have heard of the "dead lying in heaps" but never saw it till at this battle.
> Emory Upton, September 27, 1862[1]

In early September 1862, as McClellan mobilized the Army of the Potomac once more, Upton received a brevet promotion to Captain for his service during the Peninsula Campaign. Along with the promotion in rank came the assignment as commander of the Artillery Brigade, First Division, XI Corps. Upton now commanded four batteries totaling 24 guns and over 400 men whose job it was to support the First Division's 13 regiments of infantry. His batteries included the Maryland Light Artillery, Massachusetts Light Artillery, and New Jersey Light Artillery, along with his old command, Battery D of the 2nd U.S. Artillery.[2] However, Upton had only a few days to get acquainted with his new command. On the evening of September 6, orders arrived to immediately begin marching north into Maryland from the XI Corps camps around Alexandria.[3]

A Bold Strategy

Robert E. Lee's decision to invade the North in September 1862 was the product of his success against both McClellan and Pope, as well as what he saw as critical timing. Having pushed McClellan back from Richmond and defeated Pope at Second Manassas, the always audacious Confederate general saw an opportunity, one he hoped might change the course of the war and cause the Lincoln administration to enter peace negotiations.

Lee had utterly demoralized the Union armies of both Pope and McClellan, and the command situation in Washington was confused. McClellan and the Army of the Potomac had returned up the Chesapeake, and McClellan had been relieved of command. Lee felt that he needed to gain another major victory and do so now while his enemy seemed ripe for defeat. If he did not destroy the Army of the Potomac in the process, then he would almost certainly destroy the will of the Northern people to continue to fight. This loss of willpower would, in turn, allow the war to end quickly before the passage of time exposed the Confederacy's disadvantages in manpower and resources.

Lee also understood the political reasons for exploiting the opportunity he had in front of him. November would bring a new round of congressional elections in the North, and another crushing defeat might spur the election of more anti-war Democrats to the Congress. If these Democrats controlled the Congress, they could press the Lincoln administration to pursue a peaceful end to the conflict. Also, President Davis was anxious to gain recognition and possibly direct military support from either France or Great Britain. Another crushing Union defeat might bring that recognition closer to reality.

However, Lee was uncertain which way to move his army. Lee could see that his army was tired from a summer of fighting and badly in need of resupply. Union forces had stripped northern Virginia of food and supplies, so he must look elsewhere. Lee knew he could retire south and take up positions on the far side of the Rappahannock River, which would allow him to rest, resupply, and reorganize his army. But this would also allow Union forces time to reorganize, and the enemy might see it as a sign that Lee and his army were incapable of sustained operations in the field. Worst of all, perhaps, it would mean surrendering the initiative Lee had fought so hard to retain all summer. While Lee knew his army of 75,000 men was nearly exhausted, he also knew that their morale was high and that they were flush with victory. Meanwhile, his opponents hid behind Washington's fortifications, demoralized by defeat.

Lee believed he had to act and to do so with some speed. He quickly examined his options and decided that a move into Maryland offered the best chance of success. Lee envisioned a grand turning movement whose primary effects would be political and psychological. For the first time, Confederate forces would cross into Northern soil, threatening not only Washington, but also Harrisburg, Baltimore, and Philadelphia. This would spread panic in the North and almost certainly lead to demands that the Army of the Potomac leave the safety of the fortifications around Washington and attempt to expel the invader from Maryland. Lee hoped they would do exactly that and do so before the Union army was really prepared to fight.

Also, the invasion would allow Lee to resupply his army off the ripe fields of Maryland and possibly Pennsylvania, and, by drawing Union forces north, allow northern Virginia time to recover from Federal occupation. At the same time, Lee's army could interrupt the westward movement of Union supplies along the Chesapeake and Ohio Canal as well as the vital Baltimore and Ohio Railroad.

More importantly, however, Lee could retain the initiative, keep Union forces off balance, and force them to fight at a time and place of Lee's choosing. A resulting Southern victory on Northern soil would be seen as another indication of the North's impotence on the battlefield while demonstrating their inability to even defend their home ground. This could severely damage Union morale to the point that the North could not sustain the war effort against the South.

Moving Against the Invaders

Before midnight on September 6, Upton's new brigade was on the move. After quickly packing supplies, feeding and watering the horses, and limbering up the guns, his 400 men rode out of camp in Alexandria and moved north towards Washington. They crossed the Potomac via the Long Bridge, and one soldier remembered that, as the batteries crossed the river, the moon and stars shone "with a brilliancy seldom equaled, rendering the night march a pleasant one."[4] As the steady tramp of the soldiers' feet and the rumbling of wagons filled the night, hundreds of Washington's citizens crowded onto the sidewalks to watch the army pass. Many of them called out to the soldiers asking about their destination. But the only answer provided was "We are going to meet the rebels."[5]

The brigade moved through Georgetown before reaching the small village of Tenleytown (present-day section of the District of Columbia near the intersection of Nebraska Avenue

Northwest and Wisconsin Avenue Northwest). Here, Upton ordered the brigade to halt and rest for the remainder of the night. The brigade spent a quiet night and morning at Tenleytown, as orders to move onward to the north did not arrive until almost 5:00 p.m. that evening. But the march was a short one of only six miles. Once again, the entire army halted for the night. At daybreak on September 8, the army began moving again, passing through Rockville, Maryland, where they stopped after another easy march of six miles.

The main reason for these stops and starts was the lack of intelligence on Lee's move-

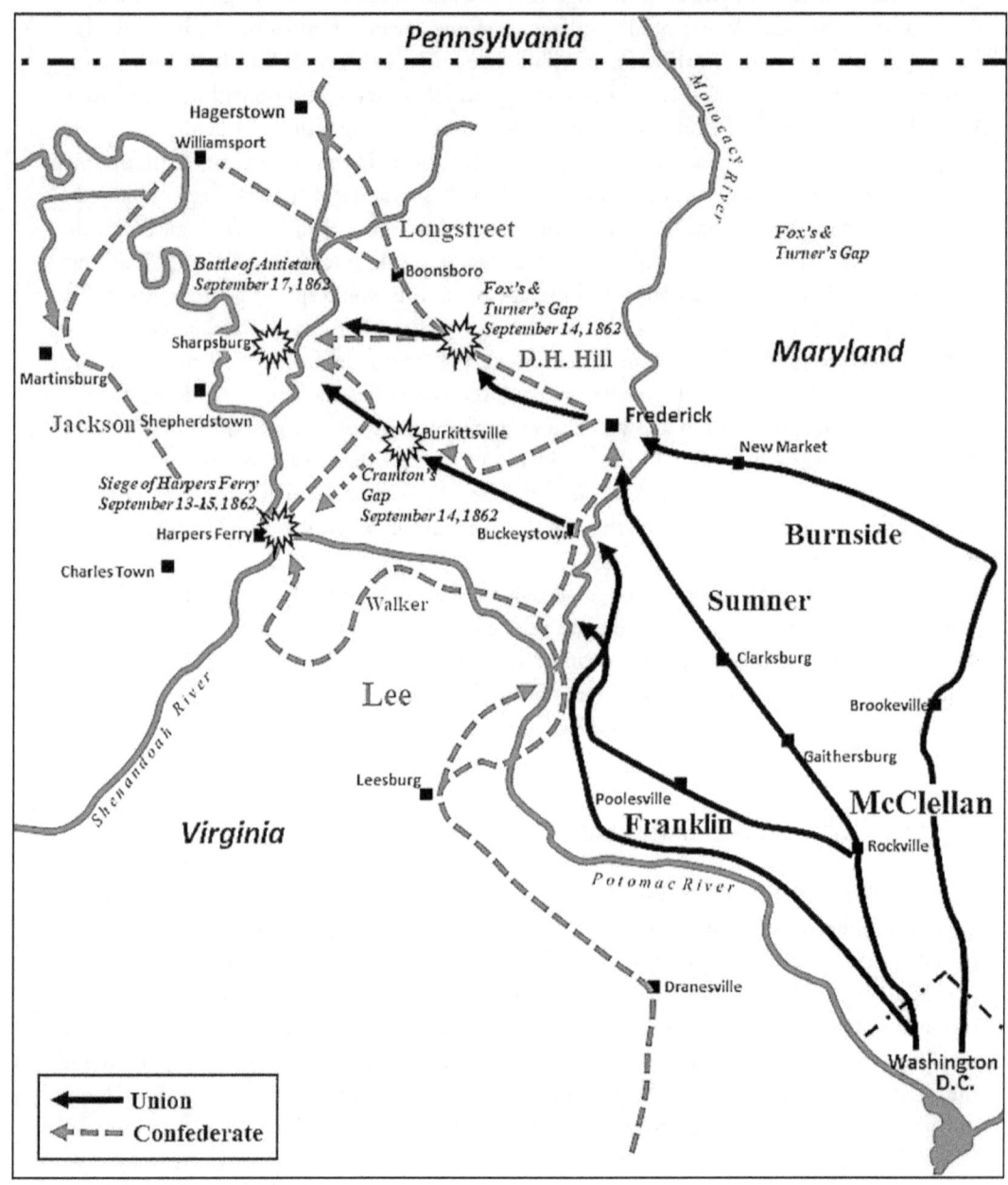

The Maryland Campaign, September 1862 (drawn by the author).

ments. McClellan had to be ready to counter potential enemy advances towards Washington, Baltimore, Harrisburg, and Philadelphia. So, he hesitated to commit to a plan until he had reliable information on Lee's precise location. In the meantime, he would have the Army of the Potomac probe steadily towards Frederick, Maryland, some 25 miles northwest of Rockville. Unknown to McClellan, Lee and his army were currently encamped at Frederick, where the Confederate general awaited word on the location of the Union army from his cavalry commander, the legendary General J.E.B. Stuart, as well as any intelligence on the Union garrison at Harpers Ferry, Virginia.

Almost as soon as the Army of Northern Virginia crossed the Potomac at White's Ford north of Leesburg, Virginia and moved into Maryland, Lee realized he had potential issues regarding his lines of communication. These lines were the pathways and routes for not only communications with Richmond but also resupply of his army and a potential path for retreat if the situation dictated. Any lines of communication east of the Blue Ridge would not be viable, as Union forces from Washington could quickly move out to cut them. So, Lee decided that his lines of communication must run west of the Blue Ridge through the Shenandoah Valley. This line, once securely established, would allow him to eventually move into western Maryland, thereby threatening Pennsylvania, and require that the responding Union army move further and further from its base of supply in Washington, lengthening its own lines of communication and making them vulnerable to attack.

But the problem with establishing any lines of communication in the Shenandoah was the presence of a Federal garrison of 12,000 men at Harpers Ferry. Nevertheless, as the campaign began, Lee was unconcerned with Harpers Ferry, as he was certain that, as soon as the Army of Northern Virginia crossed into Maryland, the Union garrison would abandon its position to prevent being cut off and isolated.

As his army pressed northward, Lee was also relying upon the Lincoln administration to provide a commander who would move out quickly from Washington and offer openings for Lee to conduct a campaign of maneuver. Lee assumed this commander would be John Pope. He had already seen Pope's inability to manage a large army properly, and he was justifiably confident he could manipulate Pope into a position where the Army of the Potomac could be destroyed.

But this assumption demonstrates the first in a series of flaws in Lee's intelligence information. Pope was in disgrace and, even as Lee crossed the Potomac into Maryland, George McClellan's return to command was already being openly discussed in Washington. While Lee felt confident fighting either Union general, he was unaware of these events. As McClellan's army camped outside Rockville, Lee had no idea the Union army was so close, much less that it was headed for Frederick with McClellan back at its head. As a result, Lee remained quietly confident that he and his army were in no immediate danger.

Meanwhile, Upton and the rest of XI Corps languished until September 12, when they marched ten miles to the Monocacy Bridge north of Urbana, Maryland. The next day, they received orders to move northwest to the town of Jefferson, where they encountered a small detachment of Lee's men and quickly drove them off.[6] The presence of the enemy was a surprise, but not the only one for Union forces. Late the previous afternoon, advance elements of the Union army entered Frederick where they fought a brief battle with skirmishers from Lee's army. After the Confederate skirmishers had withdrawn, Union officers discovered that Lee had been there since September 6 and had only left two days earlier on September 10.

But the biggest surprise came on September 13. On that day, a Union soldier discovered a small envelope containing three cigars wrapped in a piece of paper. He was likely delighted by his good fortune at finding some cigars, but he soon found a treasure even more valuable. The piece of paper wrapping the cigars was a copy of Special Order 191 issued by Robert E. Lee on September 9.

After the soldier delivered the order to his commanding officer, Union generals read it and learned that Lee had divided his army. Despite the objections of Generals Jackson and Longstreet, Lee had sent Jackson southwest with 38,000 men to subdue the garrison at Harpers Ferry while he took the remaining 28,000 men west over the mountains towards Hagerstown. Lee was certain that, as soon as Jackson arrived at Harpers Ferry, the Union troops stationed there would surrender. Jackson could then cross the Potomac into western Maryland and rejoin Lee, allowing the entire Confederate army to advance into Pennsylvania.

But as the Union army entered Frederick on September 12, Lee learned that the garrison at Harpers Ferry had not surrendered, and on September 13, his cavalry informed him that the Army of the Potomac had entered Frederick with George McClellan again in command. The first piece of news was irritating to Lee but the second genuinely shocked him. With his army divided and the enemy so close, Lee was dangerously vulnerable. He immediately turned his portion of the army around and moved to defend the passes through the South Mountain Range of the Blue Ridge, hoping to delay the Army of the Potomac until Jackson's troops could join him.

With Lee's orders in his hand, McClellan saw the opportunity in front of him. Although he still believed that Lee's army outnumbered his own, McClellan now knew that the enemy

Alfred Waud's sketch of the Army of the Potomac marching to the South Mountain passes through Middleton, Maryland (Library of Congress).

army was divided. He realized he must attack and defeat Lee before Jackson could leave Harpers Ferry and rejoin his commander. Lee, meanwhile, planned to hold McClellan at bay by defending the passes through the mountains. Once the Federal garrison at Harpers Ferry had surrendered, Lee would reunite his army at Sharpsburg, Maryland on the northern banks of the Potomac and proceed onward to Hagerstown, still free to maneuver until he could get the Army of the Potomac where he wanted it.

Unfortunately for Lee, there were five passes to defend, four of them within a five-mile front. He spread his forces among them, but McClellan wisely chose to focus his attention on only three: Turner's Gap and Fox's Gap, which were only about a half-mile apart, plus Crampton's Gap, which was six miles to the south. McClellan moved with uncharacteristic swiftness and, on September 14, Upton's battery accompanied XI Corps as it attacked Crampton's Gap while the remainder of the Army of the Potomac assaulted Turner's and Fox's Gaps.

Crampton's Gap

Upton's artillery advanced along with the rest of the corps to within a mile and a half of the pass before coming to a halt just before 6:00 a.m. With the sun rising behind him, he could see the green, heavily wooded South Mountains towering over the white houses that marked the small village of Burkittsville. From the town, a narrow road wound up the side of the mountains to Crampton's Gap. Despite the heavy foliage, he could see Confederate batteries and infantry posted behind fences and barricades, blocking the passage over the mountains. Just beyond the town at the foot of the mountains, Upton could make out the enemy's first defensive line, a stone wall defended by Confederate infantry. All in all, it was a formidable defensive position.[7]

General Franklin ordered an attack to begin about 3:00 p.m. with Upton's artillery brigade to support Slocum's division as it advanced up the right side of the road into the pass. As soon as the leading lines of Union infantry emerged from the cover of the woods and advanced on the stone wall, Confederate artillery opened fire on them. One veteran wrote, "The mountains, like huge volcanoes, belched forth fire and smoke. The earth trembled beneath us, and the air was filled with the howling of shells which flew over our heads, and ploughed [sic] the earth at our feet."[8] Upton's artillery, which was posted to the rear, tried to return their fire and silence them but the enemy guns were well hidden in the trees on the mountainside. Slocum then sent word for Upton to send one battery forward to help with the attack on the stone wall. But before the battery was in position, the Union infantry had taken the wall, and the Confederate defenders "were fleeing in confusion up the mountain, closely pursued by every regiment of the division."[9]

As the Federal infantrymen rapidly advanced up the mountainside, the Confederates reformed at the crest and attempted to make a stand. But Slocum's infantry quickly overwhelmed them, and the Confederate troops fled in panic down the west side of the mountains, retreating rapidly away across the plains on the far side.

As Upton and his artillery brigade followed, he witnessed the appalling signs of battle that demonstrated the new standard of death and destruction this war was establishing. While Upton had seen the battlefields at Manassas and on the Virginia Peninsula, this was the first time he had viewed one immediately after a battle. The dead littered the road and the narrow fields, and woods to either side and "great care was required ... to avoid treading upon the lifeless remains which lay thickly upon the ground."[10] Daniel Holt, an assistant surgeon with the 121st

New York Infantry, wrote his wife that he saw one Confederate soldier lying by the road "with his brains blown out, arms extended, and eyes protruding from their sockets," while others lay nearby "in all manner of positions—some not yet dead but gasping the few remaining breaths away in utter unconsciousness of surrounding circumstances—others mortally wounded calling for water."[11] Upton and his men could also see trees that were "literally cut to pieces by shells and bullets" as well as hundreds of enemy wounded and prisoners lining the roadside, "while knapsacks, guns, canteens, and haversacks were scattered in great confusion."[12]

Meanwhile, the rest of the Army of the Potomac achieved similar results to the north, quickly forcing both Turner's and Fox's Gaps and routing the Confederate defenders. Lee was appalled by this turn of events, and his adjutant general recorded, "The day has gone against us."[13] Lee now faced a new reality, and it was one of seeming disaster. He immediately ordered his part of the army to move south to Sharpsburg and retreat across the Potomac into Virginia. He also sent a dispatch to Jackson telling him to abandon operations against Harpers Ferry and to move to Shepherdstown, Virginia, opposite Sharpsburg, so that he could cover the Potomac crossing.[14]

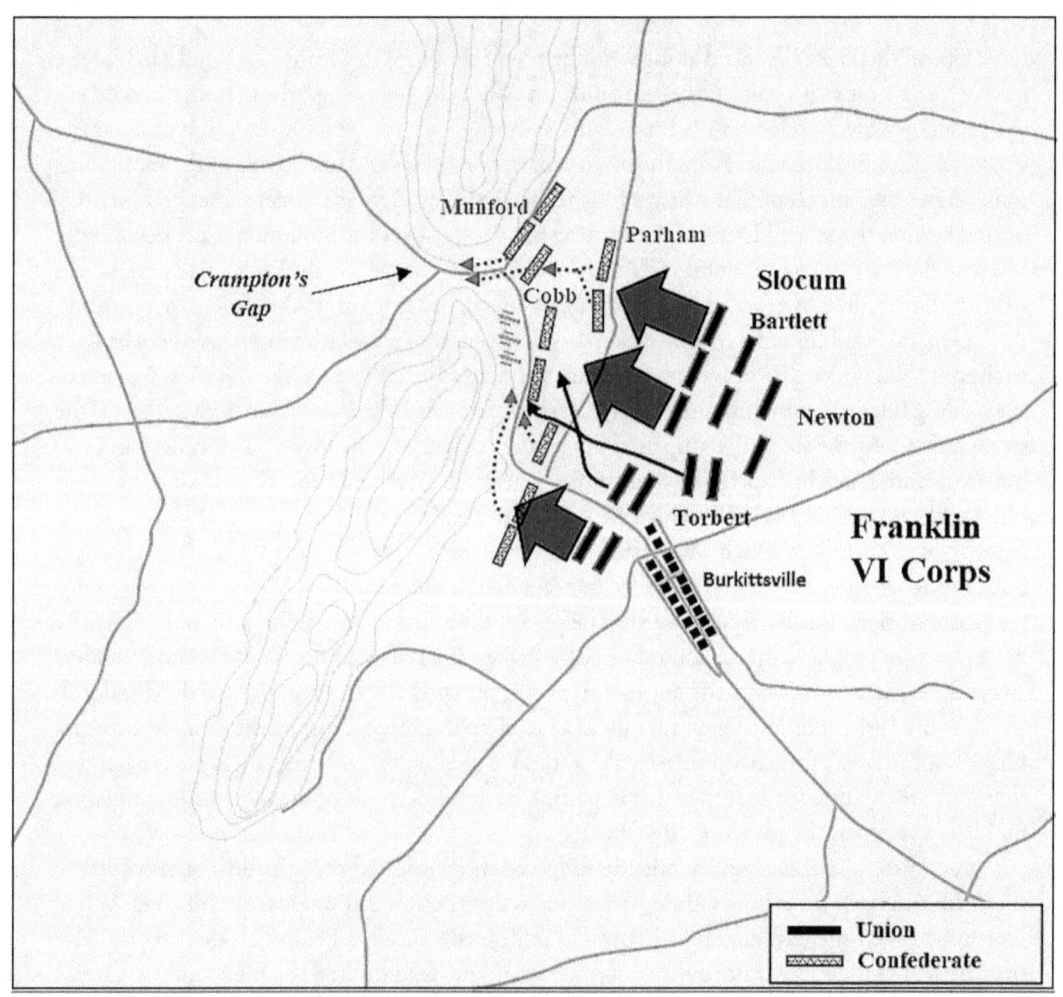

The Battle of Crampton's Gap, September 14, 1862 (drawn by the author).

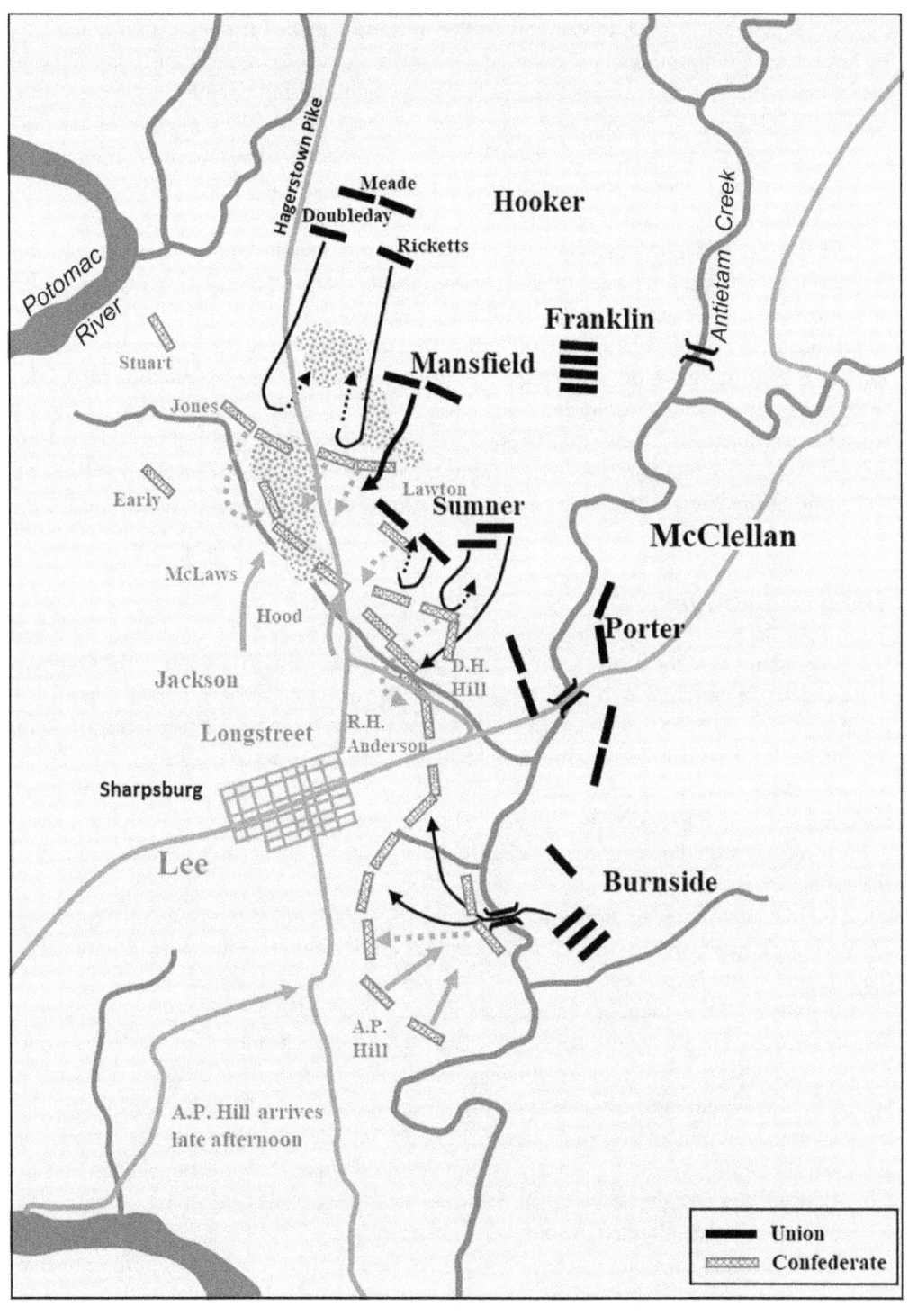

The Battle of Antietam, September 17, 1862 (drawn by the author).

On September 15, as Upton and his artillery brigade remained encamped in Pleasant Valley just west of Crampton's Gap, Lee arrived in Sharpsburg and began preparing to move across the Potomac into Virginia. But as Lee was enjoying a morning cup of coffee, a dispatch rider arrived from Harpers Ferry with a message from General Jackson. The message told Lee that Jackson expected the Union garrison to fall later that day. Suddenly, Lee saw a new opportunity. If he could make a defensive stand at Sharpsburg until Jackson could join him, he might then extract himself, move toward Hagerstown, and regain the initiative.[15]

That same day, Upton and XI Corps received orders to march south seven miles to Harpers Ferry and end Jackson's siege of the garrison. As the corps prepared to break camp, the booming of artillery could clearly be heard from the south, and the men knew Jackson must be pressing his attack on Harpers Ferry. Before the march to relieve the beleaguered Federal garrison began, the sounds of cannon fire in the distance stopped. General Franklin ordered the corps to hold its position until he determined what had happened. Within hours, a reconnaissance force returned with news that Union forces had surrendered, and Jackson was moving most of his corps to join with Lee at Sharpsburg. The XI Corps returned to camp at Pleasant Valley and awaited new orders while the rest of the Army of the Potomac converged on Lee.[16]

The Bloodiest Day

Lee did not have the best of positions at Sharpsburg. His army's back was to the Potomac River and, while he was able to take up a defensive line on a low set of hills, he did not have enough men to close his flanks against the banks of the river. Lee hoped that Jackson would join him early on September 16, which would be soon enough to allow the army to move west before it was confronted by the bulk of McClellan's army. But by the time Jackson arrived and took up positions on Lee's defensive line late that afternoon, the Army of the Potomac arrived in full force. Lee would now have to give battle, and his last real chance to maneuver and regain the initiative was lost.

The XI Corps received orders to move west to Sharpsburg before dawn on September 17. As Upton's men marched, they could clearly hear artillery and rifle fire in the distance. The fighting at Sharpsburg had begun.

In some ways, one could not have picked a more unlikely place for a bloody, pivotal battle. The area surrounding the small village of Sharpsburg was serene, beautiful, and lush. Antietam Creek wound about the town before flowing into the Potomac, its three bridges often serving as sites for local children to swim and play on hot summer days. As XI Corps approached the battlefield, they looked down from a nearby hill on what one officer described as a scene "of surpassing beauty, upon which the eye rests with untiring delight."[17] By the time Upton and XI Corps arrived, however, the beauty of the fields and meadows around Sharpsburg was shrouded by thick smoke, and death filled the once serene countryside.

McClellan's plan of attack was to pound at Lee's flanks until one weakened sufficiently that Lee would have to shift forces from the center of his line. When that occurred, McClellan would exploit the weakened center to break Lee's army in two. Throughout the morning, Union forces hammered at Lee's left flank, making repeated assaults on Jackson's corps. Lee countered these attacks with stiff defense and then counterattacks of his own. The effect of all this fighting was primarily death. No one gained much ground while thousands were killed or wounded.

Later in the morning, Union forces attacking Lee's men along a sunken country road flanked the Confederate position and drove the enemy into retreat, exposing Lee's entire center just as McClellan hoped. But rather than commit his reserves to break Lee in two, the always timid McClellan held back.

Slocum's division approached the battlefield just before noon, and McClellan ordered them to relieve the II Corps on the Union right. Upton's artillery moved down the Hagerstown Pike to take up positions near the Dunker Church. As they passed the cornfields on the Miller farm, Upton could clearly see how desperate the fighting had been thus far. During the three hours of fighting for those 80 acres of corn, more than 8,000 men were killed or wounded, and the tall green corn had been cut to the ground by thousands of bullets. Upton described what he saw in a letter. "The infantry fighting was terrible," he wrote. "I do not believe there has been harder fighting this century than that between Hooker and the rebels in the morning. I have heard of the 'dead lying in heaps,' but never saw it till at this battle. Whole ranks fell together."[18] It was a deeply sobering sight.

Late in the afternoon, Slocum sent his 2nd Brigade under Colonel William Irwin forward

Dead Confederate artilleryman lying near the Dunker Church, where they were subjected to intense artillery fire from Federal batteries, including Emory Upton's (Library of Congress).

to attack the Confederate line. But Irwin quickly found himself in trouble, as the enemy massed to throw a "powerful column against"[19] his left. The Confederate forces were partially obscured by the terrain, making it difficult to lay down an effective fire against them. Just as Irwin contemplated a withdrawal, Upton rode up and examined the ground with Irwin at his side. After a quick study of the terrain, Upton advised the colonel to allow him to bring a battery forward quickly, and he pointed to a spot where he could position the guns to counter the coming attack. Irwin could immediately see the sense of Upton's suggestion, and, within minutes, Upton returned with a battery of six guns. Irwin wrote in his after-action report that Upton's cannons went "into action very promptly, and opened with three rifled guns, which, after playing on the masses of the enemy with great effect for half an hour, were withdrawn, and their places supplied by a battery of Napoleon guns, the fire of which was terribly destructive."[20]

As Upton's batteries blasted fire at the Confederates, enemy sharpshooters opened fire on the men serving the guns from a small wood to the left front of the position. At one point in the fighting, Upton was trying to gain a view of the enemy positions using his field glasses. He decided to get a better look by steadying his binoculars on top of a fence post. He stepped behind the post and, just as he set his binoculars on it, a sharpshooter's minié ball slammed into the post just opposite his chest, which he cavalierly referred to later as "annoying."[21]

After the battle subsided, Upton's men discovered a wounded Confederate soldier lying under a fence only 40 feet in front of the guns. Upton wrote his sister about it, saying that between the roar of the Union guns and the bursting shells from Confederate artillery, "the poor fellow must have suffered beyond conception."[22]

The two armies remained in place the next day and, during the night of September 18, Lee slipped away, taking his battered army back into Virginia. What became known as the Battle of Antietam was over and, with more than 25,000 men dead, wounded, and missing, it remains as the single bloodiest day in American history. Surveying the battlefield after the fighting, Upton and his comrades from XI Corps were overwhelmed by what they saw. Surgeon Daniel Holt wrote his wife about the scene. "I have seen, stretched along, in one straight line, ready for interment, at least a thousand blackened, bloated corpses with blood and gas protruding from every orifice," he wrote, "and maggots holding high carnival over their heads.... Every house, for miles around, is a hospital and I have seen arms, legs, feet, and hands lying in piles rotting in the blazing heat of a Southern sky unburied and uncared for, and still the knife went steadily in its work adding to the putrid mess."[23]

The VI Corps surgeon, George Stevens, described the aftermath in similar terms. "The scene on the battle-field was past description," he wrote. "The mangled forms of our own comrades lay stretched upon the ground, side by side with those of the rebels. On almost every rod of ground over 100 acres, the dead and wounded." He noted that, at one point along their line, "the rebels lay so thickly as almost to touch each other." In addition, there was the broken, bloody litter left by dead animals and shattered equipment. "Broken caissons, wheels, dismounted guns, thousands of muskets, blankets, haversacks, and canteens," Stevens wrote, "were scattered thickly over the field; and hundreds of slain horses, bloated and with feet turned toward the sky, added to the horror of the scene."[24]

Despite the apparent carnage all around him, Upton's letter to his sister after the battle included the bravado typical of young men of the time. "From the time we left Alexandria ... till the close of the battle of Antietam, I never spent any hours more agreeably or enjoyed myself better," he told his sister. "We lived well, marched through a lovely country, had beautiful weather, magnificent scenery, and above all two glorious battles."[25] But as later events would show, the butchery at Antietam was just the beginning, and as the war continued, it would take a great toll on Upton. He would eventually see these deaths as needless and futile, the products of poor tactics and bad leadership.

As for Upton's small part in the battle, he received praise and thanks. Colonel Irwin wrote about Upton's support for his brigade saying he deserved "the highest commendation." "It gives me very great pleasure," he reported, "to acknowledge how much I was indebted to Captain Upton, and to the officers and men under his command."[26] General Slocum added his own approval of Upton's actions, writing that his division's artillery "was well served and did good execution."[27]

Upton's brigade moved around the vicinity of Sharpsburg for several weeks, as the corps shifted in case Lee attempted to return north of the Potomac. Finally, they settled into camp and, despite Lincoln's appeals to McClellan that the army chase Lee, the Army of the Potomac remained in place.

But Upton was not to stay with his artillery brigade much longer. His commanders had noted his abilities and, as a result, a new challenge was on the horizon.

5

Upton's Regulars

> In administration he was efficient. In action he was prompt. In danger he was cool. And under no circumstances did he show fear or lack of decision.
> Isaac O. Best, 121st New York Infantry Regiment[1]

One of the many regiments encamped near Sharpsburg in the fall of 1862 was the 121st New York Infantry. Following President Lincoln's call for an additional 300,000 volunteers in July 1862, authorities in the New York state government called for the creation of one new regiment from each of the state's senatorial districts. The 121st was recruited in the 20th Senatorial District, which included Herkimer and Otsego counties in north central New York. The governor appointed the local Republican congressman, Richard Franchot, to supervise the recruiting and organization of the regiment. With the support of special county committees, Franchot recruited 30 officers and 1,063 enlisted men.[2]

The motivations of these volunteers to enlist varied but reflected those found across the North from the beginning of the war. Among most, there was certainly the desire to have an adventure, and many likely felt the need to perform what 19th-century society saw as their "manly" duty. Some of those who would become officers also believed that a wartime service record would serve their post-war political or business ambitions. In the case of the 121st New York, there were also financial considerations. At the time the regiment was being recruited, the average yearly wage for a farm laborer in the area was about $200. However, enlisting in the 121st brought an immediate bounty of that same amount.[3] So, just by signing their names, many of these volunteers could earn a year's wage, money that they and their families likely needed.

Nonetheless, it would be shortsighted to say these were the only or even the most prominent motivations to enlist. After all, this generation of men from the North was the most well educated and well read in the nation's history up to this time. Most were voracious readers of newspapers, and it can be said with confidence that many had a clear understanding of the issues related to the war. While the majority were almost certainly not passionate abolitionists like Emory Upton, most did have a passionate belief in the cause of saving the Union.[4] They saw themselves as the guardians of the legacy left by their patriot forefathers during the American Revolution, and they sought to be "worthy of their heritage."[5]

The new regiment mustered in for duty a mile and one half south of Herkimer, New York, at Camp Schuyler on August 21, 1862. The governor appointed Congressman Franchot as the Colonel of the regiment, and the men began to receive their equipment and undergo drill instruction. However, because of the events on the Virginia Peninsula and McClellan's retreat to

Washington, they only had a few days to prepare. Franchot received orders to move the new regiment to Washington, where it would join the Army of the Potomac. On August 30, the men boarded a train for Albany and, once in the state capital, they clambered onto a boat for a trip down the Hudson River to New York. There, the regiment boarded another train, which took them south through Philadelphia and Baltimore to Washington.[6]

The regiment had barely set up camp in Washington and resumed its training when orders came for it to move out and join the main army, which was then marching into Maryland in pursuit of Lee. Originally assigned to the V Corps, Franchot leveraged a relationship with General Slocum to obtain the regiment's transfer to the 2nd Brigade of VI Corps' First Division.[7]

The regiment caught up with the brigade just as the attacks on Crampton's Gap began, but their only action in the fighting was to round up stragglers and Confederate deserters. As the Army of the Potomac pressed on to Sharpsburg, the 121st remained behind to guard enemy prisoners and missed the fighting at Antietam. They marched across the battlefield two days after the battle on September 19, and Colonel Franchot received orders to encamp along the Potomac near Bakersville, Maryland, which was about five miles north of Sharpsburg.[8]

A New Command

Shortly after the 121st arrived in its new camp, Colonel Franchot decided the military life was not for him. While he had performed admirably in recruiting and organizing the regiment, he came to realize that he simply was not qualified to command an infantry regiment nor suited to the military life, in general. Therefore, he submitted his resignation and announced he would return to Washington to assume his duties in Congress.[9]

The timing of Franchot's decision was fortuitous for Emory Upton. In mid–August, Upton received orders to report to West Point, where he was to become an instructor on the Academy staff. This news upset Upton greatly. The very last thing he wanted to do was leave the field in the middle of a war. Once the Maryland campaign ended, he left his artillery brigade and traveled to Washington to plead his case. While making the rounds in the halls of the War Department, he heard of Franchot's resignation and that the authorities in New York were trying to find a suitable replacement. Upton saw this as a critical opportunity, and he grabbed it.

Although Upton loved the Regular Army, he could see that the best path to advancement in this particular war was to transfer to the state volunteer forces. Civilian influence and participation in the war were increasing. Meanwhile, the prominence of West Point graduates, even among the generals, was being steadily diluted by the sheer magnitude of the war and the number of command positions required by the rapidly expanding Union army. But more important to Upton was the fact that the only way for officers like him to gain the opportunity to lead large bodies of troops and distinguish themselves was with the volunteers. So as soon as Upton heard about Franchot's resignation, he contacted politicians from his home state and proposed that he take command of the 121st.

While Upton might have lacked the political influence normally necessary to gain the position, the governor and state congressional delegation knew how highly those in the Regular Army regarded him. Moreover, the opportunity to have a West Point graduate from their home state assume command was just too good to pass up. The governor immediately appointed Emory Upton as a Colonel of U.S. Volunteers and gave him command of the 121st New York.[10]

Upton reported to his new command on October 23 wearing shoulder epaulets with the eagles of a full colonel. Both the regiment's officers and men were immediately impressed by their young 22-year-old commander. After first seeing him, one officer noted Upton as appearing young, with high cheekbones, a small mustache, thin cheeks, and a "strong square jaw." He also noticed the new colonels "deep blue, deep set eyes," which always seemed to be searching. His eyes combined with a dark, pale complexion made Upton seem to the volunteer officer as a "man who was deeply impressed with the seriousness of warfare and had mastered its science."[11]

Another officer, Douglas Campbell, remembered that, on Upton's first day in camp, the new colonel called the officers together and addressed them, telling them exactly what he expected of the regiment and its officers. Campbell said that, afterward, it was apparent to all the officers that "we had indeed found a man." Campbell, who held a strong belief that earnestness was the key ingredient for success, said that no man he ever knew was more earnest than Emory Upton.[12]

Upton's aptitude for command was immediately apparent. Like every good leader, he knew that his first job was to see to the welfare of his men, to ensure they were properly clothed, fed, and sheltered. When he arrived in the camp near Bakersville, he found the regiment wanting in just about everything except misery itself. Using all he had learned about navigating the army's complex channels in his preceding artillery assignments, he quickly laid his hands on the clothing and overcoats his men would need for fall's cool and rainy weather. He also made sure to improve food supplies, and most importantly, he took immediate action to recover his soldiers' health.[13]

When Upton assumed command, he found that illness had taken a severe toll on the regiment. In the rush to get the 121st New York into the field, no one had issued them with either shelter tents for the men or the large tents used for regimental hospitals. As a result, the men made shacks from fence rails, which they covered with straw and

Emory Upton after being promoted to Colonelk, ca. 1861 (National Archives).

brush. As soon as the fall rains began, these shelters became completely inadequate. Not surprisingly, illness and even death were soon the results. On the day Upton assumed command, the 976 officers and men the regiment had when it left Camp Schuyler had been reduced to only 750 present for duty, and many of them were only able to perform half their duties due to sickness.[14] The assistant regimental surgeon, Major Daniel Holt, was overcome by the sheer numbers of the sick, as well as the lack of medicine. He wrote his wife on September 25 telling her about the conditions in the camp. He reported there were 150 men on the sick list, and he expected more than 300 at the daily sick call. "Unless a change takes place soon," he wrote, "deaths will be as frequent as the most cruel enemy could wish." He concluded his description of the situation by saying, "I fear that we have only commenced to see trouble in this respect."[15]

Soon, the regiment suffered its first casualty and, as was so often the case in both Union and Confederate armies, the soldier succumbed to disease and not the actions of the enemy. Private Helon Pearsons, 23 years old, died from typhoid fever on October 2.[16] The regiment's Adjutant Clerk wrote home saying, "Helon Pearsons died last night of typhoid fever. He now lies back of the hospital tent covered with a blanket under the protection of a guard. The pioneers have made a board box and he is to be buried after battalion drill."[17]

The death of this young soldier and the rampant illness in the regiment badly damaged morale, and, when he arrived in camp, Upton knew he must act quickly. First, he moved the sick from their makeshift shelters into a brick barn that he commandeered as a hospital. He then assisted Major Holt by obtaining more medical supplies, relocated the rest of the men to a better campsite, and got them the proper shelter tents they needed. But more than that, he made it his business to learn all he could about properly organizing a field hospital. Major Campbell reported that, shortly after Upton's arrival, Campbell ran into a friend who was serving in one of the nearby Regular Army regiments. The friend approached him saying, "What is the colonel of your regiment doing? Is he studying medicine?" Campbell asked what this friend meant, and he told him that Upton had visited the Regular's hospital almost every day, talking to their surgeons, and learning all he could about their medical system.[18]

Armed with this new knowledge, Upton supported Major Holt's diligent efforts. One element of this support was to take Holt's side in dealing with the regiment's chief surgeon, Stephen Valentine. Holt complained angrily about Valentine almost from the moment the regiment was formed. Valentine was initially assigned as an assistant surgeon and, like Holt, served under the command of the regiment's first chief surgeon, William Bassett. But Valentine insisted that he be titled as the first assistant surgeon because he had a date of rank one month prior to Holt's.

This effectively placed Valentine over Holt, and Valentine used that position to make Holt's life very difficult. Then, when Barrett left the regiment on September 30, 1862, Valentine became the chief surgeon by default. Holt described Valentine as both a drunk and an incompetent physician. He wrote his wife, telling her that whenever they held sick call, Valentine would angrily dismiss every soldier who reported being ill and do so not because they were malingering, but just because Valentine was lazy and wanted to avoid the work. As a result, all the soldiers learned to turn to Holt for care.[19]

Holt soon observed that Upton had taken a quick but accurate measure of Surgeon Valentine. "Colonel Upton is down upon him [Valentine]," he wrote his wife, "and I think from the general appearance of the man that when he sets his foot down upon a matter he intends to carry it out. So I live in hope."[20] In fact, once the U.S. Army Surgeon General began tightening standards for military surgeons a few months later, Upton had Valentine called to Washington to undergo questioning about his abilities. Unfortunately, Valentine survived the inquiry and returned, much to both Holt and Upton's dismay.

All these actions, as well as Upton's general demeanor, quickly endeared him to the soldiers in the regiment. Major Campbell later wrote about an incident that showed how Upton treated his soldiers and the respect they had for him. Campbell came upon a young soldier who had been confined to his tent following guard duty. The soldier was in tears "as if his heart would break." Campbell asked what had happened, and the soldier replied that Upton had just relieved him of his duties for allowing another soldier to take his rifle while on guard duty. Apparently, the colonel had lectured him on the dangers inherent in such neglect and spoke to him harshly, as if he "were unworthy to be a soldier." While Upton had decided not to punish the young man, the soldier told Campbell that he would "prefer to spend a month in the guardhouse than for Colonel Upton to have such a low opinion of him."[21]

This brand of loyalty came despite Upton's insistence on strict discipline. "He took command without show or ostentation," remembered Isaac Best. "From the day that Emory Upton took command there was a change for the better. The camp was newly ordered and cleaned up, inspections were more rigid, and the officers were promptly taken to task for any slackness on their part."[22]

The regiment moved out of Maryland in early November, headed for eastern Virginia. As they moved slowly to the southeast, Upton took the opportunity offered by every pause in the march to make his volunteers into men that could both look and perform like real soldiers. He began a rigorous process of drilling and training that consumed every usable hour of the day. Upton had the regiment roused by reveille at 5:30 a.m. The men would quickly dress and have breakfast, followed in quick succession by the sick call, camp and company inspection, and then company drill. Following lunch, he ordered the regiment into battalion drills at 1:00 p.m. and dress parade at 4:00 p.m.[23]

During these parades, Upton had his soldiers properly dressed for the occasion, complete with white dress gloves. "I feel proud of the 121st," Captain John Kidder wrote to his wife. "It would do you good to see them maneuver on battalion drill, then march to camp at right shoulder, shift arms, every man steps at the same instant."[24] Under this intense instruction, it did not take long for the nearby veteran regiments to take notice. Soon, they began to refer to the 121st New York as "Upton's Regulars" because they marched and behaved like men from the Regular Army and not like those from an inexperienced volunteer regiment.[25]

Upton did not merely restrict his reforms and discipline to the enlisted soldiers. He moved quickly to ensure the officers were up to the task of leading their men. Because of the way states raised volunteer Civil War regiments, politics often influenced the assignment of their leadership positions. As a result, men like Richard Franchot became officers despite their lack of qualifications or even the right temperament needed to command. The fact that Franchot was smart enough to realize he did not have what it took to command the regiment and that he should resign was the great exception to the rule. Most of the officers in volunteer regiments were either political appointees who used their influence to gain a commission or men who simply were popular figures elected as officers by their soldiers. Neither made for good potential as leaders, and combat tended to weed these men out.

In the case of the 121st New York, however, there had been no battles to show who could lead and who could not. This concerned Upton deeply and, shortly after taking command, he began his own process to identify and remove those unqualified to serve as officers. First, he asked authorities in Albany not to assign any more volunteer officers to the regiment unless he personally approved them, to which they agreed. Next, Upton decided to deal with his current officers by giving them a series of tests based on West Point standards. The effects were immediate. "Some of the Officers," John Kidder confided to his wife, "have had to resign by request of the Colonel, who is a very strict man."[26] Those officers that stayed, Kidder among them, became very loyal to Upton and approached their responsibilities with great seriousness.

Fredericksburg

The 121st eventually arrived at Belle Plain Landing on the Potomac River just northeast of Fredericksburg, Virginia, in early December. As they marched towards the campsite, it began to rain hard before turning to "snow of the large, soft, fleecy flake kind."[27] The road Upton's men trudged on soon became a deep quagmire of slippery mud. Captain John Kidder wrote his wife that "Virginia is nothing but a bed of quicksand."[28] The soldiers were soon soaked on the outside by the rain and snow, while below their army overcoats, they were just as wet from perspiration. If this was not miserable enough, as soon as the sun set, a fierce wind began to blow, and

Union camps at Belle Plain Landing where Upton's 121st New York stayed in December 1862 (Library of Congress).

the temperature dropped even further. At last, they reached their designated campsite on a low flat area near the Potomac.[29]

If conditions were not already very forbidding, they now became absolutely grim. One could not have selected a worse place to make camp in the winter. The campsite was on open ground, which exposed Upton's soldiers to both high winds and extreme cold. Upton asked Colonel Cronkite, the brigade commander, if he could move his regiment out of the field where they currently camped to the comparative shelter of a strip of woods down the road. Cronkite refused his request.[30] But the next day, Upton located a nearby grove of cedar trees and was able to move the regiment there. Although it was not a perfect solution, it was the best he could do. He wrote his sister about the harsh conditions of that encampment and his concern for his men's welfare:

> When we arrived it was snowing and quite cold, and we had to encamp on the plain. There were no woods to break the wind, no wood to build fires, and the men were wet to the skin; the ground was covered with snow and water, and with but a thin shelter-tent over their heads, and nothing but the cold ground to lie on and one blanket for a covering, you can imagine how the poor soldiers fared that night. Yesterday it was clear and cold, and last night colder than any night last winter. The ice froze thick enough to bear a horse. Today I took the regiment from the plain to the dense cedar woods and a high ridge to protect them from the wind, and to-night they are very comfortable, although it is still very cold.[31]

As they camped at Belle Plain Landing, 25 of Upton's men reported to sick call, leaving only 657 available for duty. But, as Isaac Best recalled, because of Upton's hard work in training, supplying, and caring for the health of the regiment, those 657 men "were physically fit for anything that might be required of them."[32] But Upton's men also noticed that their commanding officer was more than willing to share the same miseries that they endured. John Kidder wrote his wife about Upton, saying, "Our Colonel sleeps on the ground without any tent the same as the rest of us do and is always on duty."[33]

The regiment was not in camp for long, as the move to Belle Plain Landing was part of a march by the entire Army of the Potomac towards the Rappahannock River and the city of Fredericksburg. McClellan's replacement, General Ambrose Burnside, had decided to strike Lee's army before winter fully set in, which would make any advance by the enemy impossible.

Burnside was an odd choice to command the Army of the Potomac. He did not want the job of being the army's commander and had no reluctance about saying so to anyone who would listen. He believed he did not have the talents and abilities necessary in an army's commander and would have been very happy to simply remain in charge of his own corps. But now the job was his, and he decided an offensive was the best course of action. Unfortunately, as events would soon demonstrate, Burnside's evaluation of his capabilities was very accurate.

The new commander's plan was to make a quick advance to the east bank of the Rappahannock opposite Fredericksburg. Once there, the army would immediately cross the river, seize the heights west of the city, and engage Lee's army when it arrived in an attempt to block the path to Richmond. But nothing went as planned. The bad weather delayed the arrival of the engineers and the pontoon boats required for the river crossing. By the time they arrived, the lead elements of Lee's army had taken positions west of the city, entrenching themselves on the high ground. At this point, Burnside should have realized the tactical situation had changed drastically and called off the offensive, as some of his corps commanders suggested. But he decided to press on with the attack. The pontoon bridges were erected under fire, and Burnside would send the army across to assault Lee's strong positions.

Early on the morning of December 11, Upton received orders to move the regiment forward to the Rappahannock. The sky was still cold and dark, but he ordered his staff to awake the regiment, and soon the sounds of the regiment's drummer boys beating an urgent reveille roused his men. Upton told his officers there would be no time for coffee and to immediately begin packing up. He instructed his company commanders to place everything not needed for battle, including the regiment's tents, in the supply wagons so they could remain in the rear. As the word spread through camp to douse their campfires and stop brewing coffee, Upton's soldiers began preparing to march.[34]

Unaware that a major battle was in the offing, the soldiers found the weather cool and crisp, and one man recalled that "we jogged along in eager anticipation of something better than that which we had left."[35] While the river was only six miles away, the regiment made slow progress. They often had to step off the road to let artillery caissons and wagons roll by on their way to the Rappahannock. Soon, the road was badly torn up by all the wagon traffic, and Upton's men struggled to get good footing as they continued their march. At several points, Upton and his men came upon stretches of what was called a "corduroy" roadbed. This type of road resulted from a process used by army engineers to overcome extremely muddy roads. The engineers' technique involved covering the roadbed with round pine poles laid perpendicularly across the road and then covered with brush. Longer poles which the engineers laid lengthwise and then anchored down using long pins that they hammered into the ground, held these pine poles in place.[36] It was crude by modern standards but very effective.

Finally, around noon, as Upton approached the heights above the east side of the river, he could hear cannon firing. He and his officers scaled the hills to join other officers from the brigade to gain their first view of the battlefield. Their brigade and the rest of VI Corps would cross the river at the far left of the Union line, which placed them about two miles below the city. Captain Kidder, recalling his colonel's tactics training sessions, made a deliberate and thorough examination of the ground ahead. The river seemed small from atop the hill, but it appeared to be 400 to 500 feet wide, and on the far side, there was a broad plain about three miles deep. Beyond the flat terrain were a series of ridges that sloped gradually back approximately six miles. On these distant ridges, he could see Confederate troops from Stonewall Jackson's corps who were well beyond the range of the brigade's artillery.[37]

Upton and his officers returned to the regiment, and they began marching towards the southernmost of five pontoon bridges laid across the river by Federal engineers. As they advanced, the soldiers could hear heavy artillery and rifle fire upriver off to their right, and they could just make out the tops of the spires of Fredericksburg's churches in the distance. I Corps was the first across the river just ahead of VI Corps and, unlike the fighting that occurred at the pontoon bridges leading directly into the city, there was no opposition to their crossing. As often was the case in the war, the road leading up to the bridge was littered with cast-off equipment and refuse left by the first soldiers across. But one of Upton's soldiers, Isaac Best, later wrote that his most vivid recollection of crossing the Rappahannock was "the fact that the surface of the bridge was carpeted with playing cards, and the surface of the river was almost covered with cards that had been thrown away by those who had crossed on the bridges above." To young Isaac, who would become a Congregationalist pastor after the war, this was clear evidence of men trying to throw away any sign of sin before battle. He was convinced that these men did not want "to go to certain death with gambling devices in their pockets."[38]

Like most of his men, Upton anticipated the regiment was about to see its first real combat. But no sooner had they crossed the bridge than a messenger told Upton the entire brigade would be moving back across the pontoon bridge to the eastern side of the river. Most of the officers and men were stunned by this turn of events. "Why such movements I do not understand," wrote Captain Kidder, "unless it was to deceive the Rebs."[39] Upton turned the regiment about, and they marched across the river, making camp for the night nearby on the flats.

The next morning, December 12, the brigade received orders to cross the Rappahannock once more. As Upton and his men moved across the pontoon bridge, a thick fog covered the river flats, which concealed the hills beyond and screened them from the enemy's view. Once across, Upton formed the regiment into line and began to move the men inland towards the Old Richmond Road near Deep Bottom Creek. As they steadily marched towards the heights on the west side of the river, the fog began to recede. Within minutes, Confederate artillery could see the Union troops advancing towards the hilltops, and the Southern batteries opened fire with solid shot. At first, the shells roared harmlessly overhead, and a Federal battery galloped by the 121st, setting up quickly and returning the enemy's fire.[40]

As the regiment reached their assigned position along the road, Upton told his officers to have the men lie down in the ditch next to the roadbed. This not only screened them from

The city of Fredericksburg in 1862 as seen from the eastern bank of the Rappahannock River (New York Public Library).

the enemy's view, but it also provided cover from the shells that now screamed overhead at a steadily increasing rate. As for Upton, he was the only man in the regiment mounted on horseback, making him a very tempting target. Realizing this and likely remembering what had happened to him at Manassas when he rode on horseback while in range of the enemy, he had his mount lay down in the roadway as he took cover with his men. Not long after this, a round of Confederate solid shot flew by, just above Captain Kidder's head. "I was standing on the bank [of the road] ordering my men to lay down, [when] a shell came directly over my head," recalled Kidder. "I heard and saw it coming. I squatted down and let it pass over me. It struck in the road and passed over the Colonel's [Upton's] horse, which was lying down or it would have killed him immediately."[41]

While most of the shells continued to pass overhead and did little more than throw up clouds of dirt when they struck, one caused the regiment's first combat casualty. A percussion shell landed in the roadway and, while it seemed to explode harmlessly, a fragment from the shell casing struck Private Edward Spicer in the head, killing him instantly. His comrades lifted his body out of the ditch, placed it in a shallow grave next to the road, said a prayer, and returned to their position.[42]

As the artillery batteries from both sides played out a deadly duel with one another, Upton mounted his horse once more and rode along the line "leisurely and showed no concern or fear."[43] While this may seem to have been very foolhardy, this kind of display was common practice among good commanding officers during the war. They felt that showing the men they could remain cool and calm under fire provided a good example from which their men could strengthen their own courage and resolve. It is little wonder, then, that casualties among officers were so high during the Civil War.

Upton and his men remained in their position along the Old Richmond Road all day on December 12 and into the night. The next morning, as they remained crouched in the ditch next to the road, they could hear the loud rumble of artillery and the rattle of rifle fire far to their right. It was the sound of the main Union assault against Lee's army. With his men well entrenched behind a stone wall atop Marye's Heights, Lee repeatedly repulsed attacks up the steep hillside by men from the Army of the Potomac's II Corps. While Union forces had some limited success on Lee's left, it was not exploited, and the battle turned into an ugly disaster for Ambrose Burnside. He lost almost 13,000 men and gained absolutely nothing.

On the night of December 13, the 77th New York arrived and relieved Upton's regiment. Just before sunrise, Upton and his men reached the relative safety of a ravine near the river, where they stopped, lit fires, and made themselves as comfortable as they could. They remained in the ravine until the next morning when, despite rumors that the battle was to recommence, Upton received orders to move back across the Rappahannock and make camp. Not long after the brigade and the remainder of VI Corps were on the far side of the river, he and his men watched as engineers pulled up the pontoon bridge. Shortly afterward, new orders came to Upton directing him to return the regiment to Belle Plain Landing. The campaign at Fredericksburg was over and, when Upton took stock, he found he had lost four men killed and seven wounded.[44]

Still, what Upton saw along the main line of the Union attack against Marye's Heights was deeply sobering. Years later, he described Fredericksburg as a "bloody battle," and he vividly recalled the "flashes of musketry and the roar of artillery." More telling, however, was his memory of its horrors with "ten-thousand killed and wounded stretched cold upon the plain, & writhing in their agony."[45]

Winter Camp at White Oak Church

Luckily, the regiment would not return to the frigid open ground at Belle Plain Landing. Before they arrived there, brigade officers directed Upton to file the men off the road and march them into a dense forest of massive oak trees near a ramshackle old chapel called White Oak Church. There, he had the men begin the makings of a winter camp, complete with small log shanties. But he soon realized that the dense woods had no open ground where he could continue the regiment's drill and training. So, Upton ordered his men to move the camp to the edge of the woods next to a large open field. Here, the trees would shelter them from the cold winter winds, and they could use the field for drilling.[46]

While Upton's men now had an opportunity to rest and be as comfortable as was possible in their crude winter quarters, their colonel found that, despite his best efforts to keep the men busy with drill, camp life always provided its own unique problems. The first was discipline. Volunteer soldiers seemed to chafe more about military life when they were in the relative idleness of camp, and there were repeated incidents of disobedience. The fact that his officers and enlisted men had known one another in civilian life often made these incidents more difficult to manage effectively. Soldiers sometimes took advantage of those previous relationships, and many officers struggled to maintain the somewhat distant relationship required by good military order.

Captain Kidder's experience in winter camp at White Oak Church is an example, and in this case, Kidder demonstrated what he could learn about leadership and discipline from Emory Upton. The captain's problems came in the form of two young soldiers whom he had enlisted into the regiment in New York, Charles and Edward Pattengill. In peacetime, these two brothers had been customers of Kidder's business, a wholly different relationship than that of an officer and enlisted soldier. Charles, who had attained the rank of sergeant, presented Kidder with the first issue by being absent without leave and taking a sojourn down to Belle Plain Landing. Kidder caught him returning and reported it to Upton, who promptly reduced Charles in rank to corporal. Apparently, Charles was not pleased by this demotion and became openly disobedient. Kidder wrote in his journal, "He has been a stubborn Corporal." He reported him to Upton again, and the regiment's young colonel took matters into his own hands by busting Charles all the way down to private. Kidder wrote home relating the incident to his wife by telling her, "I have had some thoughts of reducing him for disobedience of orders but the Colonel has saved me the trouble."[47]

However, right after Kidder had dealt with Charles, the other Pattengill brother, Edward, created a new problem. Kidder happened to hear an argument between Edward and another soldier in which Pattengill was accused of having an unauthorized extra piece of tent canvas. Captain Kidder confronted Edward and asked him where he had obtained the canvas, to which Edward replied that he had bought it from another soldier named George Teel. Edward added that, since Private Teel was in a hospital in Washington, he had no need of the canvas. Kidder told Edward he had no argument with the fact that Teel did not need the canvas. Rather, he pointed out to the private that Teel had no right to sell government property. He ordered Edward to deliver the canvas to his sergeant or suffer the consequences, which the private refused to do.[48]

That evening, Upton was in his headquarters tent when Captain Kidder came by to deliver his evening report, which contained mention of an issue with Edward Pattengill. Upton asked Kidder about the details of the problem, which Kidder provided. Upton agreed that Teel had no right to sell the canvas, but he told Kidder that was not the real problem. Instead, the more serious issue was Pattengill's questioning the authority of an officer, and he told Kidder to deal with it. Upton assured Kidder that his soldiers would respect him all the more for doing so. Upton then instructed Kidder to have Pattengill arrested immediately and tie him up to a tree if he had not surrendered the canvas to the Orderly Sergeant.[49]

While the matter seemed very trivial, Kidder clearly saw the point Upton was making. He returned to his company and directed his Orderly Sergeant to ask Edward Pattengill for the canvas one more time. He told the sergeant to inform Pattengill that, if he returned the canvas, all would be forgotten. But if he refused again, the sergeant was to tell Pattengill that he would be arrested and punished as Colonel Upton directed. The private foolishly resisted and soon found himself tied up to an oak tree. Kidder was concerned about how his men would react, but he soon learned that, as Upton had predicted, they approved of the way he dealt with Edward Pattengill. "The boys were all glad of it," he said in a letter home. "As our Colonel is a regular officer," he wrote, "we have to style a little and we are not permitted to be intimate with our men. I think this is a mistaken notion, but we must obey orders."[50]

Upton's next problem was maintaining proper regimental strength. As the regiment remained in camp, desertion and sickness plagued him. In one letter, Assistant Surgeon Holt stated that more than half the regiment had taken "French leave," a term commonly used to describe desertion during the Civil War. Further, he wrote, they did so "without waiting to say 'goodbye' to the Colonel, or even to call upon their Surgeon to ascertain whether he thought it would be healthy for them to leave this cold weather without purse or script."[51]

One of Upton's men, Charles Beckwith, later wrote that one of the reasons for increased desertion was pay. By January 1863, none of the soldiers in the 121st had been paid since they mustered into service the previous summer. A rumor began to spread among the regiment that, under an article of war, volunteer troops could not be held to their enlistment contract unless they were paid at least once every four months. Upton and his officers soon heard of this rumor and made sure the men knew the pay situation was not a legal cause to leave the regiment. But this only further angered some of the men. Beckwith wrote, "they, being sick of war, argued that the private soldier could get no justice; the government did not keep its contracts, therefore the soldier ought not to fight."[52]

Moreover, some of the men harbored deep resentment of the Emancipation Proclamation, which essentially made ending slavery one of the Lincoln administration's primary aims for the war. Beckwith recalled that these men said the war had become "a blanked nigger war anyway, and they were not going to fight for the negro."[53]

These disaffected soldiers also heard that there were men in the business of helping soldiers desert. For a price, these agents would provide civilian clothing, money, and a way to cross the Potomac as the deserter headed for Canada. Beckwith knew one group of soldiers planning to desert using one of these agents, and they urged Charles to come with them. "I was invited first," Beckwith recalled, "urged next, and damned last, because I would not go with them."[54] Later, one of these soldiers was shot dead by a cavalry patrol, one came back to the regiment, and the others escaped.

Upton became understandably angry at these desertions. By the end of February 1863, more than 100 men had deserted the regiment, and he sought a way to stop the steady trickle of desertion from becoming a flood. Eventually, Upton decided to try public shaming and humiliation of the deserting soldiers and their families at home by having the names of all the regiment's deserters regularly published in their hometown newspaper, the Herkimer County Journal. These lists included a harsh introduction from Upton.[55] "Sir: I forward you the following list of deserters from this Regiment, men who received nearly two hundred dollars to enlist and serve their country, and then disgracefully and cowardly deserted their comrades and the services of their Government. They are fit subjects to be published to the world and ought to be scorned by every honorable person. They have defrauded their friends at home, and cheated the Government of their services."[56]

This tactic seemed to work but, while the number of desertions decreased, the level of illness among his soldiers was not so easily solved. During the week with the longest sick list, Assistant Surgeon Holt reported over 150 men had been sent to hospitals in Washington and Alexandria.[57] A contributing issue was the lack of fresh foods, especially vegetables, which became worse with prolonged winter weather. The soldiers' poor diet, combined with cold, damp quarters, and life with hundreds of men living in close quarters, led to rampant outbreaks of dysentery, scurvy, and typhoid in all the regimental camps. The levels of illness and death soon rose to a point that left Upton's surgeon almost despondent. "The health of the regiment is bad," Holt wrote his wife in early January 1863. "Death is upon our track, and almost every day sees its victim taken to the grave." He told her he had lost two men the day before and another two that day. Referring to Charon, the ferryboat pilot of Greek mythology who ferries the dead to Hades, he wrote, "There are quite a number waiting at the river bank to be ferried over, and it makes my heart sad to think that I can in no way delay their passage."[58]

Holt also had little faith in his ability or those of his fellow military physicians to stem the tide of disease. "I have great reason to thank my Maker that I am not yet a confirmed invalid," he wrote. "I have seen and know too much of army doctoring to trust much in its efficacy. Very little can be done for a man while he lies upon the ground with typhoid fever, attended by incompetent nurses. When I order one to hospital, it seems almost equivalent to ordering his grave dug."[59]

An example of the combined effects of the fighting at Fredericksburg, disease, and desertion can be illustrated by just one of Upton's companies, Company B. Isaac Best recalled that, by January 1863, Company B had lost three men in battle, five died from disease, and four had deserted. During that same month, Best reported that only 55 soldiers were present for duty in a regiment intended to have 800. To make matters worse, Upton's persistent emphasis on professionalism and discipline in his officers continued to result in resignations.

All the while, up to this point in the war, Upton continued to maintain his strong religious faith. Isaac best noted that his commander was "strictly temperate, and decidedly religious in his conduct. He was not ashamed to keep a well worn Bible on his desk, and his conversation was always clean and without profanity."[60] He also encouraged his officers to organize a glee club that could sing hymns on Sundays. John Kidder wrote that Upton wanted them "to get up some good singing for the Sabbath."[61]

The Mud March

As mid–January 1863 arrived, rumors began to float about the army that they would soon be moving back to the offensive and, on January 16, orders arrived at Upton's headquarters tent telling him to be prepared to march. One of the actions ordered by Burnside's headquarters was to transfer all men too sick to make a march to the hospital at Aquia Creek. Upton's surgeons began examining men who had come to sick call to determine who should go to the rear. Dr. Holt determined that perhaps eight to ten of the regiment's men were too sick to move with the rest of the regiment. But Upton's infamous Chief Surgeon, Dr. Valentine, decided to send almost 80 to the hospital. When Upton received this news, he became furious. Holt wrote that the news of these men's transfer "made Col. Upton rear like a mad bull."[62] Upton, like Holt, knew exactly what Valentine was up to—the Chief Surgeon wanted to lighten his own workload at the sick call by sending any soldier who appeared even slightly ill to the rear. Holt could see that Upton was angry, and he wrote, "If he [Valentine] is not soon dismissed dishonorably from the service, I am mistaken."[63]

As early as November the previous year, Upton tried to get rid of Dr. Valentine. He wrote the medical director of the VI Corps that Valentine was "a surgeon of very little experience, no energy and no disposition to do his duty." Furthermore, Upton stated that Valentine did not bother to maintain a proper supply of medical equipment and had no concern for the soldiers' health or cleanliness. "From the large sick report we have had," Upton wrote, "I am constrained to believe that he is not stifled [sic] in his profession."[64]

As it turned out, Dr. Holt was correct about his Colonel's determination to expel Valentine. Upton had enough of his Chief Surgeon, and a few weeks later, in February 1863, he managed to get Valentine dismissed from the service under charges of "incompetency and fraudulent transactions in the discharge of his duty."[65]

On January 19, final orders arrived, and the next day, the Army of the Potomac began to

Alfred Waud's sketch of the suffering men of the Army of the Potomac during the infamous Mud March (Library of Congress).

move. Burnside's plan for this winter offensive was quite bold. His concept involved a large-scale feint by his cavalry at several fords across the Rappahannock above Fredericksburg. Meanwhile, as Lee moved towards those river fords, Burnside would take the army across the river south of Fredericksburg, then swing south and west until they could attack Richmond from the south. It was an imaginative and impressive concept.

The only problem was the weather. There was a reason that 19th-century armies usually sat idle in camp during the winter: winter meant rain and snow, which could turn roads into quagmires and make travel by men, horses, and wagons impossible. When the army marched out of camp on January 20, it was very cold but sunny and clear. The roads were frozen hard, and all looked good for a rapid advance to the river. Then things quickly turned against Burnside and his plan.[66]

In the early afternoon, a warm southerly wind began, the sky turned from clear and blue to dark and gray, and relentless heavy rain began. The frost melted, and the frozen roads thawed into deep, muddy bogs. By the next morning, soldiers struggled to move as the mud sucked the boots right off their feet, and everything with wheels sank in mud up to their hubs. Artillerymen and wagon teamsters tried doubling up their teams but, even then, many guns and wagons could not be moved. Burnside realized that any offensive would now be impossible and, conditions were so bad, he and his staff were unsure how they would get the Army of the Potomac back to its camps.[67]

Burnside assigned many regiments to either help pull stranded wagons and artillery free from the worst parts of the road using long ropes or to cut down trees and corduroy the roadbed. The 121st New York, meanwhile, was one of the few to reach the planned crossing point at Bank's Ford. Therefore, Upton was ordered to deploy his men and guard the rear at the ford as the rest of the army retreated to winter quarters. Isaac Best later wrote, "Everyone who took part in that movement must remember the misery of the two nights spent in rain and smoke, for the air was so full of water that the smoke hung close to the ground and tortured the eyes, and with what relief the army struggled back into camps to shelter and rest."[68]

When Upton got the regiment back to their warm log shanties at White Oak Church, he learned that Lincoln had dismissed Burnside as the army's commander and that the president had replaced him with General Joseph Hooker. Hooker was an interesting choice to place at the head of the army, and even Lincoln had doubts about the selection. In his memoirs, Ulysses S. Grant would write that he "regarded him [Hooker] as a dangerous man. He was not subordinate to his superiors. He was ambitious to the extent of caring nothing for the rights of others."[69] But at this point, all Lincoln asked for were victories, and he thought Hooker, who had been a competent corps commander, might be the man to provide them.

Hooker's first move was to improve food and supplies for the troops and offer the opportunity for furloughs, allowing soldiers to have a brief visit with loved ones at home. Morale improved quickly, and most of the army's men hoped Hooker would bring them victory. Upton took advantage of the new emphasis on improved living conditions for the troops. One soldier wrote that "Colonel Upton exerted himself to the utmost to provide the regiment with every advantage possible, both for comfort and health. Food and clothing of good quality and in sufficient quantity were insisted upon and the regiment rapidly recovered from the effects of the 'Mud March.'"[70]

The new commanding general also reshuffled the men commanding the seven corps that comprised the Army of the Potomac. As part of this process, Hooker chose General John Sedgwick to command VI Corps. Sedgwick was an 1837 graduate of West Point and a solid, competent soldier. He would become very popular with the men of the corps, who came to call him "Uncle John."

Hooker also implemented a system of corps badges, which not only allowed officers and men to more readily identify different groups of soldiers during battle, but also provided a source of unit pride and esprit de corps. The VI Corps was assigned the Greek Cross as their badge with a different color for each division. Since Upton's regiment was in the First Division, they wore a red cross, which the men had sewn onto the tops of their caps.[71]

As spring arrived, Upton knew a new campaign was almost certainly in the offing. This likelihood demanded that he act to replace the nine officers who had resigned during the fall and winter. The Adjutant General in Albany complained to Upton about his slowness in promoting new officers. While the state had given Upton permission to select and approve all new commissions, they still became impatient when he did not move to immediately replace the regimental officers who had left service. But Upton was undeterred, and he insisted on being very deliberate in his selection process. In response to growing pressure from Albany, Upton wrote the Assistant Adjutant General of New York in April 1863: "There are about ten vacancies in the Regiment and the only reason they have not been filled is because I have not found men with the requisite energy, firmness and intelligence to make good officers. As fast as men have exhibited their qualities I have forwarded their names. I trust Gov. Seymour will allow me to fill the vacancies in the manner proposed and when filled, I will promise a Regt. which will be not only an honor to the State, but to the whole country."[72]

After carefully screening the available candidates in the regiment, Upton promoted seven of his sergeants to lieutenant. But he also went outside the regiment to find one officer. In an obvious act of nepotism, Upton had his brother, Henry, transferred from the 104th Illinois to the 121st New York. Henry, who had only been a private in the Illinois regiment, was made a second lieutenant in Company G. However, this act of family favoritism did not seem to upset anyone, and Captain Kidder admitted that Henry was a very good officer.[73]

Major General John Sedgwick, the VI Corps commander, affectionately known to his soldiers as "Uncle John" (Library of Congress).

Salem Church

As spring arrived, General Hooker began planning for the offensive Upton anticipated was coming. The strategy Hooker developed was actually quite brilliant and, as other plans before and after, was designed to get the Army of the Potomac between Lee and Richmond, forcing the Confederate general to fight at a point of Hooker's choosing.

In this instance, Hooker's plan called for his I, II, and VI Corps to confront Lee's army by massing opposite Fredericksburg. Then, as Lee watched his front, Hooker would march the other four corps of the army far to the right, crossing the Rappahannock at Kelly's Ford, and then advancing quickly across the Rapidan River at Germanna and Ely's Fords to a point near the crossroads at Chancellorsville. Once most of his forces were in place there, Hooker would also shift I and II Corps across the Rappahannock to join them, leaving only Sedgwick's VI Corps in front of Lee's army.

If the plan worked, by the time Lee realized what was happening, the bulk of the Army of the Potomac would be in his left-rear threatening the path to Richmond. His only choice would be to withdraw from Fredericksburg and attack Hooker's superior numbers, leaving VI Corps free to advance and attack Lee's rear. The plan was audacious, and Hooker was very confident of its chances for success.

At first, all went as planned. On April 27, Upton received orders to move the 121st New York along with the rest of the brigade and First Division of VI Corps. The regiment broke camp and once again began moving towards the Rappahannock. Early on the morning of April 29, the First Division began crossing the river. It was a very foggy morning along the Rappahannock, and Upton ordered his men to move as quietly as possible to avoid alerting the Confed-

Alfred Waud's sketch of the VI Corps First Division crossing the Rappahannock during the Chancellorsville campaign (Library of Congress).

erate skirmishers on the far side. Officers and sergeants gave all their orders in a whisper, rifles were left unloaded, and bayonets remained in their scabbards. The horses that had pulled the boats to be used to cross the river were left behind, and soldiers brought the boats to the shore by hand and quietly placed them in the water. Then, Upton and his men began to silently file into the boats and rapidly row across the Rappahannock.[74]

The enemy pickets did not hear the Union soldiers' approach until the first boats arrived at the west bank of the river. They began to fire blindly into the dense fog, and the rest of Upton's men who were following in the second wave of boats could hear the enemy bullets harmlessly splashing into the river nearby. The Confederate pickets began to run to the rear, pursued by the lead elements of the 121st until the regiment reached the Old Richmond Road, where they had been during the battle in December.[75] The remainder of the VI Corps soon crossed and faced the entire Army of Northern Virginia. The men dug in just west of the river and spent most of the next four days dodging sporadic enemy sniper fire.

Meanwhile, the remainder of the Army of the Potomac advanced as planned, arriving at Chancellorsville on April 30. When scouts informed Lee of Hooker's arrival in his rear, the wily Confederate general was surprised but not panicked. As Hooker thought he might, Lee pulled his army away from Fredericksburg and advanced to meet Hooker. But, unlike the move in Hooker's plan, Lee chose to divide his army, leaving a substantial rear guard to block VI Corps.

The hard fighting at Chancellorsville commenced on May 1, and Union forces seemed to quickly gain the advantage. General Meade's V Corps and elements of General Couch's II Corps fought fiercely and were steadily pushing Lee's men back when Hooker ordered them and all the other corps to fall back towards Chancellorsville. It seems that, while Hooker's planning was brilliant, his execution was not. Hooker might have been a solid corps commander but leading an army in battle was beyond his capabilities. With much of the army out of his direct sight, he had to rely on messages from his corps commanders to develop a picture of the battle. This caused Hooker to become hesitant, and he was unable to direct the battle from a map. By ordering his advancing troops to withdraw, he surrendered the initiative to Lee, which was a fatal error.

The two armies battled throughout the day on May 2. But as the fighting continued, Lee prepared to strike a fatal blow. He divided his army one more time, sending Stonewall Jackson's corps on a long march around Hooker's right flank. No one in the Union army detected this move, and Jackson was able to make a surprise attack against the XI Corps in the late afternoon. This attack shattered Hooker's army and sent them in full retreat to a defensive position along the Rappahannock.

That night, Hooker sent orders to General Sedgwick to move VI Corps through the enemy units to his front and join the rest of the army. The corps moved out at mid-afternoon and quickly overran the Confederate troops and batteries atop Marye's Heights. Upton's regiment and the rest of First Division had remained on the left of the VI Corps' line but now advanced as the lead element of the corps over the heights and west onto the Orange Plank Road towards Chancellorsville. As they moved forward, the 2nd Brigade and the 121st advanced in a column of fours south of the road across a field, with the 1st Brigade to their right on the north side of the road.[76]

Upton rode alongside the regiment on horseback as he sent his own skirmishers forward to join those from a New Jersey regiment. The two groups of skirmishers moved steadily towards a heavy line of trees about a mile ahead. He then ordered the main body of the regiment out of column and into line of battle. After quickly reforming, Upton advanced them slowly until they were about 300 yards from the trees. At that point, the skirmishers engaged enemy pickets deployed in the woods, and the firing between the two sides became steady. As the Union skirmishers advanced into the trees, Upton halted the regiment at a rail fence and ordered them to lie down and take cover.[77]

As the sounds of rifle fire continued in the woods, a Federal battery deployed on the road and briefly exchanged fire with a Confederate battery to the west before driving the enemy guns away. The 121st New York had been in the lead when it reached the fence, but now the 96th Pennsylvania moved in on their left, and the 23rd New Jersey aligned on their right. About 5:30 p.m., a dispatch rider delivered orders for Upton to move the regiment forward and attack an enemy line reported to be withdrawing from positions around Salem Church, which consisted of a brick chapel and schoolhouse on the far side of the woods. The 121st New York was about to see its first true fighting.[78]

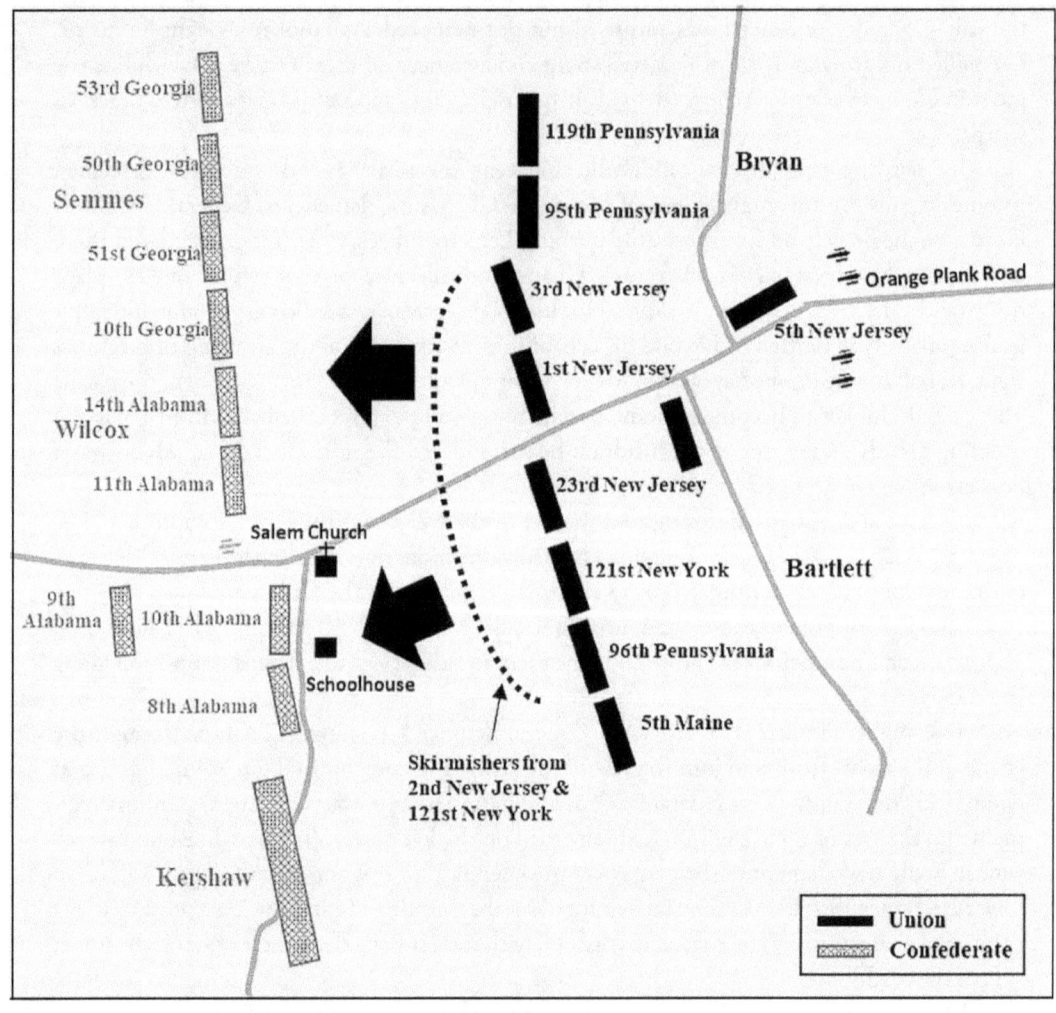

The Battle of Salem Church, May 3, 1863 (drawn by the author).

The regiment stood up at Upton's orders and advanced at a deliberate pace about 70 yards into the woods. Thick secondary growth underbrush filled the woods, but the regiment continued forward despite having to wade through the bushes. The men were very quiet, and there was no sound from them except for the occasional soldier swearing when the man in front of him pushed aside a bush, which then swung back and swatted the trailing soldier in the face.[79]

The regiment soon caught up with their skirmishers, and Upton ordered the men to "fix bayonets and forward, double quick, charge."[80] The men proceeded to run forward as ordered for about 100 yards when a line of Confederate infantry rose up in front of them "as if by magic" and delivered a volley of rifle fire described by one man as "terrific."[81] The enemy had not withdrawn after all.

In addition to the enemy infantry deployed directly in front of the regiment, the Confederates had men stationed in the church firing from the upper story windows using smoothbores loaded with three buckshot and a bullet to each charge.[82] As Upton's men fell by the dozens, Confederate bullets wounded his horse and cut the reins. The horse bolted toward the enemy lines, and Upton had to leap from his back to escape being killed or captured.[83] With Upton now leading the regiment on foot, the 121st continued moving forward, advancing about 20 yards farther, as the Confederate line opposite them broke. The regiment continued to advance, surrounding the school briefly before the enemy rallied again about 20 yards away. At this point, Upton's position became untenable because, while the 96th Pennsylvania had advanced close to his left, the 23rd New Jersey had refused to charge and, in the words of Captain Kidder, the 23rd "immediately turned and ran like sheep."[84]

This left Upton's right flank unprotected, and the Confederates soon advanced on that

Salem Church as it looks today (National Park Service).

side, pouring a terrible enfilading fire into his exposed flank. He ordered his men to begin falling back into the woods and to rally in the field where they had begun their advance. After the men came out of the woods, they retreated about 300 yards before gathering around Upton, who stood nearby with the regimental colors. As the enemy emerged from the woods in pursuit, about 75 men from the 121st and 15 soldiers from the 96th Pennsylvania opened fire and drove them back into the trees.

That night, the 121st moved into a defensive line with the rest of VI Corps, with their backs to the Rappahannock. Upton, who Kidder remarked was "one of the best and bravest hero,"[85] was noted by the brigade commander as having "led his regiment into action in a masterly and fearless manner, and maintained the unequal contest to the last with unflinching nerve and marked ability."[86]

While Upton's official report stated the regiment "came out of the action without any demoralization, and is again ready for any service that may be imposed upon it,"[87] he likely found little satisfaction in the results of the engagement. He reported his losses as 44 killed, 115 wounded, and 110 missing, making a total of 269 men lost out of 453 who went into the battle at Salem Church.[88] In the words of Surgeon Holt, "The 121st exists no more in fact [italics in original]."[89]

Among the badly wounded was Upton's brother, Henry. The young lieutenant was shot through the shoulder and upper portion of his right lung. He had laid wounded near the woods as the regiment retreated and was soon taken prisoner by the Confederates. He and all the other Union wounded were taken to the church, where they were soon joined by Surgeon Holt, who had also been captured during the fighting. Holt treated Henry and the others as best he could, given that he had almost no medical supplies on hand. On May 7, the Confederate troops moved off, and Union forces arrived to evacuate the wounded.[90] Henry was sent home to recover, and for the next few months, Upton's letters enquired about his health and recovery. "How is brother Henry's shoulder," he asked his sister in a July 1863 letter. "Have him keep perfectly quiet, and not think of returning until able to do duty."[91]

The 121st New York suffered an appalling 59 percent casualty rate at Salem Church, the worst of any Union regiment in the Chancellorsville campaign.[92] While not apparent at the time, the fighting at Salem Church would become a seminal event in Upton's life. This was Upton's first experience going into battle with infantry employing the prevailing tactics of the time. There had been little advance preparation and almost no artillery support. It had been an infantry charge at the double-quick step in line formation against a well-positioned defensive force. The results were horrific, but, sadly, very common in this war. Upton saw firsthand the slaughter exacted by 19th-century rifles, and he saw the price paid by his own men. From this point forward, he would never make a frontal attack in daylight without careful preparation and proper support. Even more so, the events at Salem Church began a professional journey for Upton that would last the remainder of his life, that of a passionate reformer who was determined to change the army's professional culture and tactics.[93]

Recovery

As the Army of the Potomac once more retreated in defeat, Upton returned with the regiment to their old camp at White Oak Church. With his ranks decimated at Salem Church,

Upton had to find replacements. Many of the wounded were to be discharged, while others were transferred to the Veteran Reserve Corps, where they would only perform light duties for the remainder of their enlistment.[94] Fortunately for Upton, there were soldiers readily available.

Four New York infantry regiments were disbanding because most of their men had now served their two-year enlistments and were heading home. However, there were others within their ranks who had not served two years and were considered to be three-year recruits. They were told they would be transferred to fill the depleted ranks of other New York regiments such as the 121st.[95]

This did not go over well with the transferred soldiers assigned to Upton. Most of these men felt they had only signed to fight with their original regiments, and that they ought to go home with their comrades. Further, they argued that they had not been told they were signing three-year enlistments when they joined their original regiments. John Kidder wrote his wife about the situation, telling her, "They are disposed to be mutinous. I am fearful we shall see trouble with them as they say that they will not go into a fight."[96]

Upton did his best to calm the situation. He called the new men together and "explained to them their position and the position of the government, and his determination to enforce rigid compliance to orders, and at the same time appealed to their pride and patriotism."[97] This approach worked with the majority of the soldiers, who then did their best to integrate themselves into the regiment. However, others still protested and sent a formal complaint to the War Department. But the Secretary of War, Edwin Stanton, denied their request for discharge, saying, "Might as well disband the Army." In the secretary's opinion, these men had been duped by their enlistment agents and that the government was not responsible for their illegal acts or the false promises they had made.[98] Unfortunately, no sooner had Upton quelled the uprising from some of the transferred soldiers than a new problem appeared. But this time it was among his officers.

During the fighting at Salem Church, Upton had a captain and two lieutenants killed in action and another wounded captain died on May 18. Additionally, his brother Henry was at home recovering from his wounds, and another of his captains had been captured. In fact, only one wounded officer, Captain Mather, returned to duty quickly. Upton needed to fill these positions as soon as possible, as Lee might decide to go on the offensive at any time.[99]

His first act was to promote three of his lieutenants to captain, which was applauded by all his officers. "This is as it should be," wrote Henry Kidder. "We are all glad to see such men promoted as they are worthy of it."[100] However, the young colonel created discontent when he arranged the transfer of three officers from the 27th New York into his regiment. Most of his officers felt the additional replacements should be found by promoting noncommissioned officers within the 121st.

Before this action even had time to settle, Upton made matters worse. One of his majors, Egbert Olcott, was moved up the chain of command, creating a vacancy. Being promoted to major was seen as a significant step up the ladder by Upton's captains, and they anxiously waited to see who he would promote into the vacant position. But once again, Upton went outside the regiment, transferring Captain Robert Wilson over from the 16th New York to serve as a major in the 121st. At this point, one of his officers, Henry Galpin, turned in his resignation. Galpin was a popular choice for the major's position among the other captains in the regiment, who were very upset he was not promoted. Upton refused the resignation and Galpin forwarded it directly to the War Department. Upton called his officers together and tried to quell this small rebellion. Unfortunately, his efforts fell flat. Perhaps it was because, as an officer from the Regular Army, Upton saw things differently than his volunteer officers. His only criteria for selecting officers was to find those he felt were the most qualified, whether they came from within the regiment or not. Henry Kidder recalled that Upton told them "to smother their feelings or leave the service as he said that having Wilson for Major added another brave and good officer."[101]

This turbulent situation became even worse when Captain Wilson arrived. As soon as he saw how unhappy the other officers were with his promotion, Wilson immediately resigned the position. Confident that Galpin would now be promoted, the officers seemed content to drop the matter completely. However, Upton decided to promote Captain Mather to major. Mather was a member of the 121st but was junior in rank not only to Galpin but to three other officers as well. Several more officers turned in resignations, and Upton refused them all.[102]

He called another meeting with his officers where he told them he had passed over Galpin because he, like many others among the officers, was far too familiar with his men. Again, as a Regular Army officer, Upton apparently did not realize his comment made him seem more than a little oblivious to reality. After all, this was a volunteer regiment where many of the officers had not only recruited the men, but they had also known them for much of their lives. As such, it was almost impossible to achieve the kind of distance Upton thought necessary in the relationship between an officer and his soldiers. Further, many of the officers believed the reason Mather seemed less familiar with the men of his company was that he was very pretentious and "all fop, all dress."[103] In the end, no one else resigned, and the regiment's officers seemed to accept the situation, although with strong reservations.

The regiment spent the month of June recovering from Salem Church and the upheaval caused by the staff promotions controversy. But Upton and his men soon would be on the move again, and Upton would find himself moving up the chain of command once more.

6

Brigade Commander

> And it is just and fitting here to acknowledge the soldierly conduct and valuable assistance of Colonel Upton and his gallant regiments, the Fifth Maine and One hundred and twenty-first New York. Prompt in their support, they deserve our heartiest thanks, as by their bravery they won a large share of the honors of the day.
>
> —General Orders No. 51, 3rd Brigade,
> First Division, VI Corps, November 9, 1863[1]

Gettysburg

No one could ever accuse Robert E. Lee of resting on his laurels. As he had done following Second Manassas, the always audacious Lee saw his victory at Chancellorsville as an opportunity to strike a final, mortal blow against the Army of the Potomac. He also saw how badly Hooker performed as an army commander and thought the morale of his opponent's men might be very low. He decided that he must once again move across the Potomac and invade the North. But this time, he would be even bolder than he had been the year before and penetrate Pennsylvania. Hooker would have to pursue and engage the Army of Northern Virginia, providing Lee the chance for a knockout punch that could end the war on the Confederacy's terms.

On June 4, 1863, the Army of Northern Virginia began to move towards the Blue Ridge, intending to cross the mountains and move north up the Shenandoah Valley where it would be difficult for Hooker's cavalry to observe them. To keep his Union counterpart confused as long as possible, Lee ordered General A.P. Hill to move his corps into Fredericksburg and to make "such disposition as will be best calculated to deceive the enemy, and keep him in ignorance of any change in the disposition of the army."[2]

As Lee organized for his campaign, Hooker did very little planning and simply went into a reactive posture. He had surrendered the initiative to Lee at Chancellorsville and seemed to have no intention of recapturing it. On the same day Lee's army began its march north, Union scouts informed Hooker that some of the enemy camps were empty.[3] But Hooker did not seem to know what to make of this information. As Lee hoped, Hooker remained confused for several days. At first, he was certain that Lee planned to unleash Jeb Stuart in a cavalry raid, and that the rest of the enemy army had merely repositioned their camps.

On June 6, Hooker ordered the 121st New York and the rest of VI Corps' First Division to cross the Rappahannock and confront A.P. Hill's corps at Fredericksburg. Upton had his men dig in as soon as they were across the river near the same place they initially occupied in May.[4] They awaited an attack, but none came, as Hill was content to merely observe the Union army's movements until he too began the march away towards Pennsylvania. After a few days, it became apparent to Hooker that Hill had left Fredericksburg, and he ordered the First Division to re-cross the river.

It was June 13 before Hooker realized that Lee's entire army was now marching north through the Shenandoah Valley and that he must start moving the Army of the Potomac north in parallel on the east side of the mountains. The army had lost precious time, and it would have to make forced marches to catch up to Lee. That night, Hooker ordered the army to move north and directed that VI Corps leave their camps last, acting as a rear guard.[5]

On June 14, Upton had his regiment in motion, bringing up the rear of the army. Being the rear guard is never a desirable assignment when an army is on the move, especially when it is trying to move quickly. As one of Upton's soldiers later wrote, "The position of rear guard is always a wearisome one, because of the fact that the uncertainty of the movement of the troops ahead often leaves long distances between the different corps which must be closed by forced marching by those in the rear."[6] In this case, the situation for Upton and his men was made worse by a late night start and bad weather. The regiment did not step off until nearly midnight and, almost as soon as they started, a fierce thunderstorm began. In pouring rain and deep darkness "lit only by vivid flashes of lightning with accompanying peals of thunder,"[7] his men trudged through deep mud, passing abandoned burning camps of the corps that marched ahead of them. As soon as the rain stopped, the red clay roads dried quickly, which, while it made for easier walking, soon produced clouds of choking dust.[8]

The 121st New York marched to Stafford Court House and then Dumfries before reaching Fairfax Station on June 17. Once there, orders came down saying the regiment could rest for a day.[9] But before resuming the march the next day, Upton and his officers learned for the first time that Lee's army had already crossed the Potomac, moved through Maryland, and entered Pennsylvania. At this stunning news, one officer commented, "This accounts for our hard marching."[10]

On June 18, Upton moved his men to Germantown, followed by rapid marches through Bristoe Station and Centreville to Dranesville. On June 27, the 121st crossed the Potomac at Edward's Ferry, and their arrival in Maryland was greeted by another batch of fierce thunderstorms followed by hot, dusty roads as they marched through Poolesville, Maryland and then on to Hyattstown. Here, orders came down from VI Corps headquarters to increase the pace of the march. The regiment marched to New Windsor on June 29 and then made a remarkable 28-mile trek to Manchester on June 30, moving as fast as five miles per hour. Upton and his men knew this increased pace meant something serious, and he urged them to keep their ranks closed up. As soldiers often do in times like these, they resorted to humor to make the march easier. Since the officers were riding their horses while the men walked, they began making jokes loud enough for the officers to hear, saying that the horses would soon play out, and then the troops could rest.[11]

Once the regiment arrived in Manchester, Upton ordered the men to make camp and rest for the night. It was a lovely place to camp, and the soldiers quickly spread their blankets under the shade of nearby trees. The men started fires and enjoyed a hot meal for the first time in days. However, just as the men prepared to sleep, a dispatch rider arrived with a message telling Upton to get the regiment back on the road immediately. More ominously, it directed him to distribute 60 rounds of ammunition and three days' rations to every soldier. This message clearly meant that a battle was not too far off.[12]

He called his company commanders together and gave them the news. Naturally, everyone wanted more information on where the battle might be, but at this point, Upton knew no more than they did. Then he provided the startling news that President Lincoln had relieved General Hooker of command and that General George Meade had replaced him.[13]

Unknown to them, Hooker had compounded his erratic behavior regarding Lee's movements by starting a running argument with the president and the general-in-chief, Henry Halleck, regarding the disposition of the Federal garrison at Harpers Ferry. Conducted via a series of messages, Hooker continued to demonstrate just how unsuitable he was for command of one of the Union's most critical armies. Hooker wanted the garrison to abandon Harpers Ferry, while both Lincoln and Halleck insisted the garrison remain in place. Finally, Hooker sent a message saying he would resign if Harpers Ferry was not vacated, and the president was all too happy to take him at his word. On June 28, Lincoln accepted Hooker's offer to resign and immediately appointed Meade as his replacement.

Upton had his men on the road within an hour, and they marched into the night of July 1. While they trudged north, the fighting had already begun at Gettysburg when Lee's army converged on the town from the west and the north. Thinking the town undefended, they were surprised to find Union cavalry under the command of General John Buford awaiting their arrival. Buford's scouts told him that Lee was coming and, as a veteran soldier, Buford could see the potential value of the high ground just to the southeast of Gettysburg. He was determined to slow Lee down, allowing the rapidly converging infantry from Meade's army to take a position there. He achieved his goal by defending the terrain west of the town until infantry from I and XI Corps relieved his cavalry brigade. But the Union infantry could not hold for long against superior numbers, and Lee pushed them back through Gettysburg to Cemetery Hill. Here, the Union soldiers took strong positions, and, as more Federal troops arrived, they aligned themselves along the high ground Buford had chosen for the coming fighting on July 2.

As a result, on the night of July 1, Meade told General Sedgwick to move VI Corps forward as fast as possible. "Your march will have to be a forced one to reach the scene of action," wrote General Daniel Butterfield, Meade's chief of staff, "where we shall probably be largely outnumbered without your presence."[14] As Sedgwick dispatched orders to his division commanders, he directed Upton's brigade commander, General Joseph Bartlett, to take command of the First Division, which meant Bartlett needed to appoint a replacement to lead the 2nd Brigade quickly. The general did not hesitate, ordering Upton to take command of the brigade.

The transfer, which was made permanent three days later, marked an incredible climb up the chain of command for Emory Upton. In just two years, he had gone from command of a six-gun artillery battery to command of an infantry regiment, and now he found himself leading a brigade consisting of four regiments, the 121st New York, 5th Maine, 95th Pennsylvania, and 96th Pennsylvania. When Upton wrote his sister after Gettysburg, he told her with much-deserved pride, "The command of a brigade is a half-way step between colonel and brigadier-general, and I shall try to take the full step in the next battle."[15] However, as events would prove, merely performing well in battle would not be enough to attain a brigadier general's star.

Route of Upton's 121st New York as it marched to Gettysburg, June 14–July 2, 1863 (drawn by the author).

6. Brigade Commander

After only a short rest, Upton moved his brigade onto the Baltimore Pike, and they marched all through the night towards Gettysburg. At daylight on July 2, he began to see the first signs of the fighting up the road. Wounded men, hospital and supply wagons, and the inevitable stragglers that every battle produced filled the roadside. Upton pushed the brigade hard, not allowing any stops to eat or rest. One soldier recalled that "many men became exhausted and dropped down from fatigue in spite of the energetic efforts of the officers to urge them on. Orders were given the officers to shoot stragglers, and every man was impressed with the seriousness of the situation."[16]

As Upton's brigade approached Gettysburg, they could hear artillery and rifle fire in the distance. Charles Beckwith later wrote that "from its weight and volume we knew a terrific combat was progressing."[17] In the late afternoon, Upton and his men arrived on the battlefield having marched 32 miles in about six hours. The brigade crossed Pipe Creek, and, soon, Upton could see the Federal batteries that were rapidly firing barrages from Cemetery Ridge trying to beat back a massive attack on the Union left by Longstreet's corps.[18] With the sun moving lower in the western sky, the firing subsided as Longstreet's men fell back from their unsuccessful attempt to break the Federal left flank at Little Round Top.

General Bartlett directed Upton to move his brigade to relieve the defenders of Little Round Top. Upton deployed his new command into an advanced position in some woods on the slope of the hill, with numerous large rocks to provide cover. Once in position there, the men finally had a chance to rest. Knowing how exhausted his men were and fearing a renewed enemy attack on Little Round Top, Upton decided to address his men. He felt the fate of the nation might well depend on the outcome of this battle, and the words seemed to pour directly from his heart. "In a few words," he wrote his sister, "I told them how momentous was the issue, how much the country expected of us." Upton went on to appeal to the men's pride and patriotism, "I promised to lead, and asked them to follow," he later wrote. As he spoke, Upton saw his men shed their fatigue and, when he was done speaking, they burst into a loud cheer that "would have raised the hair of a confronting rebel."[19]

The next day, July 3, his brigade saw no fighting, but they were able to observe Lee's final desperate attempt to break the Army of the Potomac. Along with his soldiers, Upton watched from a distance as General Pickett's division marched across open ground to attack the Union II Corps on Cemetery Ridge. Pickett's men endured heavy artillery fire almost from the moment they stepped off. The few Southern soldiers who reached the Federal lines broke through briefly before being driven back by a fierce Union counterattack. In describing the attack in a letter to his sister, Upton wrote: "For about ten minutes I watched the contest, when it seemed that the weight of a hair would have turned the scales. Our men fought most gallantly. The rebels began to give way, and soon retreated in utter confusion. Shortly after, the enemy on our left also retreated. I think Lee will evacuate Maryland and Pennsylvania at once. He sought this battle, and was badly whipped."[20]

Pursuing Lee

Upton was right about Lee's next move. It began to rain on the night of July 3, and Lee ordered his battered army to prepare for a retreat the next day. As Lee moved south on July 4, Meade made no move to pursue the Confederate army, preferring to rest and recover for at least one day. On the morning of July 5, Meade ordered VI Corps to lead the army out of Gettysburg in pursuit of Lee. Upton's brigade took the first position in line and marched to Emmitsburg, Maryland, some ten miles south of the battlefield. Here, the brigade found that many Confederate wounded had been left behind, and the Sisters of Charity, who had a house in Emmitsburg, were caring for them. Surgeon Couch remarked on the care being given, writing that the Sisters came out "in great numbers to administer to the comfort and wants of the wounded and dying; while the Catholic Priests mixed freely up with both loyal and disloyal consoling and granting absolution."[21]

The next day, Meade ordered the brigade to turn to the west and march over Crampton's Gap to Middletown. Lee was on the far side of South Mountain, heading for the Potomac at Williamsport. The march over the pass was very difficult, as another heavy rainstorm appeared. The men leaned into the steady downpour late into the night. Before they had completed the march over the mountain, Upton called a halt to allow the men to eat and rest a little before continuing. Early the next morning, Upton had the brigade moving again, and they completed their ascent, descended the western slope, and arrived in Middletown that evening. Here, Upton halted again for rest and resupply.[22]

The next day, July 9, the brigade was on the march at 5:00 a.m., moving slightly northwest towards Boonsboro, which was 12 miles away. Five hours later, as the brigade approached Boonsboro, they made contact with enemy skirmishers. Upton deployed the brigade for battle, but before the men were in line, the Confederates at their front chose to withdraw. Oddly, at this point, with an indication the enemy's rear guard might be nearby, Upton received orders from General Bartlett to make camp for the night.[23] Had the brigade moved out promptly in pursuit, they might have caught Lee. It was these kinds of acts that would anger President Lincoln and cause him to chastise General Meade for not making a more energetic effort to chase and destroy the Army of Northern Virginia. The march continued the next morning, and there were a couple of minor clashes between skirmishers over the next two days.

On July 12, the brigade and the rest of VI Corps passed through Funkstown and found elements of Lee's army deployed in a wheat field and along a rocky ledge. The brigade deployed,

Edward Forbes' drawing of the VI Corps pursuit of Lee's army campaign (Library of Congress).

and Upton was told to advance skirmishers to drive the enemy back before sunset. He deployed his skirmish line and instructed the men not to fire until they had crossed the last in a series of fences between them and the ledge. The men performed Upton's orders with precision, taking the position with a loss of only eight wounded.[24]

After sunset and through the next day, VI Corps dug rifle pits and prepared for an assault on the morning of July 14. However, when they advanced towards Williamsport, they did not find any of Lee's army in front of them. General Bartlett sent out a small reconnaissance party who came back to report Lee was gone.[25] He moved his entire army across the Potomac the night before and was now marching away up the Shenandoah Valley. The Gettysburg campaign was over.

Occupying Northern Virginia

Upton's brigade and the rest of the Army of the Potomac moved back into northern Virginia as Lee and Meade played a chess game against one another throughout the fall of 1863. Lee would make a move, Meade would counter, and, while there might be a brief cavalry skirmish between the two sides, no major battles occurred.

The brigade encamped near Warrenton, Virginia, in August, during which Confederate guerrilla forces under Colonel John Mosby plagued the Army of the Potomac. They stole badly needed supplies, ambushed Union patrols, and kidnapped soldiers who strayed too far from camp. As his raids increased in number and boldness, Mosby became a thorn in George Meade's side, and he and his Partisan Rangers became much-beloved figures among the population of Loudon County in northern Virginia, whose hatred for the Army of the Potomac was palpable. A slight man weighing only 125 pounds, Mosby was far from the imposing figure his reputation might have indicated. Yet he was daring and brilliant, either planning and executing raids that struck hard and fast or concocting schemes that confused and bewildered Federal authorities.[26]

In August 1863, Emory Upton was the target of one of Mosby's schemes. Shortly after the brigade arrived in Warrenton, a local woman appeared in camp requesting to speak with Upton. She was ushered into his quarters, whereupon she asked him if he would provide a guard to protect her person and property from wonton acts by Union soldiers. As her home was only about a half-mile from the camp, Upton agreed and dispatched his aide and one soldier to perform guard duties. However, as soon as the two men arrived at the woman's house, a band of Mosby's men seized both. They had been hiding there, waiting for the woman's return, and she had been a willing participant in their plan. But rather than being content with the capture of the two soldiers, the woman returned to have another audience with Upton. This time, she "blandly informed" him about the capture of his men and asked that he send more men to her aid. Now suspecting her motives, Upton flatly refused her request and sent her home.[27]

Not long after this embarrassing incident, Mosby raided the headquarters of General Bartlett. This was too much for Upton to tolerate, and he decided to lead a small expedition out into the countryside to capture Mosby. Selecting his old regiment, the 121st New York, for the job, Upton divided the men into two wings. He would lead one wing towards Middleburg, about 20 miles to the north, while Lieutenant Colonel Olcott took the other wing towards the small village of Salem, which lay about 12 miles to the north-northwest. The two wings would march quietly out of camp at 3:00 a.m., using the darkness to cover their departure.

The men stumbled through the night until they reached White Plains, a distance of nine miles, where Upton called for a brief halt to rest. The soldiers then proceeded on towards Middleburg, which they reached the following evening. Upton ordered the men to surround the town and prevent anyone from leaving. With that accomplished, he moved his soldiers into the town where he had every house and building searched. He ordered the confiscation of all weapons and horses but decreed that there would be no violence or destruction of property unless provoked. "If we were fired upon from any house," Captain Kidder later wrote, "we were to order the in mates [sic] out and then burn it to the ground." Furthermore, he reported that Upton told them that, if they found any of Mosby's men, they "were not to take them alive" if they could help it.[28]

One woman attempted to block the gate to her home, refusing to allow Kidder's men to search the house. When a shoving match ensued, she lodged a complaint with Captain Kidder, demanding that the captain discipline the corporal who shoved her and that his soldiers leave her property immediately. Kidder's suspicions were aroused by her ardor. He told her that the corporal was acting on his orders and that, if she did not want to be pushed away, she should not resist. The Union soldiers proceeded to search the house where they found her brother hiding. He was suspected of being one of Mosby's men and was taken into custody.[29]

The raids on Middleburg and Salem did not result in Mosby's capture and, while several suspected guerrillas were taken prisoner, all but one was eventually released. All Upton could show for his foray were 40 horses and lots of turkeys, chickens, and ducks deemed as the "contraband of war."[30]

As the brigade remained near Warrenton in early November, Upton wrote his sister once more. He mused about his impatience with the course of the war, saying, "I sometimes get discouraged because of our not accomplishing decided results, but patience is a military as well as a social virtue, and therefore I continue to hope."[31]

Next, however, he related his feelings about the quality of the army's soldiers and what he had begun to see as a lack of leadership. "No soldier in the world can equal the American, if properly commanded," he wrote. Upton told his sister that the Union soldier only wanted "a general who can call out his good qualities, or one who comprehends his nature." Upton felt that this vital leadership quality seemed totally lacking in most of the army's generals, who seemingly displayed "total ignorance of human nature." Upton had repeatedly seen how strong encouragement from a commander could influence soldiers' conduct when under fire. "I have never heard our generals utter a word of encouragement," he wrote his sister, "either before or after entering a battle." He complained that he had not once seen them ride along the lines to "tell each regiment that it held an important position and that it was expected to hold it to the last." Perhaps worst of all, he said that he had never "seen a general thank his troops after the action for the gallantry they have displayed."[32] This concern about poor leadership would increase in the coming years and become a key factor in Upton's professional life.

While the brigade encamped, Upton received a pleasant surprise. The enlistments for original members of one of his brigade's regiments, the 95th Pennsylvania, were due to expire.

Given all the issues he had seen before with maintaining proper unit strengths, he likely was certain he would be losing these valuable veteran soldiers. But to his delight, he learned that all remaining 245 veterans in the regiment had re-enlisted. They were the first regiment in the Army of the Potomac to achieve a 100 percent re-enlistment. When their paperwork crossed his desk, Upton added a strong endorsement of their action before forwarding it up the chain of command.[33]

Rappahannock Station

Lee and Meade's maneuvering finally subsided with Lee taking a strong position at Rappahannock Station, where a railroad bridge had once crossed the Rappahannock River north of Fredericksburg near Kelly's Ford. Lee not only placed men on the south bank of the river, but he also dug and manned a strong set of fortifications north of the river. These protected a pon-

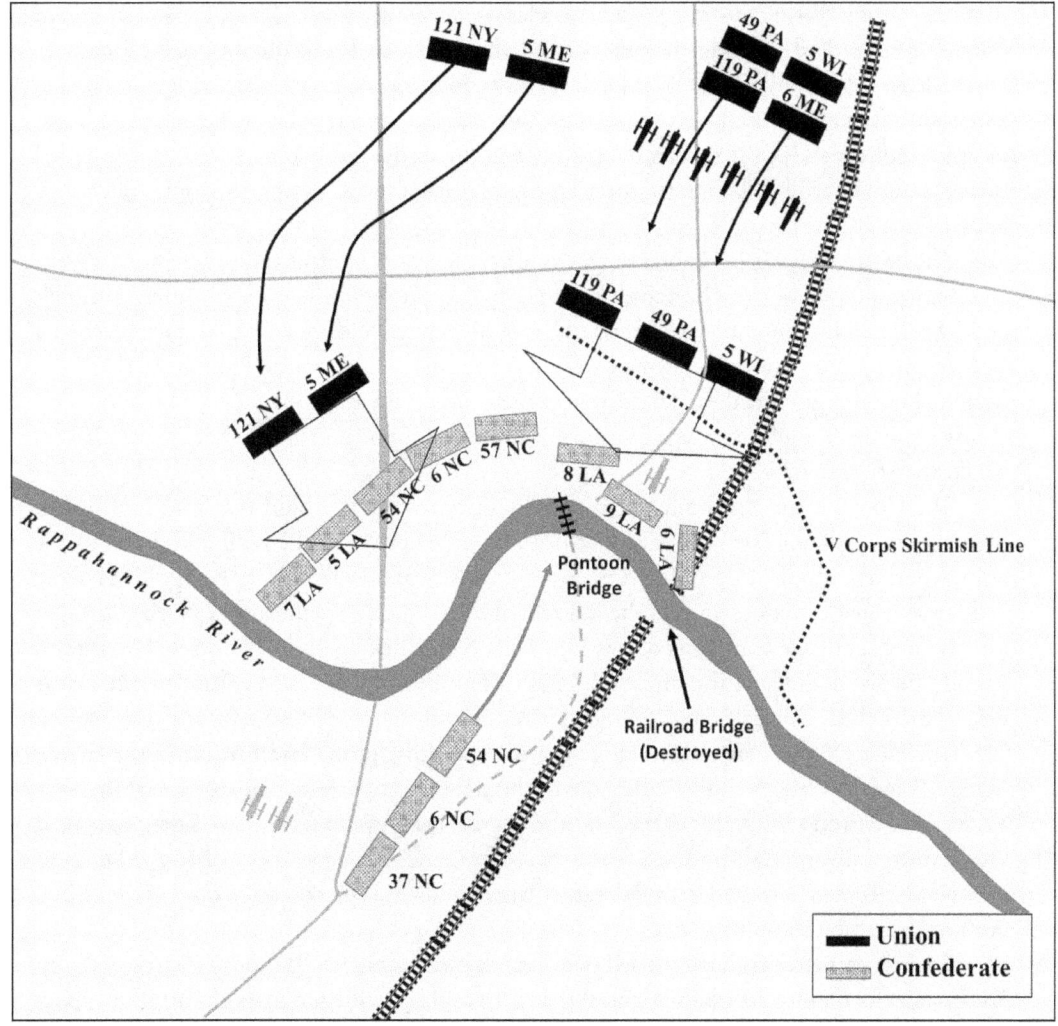

The Battle of Rappahannock Station, November 7, 1863 (drawn by the author).

toon bridge over the Rappahannock, which provided Lee with a bridgehead he could use to quickly get his army north of the river to strike the Army of the Potomac's flank.[34]

Meade had been under considerable pressure from both President Lincoln and the Congress for his failure to prosecute an aggressive pursuit of Lee following Gettysburg. Given that Lee's new position on the Rappahannock posed a credible threat to his army, he decided to move against it.

On the evening of November 6, not long after Upton had posted his latest letter to his sister, he received orders to prepare his brigade to march early the next morning. He called his regiment commanders together and relayed the word of the new movement, which they then sent throughout the camp. Soldiers began to break down their tents and pack up their meager belongings in preparation before grabbing a few hurried hours of sleep.[35]

Upton and his brigade were on the road heading south at 7:00 a.m. on the morning of November 7. The weather was beautiful and just cool enough to make the rigors of marching less challenging. One soldier recalled that the brigade's men "moved on with the usual route step, conjecturing, querying, and speculating"[36] about their destination. Shortly before noon, Upton halted the brigade and ordered that the men break out to rest and prepare lunch. The soldiers built small fires quickly, and soon were cooking a meal with pork, bread, and coffee as common items on the menu. They relaxed, and the day so far seemed almost pleasant. But the sudden rumbling of artillery and the rattle of rifle fire in the distance ended their relaxation, telling them that the purpose of their travels was more serious than they hoped.[37]

The brigade quickly fell in on the road and set out again, but this time, there was no jocular discussion on what might lie ahead. For an hour, Upton and the brigade continued through heavily forested terrain until the sounds of battle died away. Shortly after that, they reached a clearing, and Upton saw that they had arrived at the edge of the woods. From here, there was nothing but open ground ahead all the way to the banks of the Rappahannock, which he could clearly see in the distance. The view also afforded him the opportunity to see Lee's fortifications, which were considerable.[38]

The Confederates had built a strong redoubt on top of the bluff that rose high above the river. The redoubt extended for one-third of a mile upriver to the right and down to the point where a pontoon bridge crossed the river at the site of the old railroad bridge. The enemy had positioned a battery of guns in the redoubt along with three regiments of North Carolina infantry and a brigade consisting of five Louisiana regiments. The breastworks and a series of strong rifle pits dominated the surrounding open terrain and provided Lee's men with a clear field of fire against any attackers.[39]

The First Division formed in line in the woods with Upton's 2nd Brigade in the center, the 3rd Brigade to his left, and 1st Brigade to the right. Around 3:00 p.m., the entire division advanced to within 1,000 yards of the redoubt. For the next few hours, the two sides exchanged artillery fire, and Union skirmishers sent forward by General David Russell, the First Division commander, traded shots with Confederate riflemen in the rifle pits that stretched in a long line just forward of the redoubt.[40]

As dusk gathered, General Russell sent the 6th Maine and 5th Wisconsin regiments from 3rd Brigade forward to attack the right of the redoubt. He decided to mask the attack by making it appear the new regiments were simply men coming to relieve the current Union skirmishers. As Upton later reported the events to his sister, "The enemy saw the whole operation, but supposing it simply a relief, paid but little attention to the matter. The first or old line of skirmishers were notified of the intention, the second line came up to where the first lay, when both rushed upon the enemy's redoubts, and were almost inside before the enemy recovered from his astonishment."[41] The fighting inside the redoubt was brutal hand-to-hand combat using bayonets and rifle butts. While the men from Maine and Wisconsin managed to drive away the defenders on that flank of the redoubt, their losses were severe. The 6th Maine alone lost 139 men.[42]

The enemy now launched a furious counterattack trying to drive the Union troops out of the redoubt. General Russell sent orders to Upton directing that he immediately deploy two of his regiments to support the 6th Maine and 5th Wisconsin. Upton saw that the 5th Maine and his old 121st New York were first in line, so he rode over to them. "I immediately ordered them forward," he later wrote his sister, "and, to avoid any delay, directed them to load while marching."[43] With Upton leading on horseback, the two regiments moved off at the double-quick, passing over some swampy ground as they approached the redoubt.

As soon as Upton reached the line of battle, General Russell rode up, pointed to a Confederate rifle pit on the right, and told Upton to take the position. Upton could see that this position allowed the Confederate troops to pour a deadly enfilading fire into the Union soldiers. He could also see that they had a considerable force there. "The work was on the summit of a gently rising knoll," he wrote to his sister. "Their banners could be plainly seen outstanding against the sky, while their saucy heads appearing everywhere above the parapets forewarned us how deadly might be our task."[44]

The sun had since set, and pronounced darkness had replaced it. One soldier remembered that there was "no moon to light up the surroundings" and that the "stars themselves seemed to hold back a little of their usual radiance, lest too much cheer might surround us."[45] But as that same soldier pointed out, the deep darkness "proved to be the instrument of our salvation."[46] The reason for that was that Upton chose to use the darkness as a tool and modify his tactics to take advantage of it.

He ordered the two regiments to unsling their knapsacks and fix bayonets. Then he directed that no one was to fire a shot until the enemy engaged them. With whispered orders to advance, the men ran forward and, when they were only 30 yards away from the rifle pits, Upton gave the order to charge. The blue line swept over the knoll and into the rifle pits. One soldier from the 121st New York recalled that they went "forward on a run, with a yell" before jumping into the rifle pits where "the Rebels in them began to run. We did not fire until we got inside the rifle pits, and the fire of the enemy was not very severe."[47]

While Upton had achieved the objective in the general's orders, he quickly determined there was more they might accomplish. His officers told him the enemy to their right seemed to be in confusion and might be trying to fall back across the river. He could see the timing was ripe to continue their attack. He sent one of his staff officers off to tell General Russell that they had taken the rifle pits and were now going to press the attack into the redoubt itself. Upton then ordered Major Mather to take part of the 121st New York towards the pontoon bridge and cut off any enemy retreat. Mather and his men set off at a run, found the bridge, and halted some retreating Confederates just as they arrived.[48]

Upton then ordered the 5th Maine and the remainder of the 121st New York to form up for another advance. The 5th Maine was aligned on the right in a single line of battle formation, with the 121st New York on its immediate left. But with the 121st, Upton decided to improvise.

Rather than forming them in the standard line formation, he put them in a close column formation that presented a very narrow front to the enemy's line.[49]

Upton had been carefully considering the use of a column formation as a new tactic and would soon become its leading advocate. To be sure, it had its disadvantages. The biggest of these was that, first, most of the attacking troops could not fire, because friendly troops were in front of them, and, second, they could be exposed to deadly enfilading fire on their flanks. However, at the same time, there were tremendous advantages to a column assault. First, because the column began its attack close to the enemy works, the attacking force was exposed to fewer enemy volleys. At the same time, the sheer weight of the rapidly advancing column could quickly breach the enemy's lines, which they could then exploit by creating flanks where none had existed before. Further, the attacking column could rapidly put a large number of troops into the enemy lines, allowing the attackers to hold onto the captured position.[50]

With his men now aligned for the attack, Upton whispered orders that, again, no one was to fire until they were inside the enemy's lines. These orders went down the line through the two regiments in hushed tones. Then, just as the men were set to move off, Upton decided to engage in some psychological warfare. He raised his voice and began to give a speech so loud that the enemy was sure to hear it. "Men of the 121st New York," he shouted, "your friends at home and your country expect every man to do his duty on this occasion. Some of us have got to die, but remember you are going to heaven. When I give the command to charge move forward. If they fire upon you, I will move six lines of battle over you and bayonet every one of them."[51] Of course, Upton did not have any force close to six lines of battle.

The men began to move forward up the gentle slope in total silence. One Maine soldier said their "hearts almost cease to beat" and the "eye strains to pierce the darkness." Officers whispered "steadily" encouraging the men to continue to creep forward. Suddenly a single shot rang out in the dark from the enemy, and Upton's men could hear Confederate soldiers shouting the alarm inside the redoubt. As the enemy fired another shot, officers ordered the Union troops to lie down just before a full volley blasted at them from the enemy line. But the shots went harmlessly over their heads.[52]

At that moment, Upton shouted, "5th Maine and 121st New York, honor the flag of the United States; forward!" The order to "double quick, charge" rang out from the regimental officers and the blue troops swarmed forward up the slope and over the redoubt with a deafening

Alfred Waud's sketch of the nighttime fighting by Upton's brigade at Rappahannock Station (Library of Congress).

yell. Convinced that an overwhelming force was coming, the Confederates inside the redoubt began to call out for quarter immediately, surrendering by the hundreds. Upton's speech had done the trick.[53] The Southern colonel commanding the position surrendered personally to Upton,[54] and many enemy officers stated they truly believed a mass column of thousands was coming at them.

Upton's attack at Rappahannock Station was one of the most remarkable in the war to date. Unlike the action at Salem Church, he decided to innovate on the spot, using the advantage of the darkness to employ stealth and a fast-moving column formation, combined with a little deception. The result was that an attacking force of only 568 men captured 133 enemy officers, more than 1,300 soldiers, and over 1,200 stands of arms in an action that lasted just minutes.[55] The attack also demonstrated that there was no need to rely on standard tactics and that innovation could achieve remarkable success with minimum casualties.

If anyone was paying attention, it also pointed out that young Emory Upton was a force to be reckoned with and the source of the kind of innovation the Union army badly needed.

7

Into the Wilderness

> I shall do my duty faithfully, and I shall leave behind a record to which you can always refer with pride and satisfaction.
>
> Emory Upton, April 25, 1864[1]

Fighting for Promotion

While the accolades for his conduct at Rappahannock Station were still fresh, Upton and many of his supporters in the army's chain of command pressed for his promotion to Brigadier General of Volunteers, the rank typically given a brigade commander. This was not the first time this had happened. In September 1863, his superiors strongly recommended him for promotion as documented in letters written to General Henry Halleck, the U.S. Army's general-in-chief, Secretary of War Edwin Stanton, and even President Lincoln, all of which General Meade heartily endorsed. These letters heaped praise on Upton and recounted his numerous successes in the field since the beginning of the war. General Bartlett, the commander of the 2nd Brigade, First Division, VI Corps, noted Upton's "coolness and bravery under fire,"[2] while General Robert Schenk, commander of the VIII Corps, described him as being "remarkable for his zeal, intelligence, and gallantry."[3]

The strongest endorsement came from General Daniel Butterfield, who had been Meade's Chief of Staff in the Army of the Potomac. Butterfield had worked with Upton in 1861 just after he first reported for duty fresh from West Point. The young officer made an impression on Butterfield that only grew stronger as the war continued. In his letter to Secretary Stanton, which General Hooker further endorsed, Butterfield wrote of Upton, "He possesses skill, energy, devotion and bravery. His presence has been felt in whatever position he has served. He has been noticed for gallantry on every field where he has been engaged."[4]

More recommendations were submitted on his behalf in November 1863, but all these commendations seemed to fall on deaf ears in Albany, where state officials held the responsibility to promote Upton. In April 1864, his fellow officers from Michigan wrote their governor, Edward Morgan, urging his support for Upton's promotion, which prompted the governor to write President Lincoln on Upton's behalf.[5] Despite all efforts, Upton remained a Colonel of Volunteers. Not surprisingly, while he kept his disappointment to himself when among his fellow officers, he complained somewhat bitterly to his sister. In early April 1864, he wrote to his sister about his frustration at being passed over:

> My Dear Sister: My long-expected promotion is not forthcoming. General Meade has informed me that without "political" influence I will never be promoted. This consolation, however, remains, if justice has not

been done, I have ever performed my duty faithfully and without regard to personal safety. The recommendation of those officers whose lives have been periled in every battle of the war have been overweighted [sic] by the baneful influence of the paltry politicians. General Sedgwick has urged my claims, and stated that they were superior to those of any other in his corps, yet two colonels have been appointed over me.[6]

Just over a week later, he wrote again, saying that, while he had not given up, he had "despaired of receiving promotion in the manner honorable to a soldier." He noted the perverse irony that promotion was "now solely the reward of political influence, and not of merit, and this when a government is fighting for its own existence."[7] His sister apparently responded with encouragement, and in his reply, Upton thanked her for her expressions of "sisterly affection."[8] But he went on at length on his deep feelings regarding his sense of duty despite this obvious snub:

> You must remember that to expose one's self simply to get promotion would be an unworthy act, and therefore, in the future as in the past, I must do my full duty with equal fearlessness. I have received of late many gratifying proofs of the confidence and esteem of both officers and men under my command, and not only in my command, but outside of it. The officers of the 1st Brigade of this division were nearly unanimous in recommending me for promotion, in the hope I might be assigned to that command. Considering that their lives to a great degree would be in my hands, especially in battle, and that no motive other than their safety and welfare could prompt such action, is it not the highest tribute men can pay me, that they should select me as their chosen leader in the hour of battle? The compliment is the more gratifying as coming from the New Jersey brigade, preferring me over every colonel from their State. The recommendation will not be forwarded, but it will serve to show the opinion of the officers of this division. Would the President consult the views of my superior officers, whose reputation depends upon my conduct to a certain degree, or those officers whose lives are in my hands in action, my promotion would not be withheld. I ought to have had it a year ago.[9]

Yet even as he wrote his sister, events were transpiring that would dramatically change Upton's fortunes, as well as those of the Army of the Potomac and the entire cause of the Union.

A New General-in-Chief

In February 1864, President Lincoln implemented a process to appoint Major General Ulysses Grant as the new General-in-Chief of the Armies of the United States. Grant had produced a brilliant series of victories in the Western Theater of the war and had done so at virtually every level of command. He was aggressive, innovative, and the master of the calculated risk. To place Grant in this position, Lincoln and the Congress created and passed a bill that restored the grade of lieutenant general, a rank previously held only by George Washington. Lincoln signed the bill into law on February 26, 1864, Grant was nominated to the Senate on March 1, confirmed by that body on March 2, and ordered to Washington the next day. He would receive the commission from President Lincoln on March 9.

This was the culmination of a long process. It was the end of a search, a quest, even, by the president to find a commander who would not only fight and win but who also had the strategic vision, as well as the political acumen, to effectively command all the nation's armies. The former had repeatedly been proven by Grant, but the latter would only be demonstrated with time. Grant would first have to develop a strategy to achieve Lincoln's war aim to reunify the nation on the president's terms, which meant the complete political and military defeat of the Confederate States of America. Then, Grant would have to accomplish the most daunting task of all by successfully executing that strategy to its ultimate conclusion.

Grant decided that his new strategy must use an entirely different approach, one that was more comprehensive, and one that reflected all he had learned during the war. His experience in the West, with its vast expanse of Southern territory, its unrepentant population, and the resilient armies of the Confederacy, made him understand that the North's war was with an entire people, their society, and their armies. Therefore, victory would only be achieved by making war on every one of those elements. However, to Grant, what would be a complex strategy had a very simple, common sense basis. As he once told a staff officer who asked him his opinion of the book on strategy written by the great French strategist Baron Jomini, "I have never read it carefully; the art of war is simple enough. Find out where your enemy is. Get at him as soon as you can. Strike him as hard as you can, and keep moving on."[10]

The first element of Grant's strategy focused on the major Confederate armies, and that was the basic foundation of his entire approach. As he later wrote, "My general plan now was to concentrate all the force possible against the Confederate armies in the field."[11] Grant planned to place unrelenting pressure on both Lee's Army of Northern Virginia and Joe Johnston's Army of Tennessee in Georgia and, if possible, draw them into the open and destroy them via one massive climatic engagement or a series of engagements.

Furthermore, while the central idea was to destroy the two major Southern armies, if they could not be destroyed in a major battle or battles, Grant would effectively use his advantage in men and resources against the South's decided disadvantage by continuously hammering at their armies in such a fashion that attrition would weaken them to a point where they either could be easily pushed aside or forced to capitulate. Therefore, his strategy was brutally elegant in that it might allow him to annihilate his enemy's military forces or, lacking that opportunity, he could exhaust the enemy logistically, economically, and psychologically.

Using what he would call the idea of "hard war," Grant

Lieutenant General Ulysses S. Grant outside his tent at Cold Harbor (Library of Congress).

was ushering in the first use of a philosophy of total war. He saw war as a brutal and unpleasant business that should be brought to a quick and speedy conclusion. The best way to do that was to simultaneously assault all elements of the Southern war effort with massive and unrelenting force.

The key element in this strategy would be the Army of the Potomac. It would draw the assignment of bringing Robert E. Lee's Army of Northern Virginia to battle and destroying it. To the surprise of many, Grant elected to keep General Meade in command of that army. But Grant also decided to accompany Meade and his army in the field. This would create friction between his staff and Meade's in the coming campaign as well as create confusion as to who was actually commanding the Army of the Potomac.

The Grand Campaign Begins

Upton made his headquarters for the winter of 1863–1864 in a small mansion just north of the Rappahannock River called Presq'Isle (near present-day Remington, Virginia). With the arrival of spring, everyone, including Upton, anticipated a new campaign would begin soon, and expectations were high with Grant in command of the nation's armies. "The spring campaign will soon be inaugurated," he wrote his sister in early April. "I trust General Grant will sustain his former reputation, and administer to General Lee such heavy blows that he may never recover."[12] He later added that he did not anticipate the campaign to begin before May 1 or possibly even mid–May. But, he continued, "we all are convinced that either a most glorious or a most disastrous one awaits us."[13] Little did he know that what lay ahead would contain some of both.

In what would be his final letter before the campaign began, he told his sister, "We are expecting to move soon. Our army is in fine condition, and I have no doubt that the bloodiest battle of the war will be fought in a few days. General Grant is well liked, and, as he is taking time to prepare his campaign, there is strong probability of his success."[14]

Unknown to Upton, the wheels for Grant's grand campaign, which became known as the Overland Campaign, were already in motion. On April 9, 1864, Grant sent Meade a dispatch outlining the coming campaign and asked that he keep its contents confidential. As with all Grant's communications, it was succinct and concise. He informed Meade that "Lee's Army will be your objective point. Wherever Lee goes there you will go also."[15] Grant's plan called for speed, the sort of speed he had come to expect from his western armies. However, Grant would soon discover that, as far as moving rapidly on the march, the Army of the Potomac was, perhaps, not made of as stern stuff as the men he had commanded in the West. Instead of being the lean, swift instrument of war he had led in Mississippi and Tennessee, this army was like a leviathan—powerful to be sure, but also ponderous, slow, and unwieldy.

Grant had decided that he would move by Lee's right flank, which would allow the army to be resupplied via the York and Pamunkey Rivers. His plan was to swiftly move past Lee's army, which was entrenched along the Rapidan, to get between the Army of Northern Virginia and Richmond, forcing Lee to come out and fight in the open or fall back into the fortifications around the Confederate capital. But he made it clear to his staff that Richmond was not their objective: "I shall not give my attention so much to Richmond as to Lee's army, and I want all commanders to feel that hostile armies, and not cities, are to be their objective points."[16]

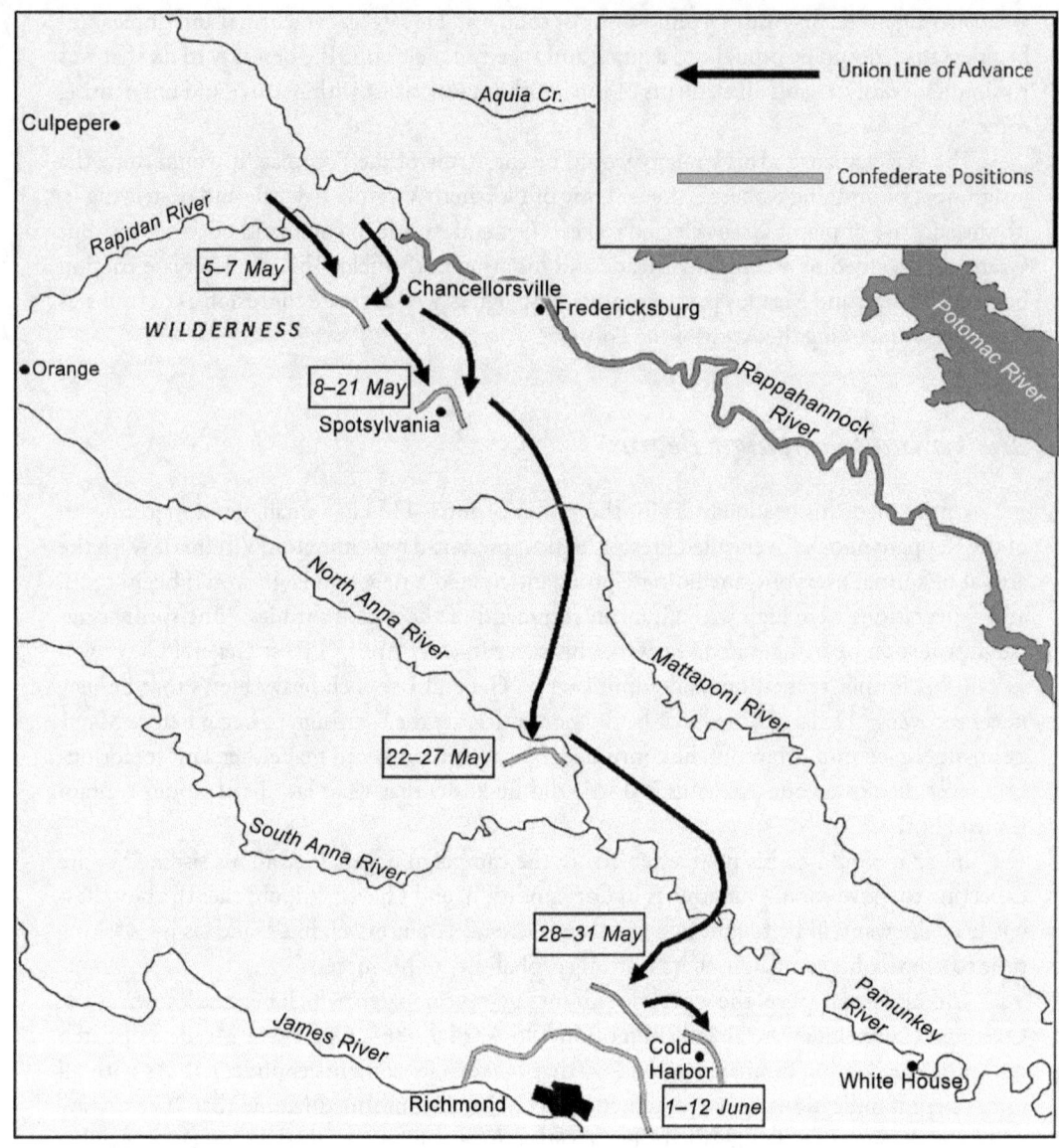

Map of Grant's Campaign (drawn by the author).

The route selected by Grant required that Upton's brigade and the rest of Meade's army traverse an area of dense forest and tangled undergrowth appropriately referred to as the Wilderness. The army had been in this unforgiving region before, having fought Lee unsuccessfully there a year earlier at Chancellorsville. The biggest challenge to any army transiting the Wilderness was the absence of good roads. The impenetrable forest was crossed from a generally north to south direction by the Germanna Plank Road, which first intersected the east to west route of the Orange Turnpike at the Wilderness Tavern before coming to a stop at its juncture with the perpendicular course of the Orange Plank Road. The other north to south thoroughfare was the Brock Road, which began immediately east of the Wilderness Tavern, crossing the Germanna Plank Road just north of its intersection with the Orange Plank Road, then continuing south, towards Spotsylvania Court House. Beyond those roads, there was no other way to move an army through the region.

On May 2, 1864, Meade's staff issued detailed marching orders for the Army of the Potomac, informing the corps commanders that the movement against Lee would begin at 2:00 a.m. on the morning of May 4. Led by General Phillip Sheridan's cavalry, who would begin moving towards the Rapidan on May 3, the infantry would cross the Rapidan at Germanna Ford beginning with two divisions of Warren's V Corps. They were to move on the Germanna Plank Road and Orange Turnpike to the vicinity of Parker's Store, with Upton and all the VI Corps following close behind. Hancock's II Corps, meanwhile, would cross the river at Ely's Ford, move quickly east towards Chancellorsville, and then turn south to link up with the remainder of the army. Finally, Burnside's IX Corps would move to Germanna Ford and follow the main force into the Wilderness.[17] Grant was planning for both surprise and speed. However, as events proved, he would get neither.

As the orders came down to begin the great movement south on the morning of May 4, the Army of the Potomac's camps became beehives of activity. One VI Corps officer recalled, "A part of the army moved to-day, and no doubt we shall go tomorrow; received orders at 6 o'clock p.m. to march at 4 o'clock a.m. tomorrow. All is confusion in camp."[18]

As scheduled, reveille sounded around 3:00 a.m. in the camps of Upton's brigade, and, by

This rare on-scene action photograph shows the VI Corps crossing the Rapidan River into the Wilderness (Library of Congress).

4:00 a.m., his men were marching south toward the Rapidan. As the brigade moved towards the river, the weather became increasingly warm and decidedly spring-like, which seemed to buoy many soldiers' spirits. VI Corps surgeon George Stevens wrote, "It was a lovely day, and all nature seemed rejoicing at the advent of spring. Flowers strewed the wayside, and the warble of the blue bird [sic], and the lively song of the sparrow, were heard in the groves and hedges."[19]

As was common when the army set out on the march after a long period in camp, the roadside to and beyond the Rapidan became strewn with clothes, boots, and other supplies. In this case, it was even worse than usual because the army's ranks had been filled during the winter months with new, young recruits. These inexperienced soldiers were quickly learning that one simply could not carry everything the army issued you into battle. The loads began to feel even heavier as the day grew warmer, causing many soldiers to cast off the excess, which one soldier remembered included "blankets, musical instruments, spare boots, and innumerable articles of doubtful utility."[20]

Just before 2:00 p.m., the first elements of V Corps began an uncontested crossing of the Rapidan over the pontoon bridges erected by the army's engineers. Upton's brigade followed and briefly made camp near Hazel Run as they awaited the units ahead of them to clear the Rapidan. Around 4:00 p.m., Upton ordered the brigade back onto the road, and they soon made their own crossing of the river before camping for the night two miles from the Rapidan along the Germanna Plank Road. Everything seemed to be going according to Grant's plan. However, no one realized that Lee was already on his way to meet the Army of the Potomac.

Lee had been anticipating a spring offensive by Grant and Meade, and Confederate scouts on Clyde's Mountain first observed movement in the Union camps on the night of May 3–4. Then, once the Union army was on the march, those scouts could clearly see the Federals moving across the river in the morning. As soon as Lee heard the news, he issued orders to General Ewell to move his corps rapidly east down the Orange-Fredericksburg Turnpike while Hill and Longstreet's Corps followed, moving in parallel via the Orange Plank Road. Lee planned to blunt this new Federal offensive as quickly as he could. He knew that the terrain in the Wilderness would mitigate the Union advantage in manpower and that the power of the Federal artillery could not be brought to bear effectively in the dense forest—the odds would be evened.

Had the Army of the Potomac moved as Grant had hoped, they would be out of the Wilderness before Lee could make contact. However, by nightfall on May 4, Warren's V Corps had barely made it to Wilderness Tavern, Upton and the rest of VI Corps were strung out on the road behind V Corps all the way back to Germanna Ford, Hancock's II Corps was still at Chancellorsville, and Burnside's IX Corps was not yet across the Rapidan. As darkness fell, Lee quickly closed the distance from the west, making a collision inevitable.

Confrontation in the Wilderness

On the morning of May 5, Upton had the brigade up early and moving south down the Germanna Plank Road. About 7:30 a.m., not long after they began their march, they heard scattered shots ahead in the distance, which soon increased in frequency and became louder. The two armies had found one another.

Confederate forces had suddenly appeared in front of Warren's V Corps as the Union troops moved along the Orange Turnpike. Meade ordered Warren to attack them and directed Hancock not to move II Corps past Todd's Tavern in case Warren needed his support. At first,

Meade believed that this was nothing more than a delaying action by a small detachment and not a major force intent on giving battle.[21] Within hours, however, the battle would begin in earnest along the turnpike between Warren and Ewell's Corps. Hill and Longstreet were still behind, moving east up the Orange Plank Road, and Lee had hoped to avoid a general engagement until they could arrive. But the collision between the two opposing armies had made that impossible.

As the fighting increased between V Corps and that of General Ewell, Upton received orders to turn his brigade down a dusty dirt path, the Spottswood Road, to cover the right flank of the VI Corps as it moved down the Germanna Plank Road. After the rest of the corps had passed, Upton formed his brigade on the far left of VI Corps. About 11:00 a.m., he received orders to advance to the support of V Corps, which was engaged with Ewell along the Orange Turnpike about two miles from Wilderness Tavern.[22]

The VI Corps advance was made by the right of wings because the dense forest and undergrowth made it utterly impossible to march in line of battle. What Upton referred to as "nearly impenetrable thickets"[23] caused the fighting to be more like a confused brawl than an organized battle. Men groped through the heavy woods and brush, while the trees and undergrowth broke up their regiments as they collided with an enemy who was just as confused and disorganized as they were.

Once VI Corps connected to the left flank of V Corps, Upton led the brigade forward into the thick woods ahead. The going was slow as his men tried to maintain some semblance of a line of battle in the dense brush and trees. As they approach a low hill to their front, the

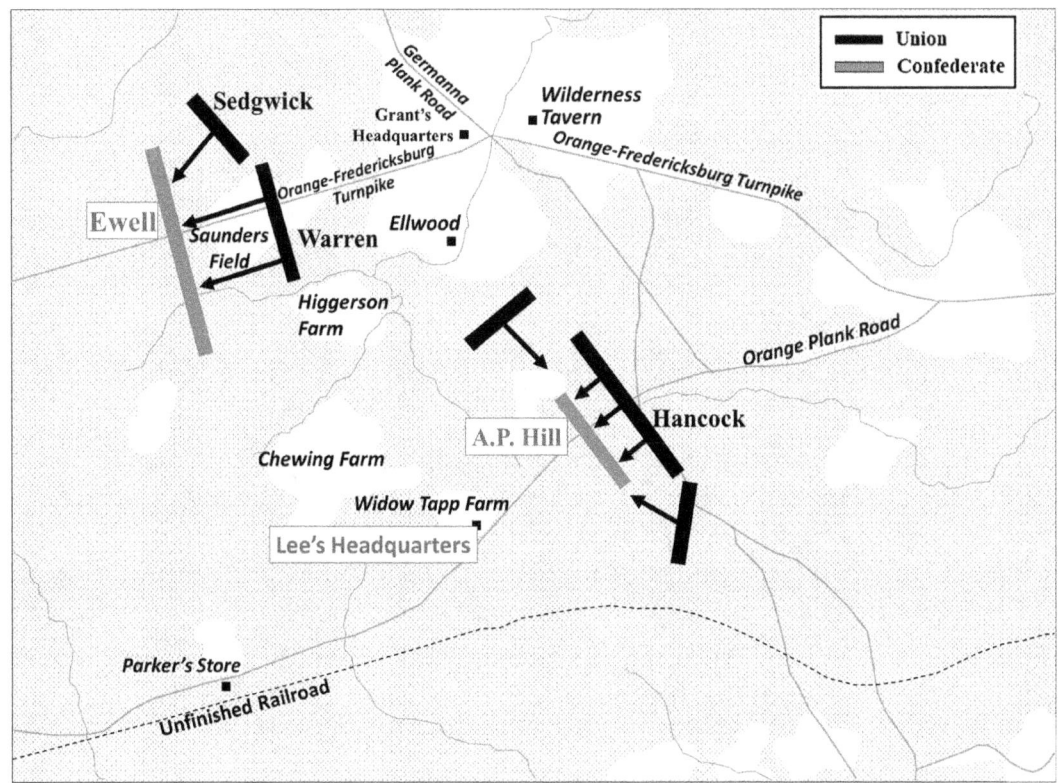

Fighting in the Wilderness, May 5, 1864 (drawn by the author).

hidden enemy opened fire, killing Lieutenant Colonel Edward Carroll, the commander of the 95th Pennsylvania. Three companies from the 95th immediately pressed forward in a charge, driving the enemy from the hill, securing the position, and capturing 30 Confederate soldiers in the process. While Upton's new position on the hill was 200 yards forward of the V Corps' line, he deemed it critical to hold and established his line there. Soon, the Third Division moved up and connected to Upton's right, securing his exposed flank.[24]

Throughout the afternoon, sporadic rifle fire popped up and down the two opposing lines, occasionally building into full volleys, but no more charges or countercharges took place. Still, all that shooting made for some discomfort among Upton's men. One soldier from the 5th Maine wrote, "There was considerable sharp rifle practice during the remainder of the day, which made it a little more safe to be behind shelter than to be exposed to rebel bullets."[25]

As night fell and the firing continued, an event occurred that added to the horrific nightmare that the fighting in the Wilderness became in the minds of many soldiers on both sides. Because of the dry spring weather, rifle fire started numerous brush fires between the opposing lines of the armies. Upton later noted in his official report that this "ground had previously been fought over and was strewn with wounded of both sides, many of whom must have perished in the flames."[26] One soldier recalled the fires that swept between the lines and the wounded who "moaned piteously"[27] as the flames approached them. He remembered that these wounded clutched their rifles close, intending to use them to end their lives before the fires reached them. He wrote of one of these men "both of whose legs were broken, lying on the ground with his cocked rifle by his side and his ramrod in his hand, and his eyes set on the front. I knew he

Alfred Waud's dramatic sketch of wounded Union soldiers being rescued from fires in the Wilderness (Library of Congress).

meant to kill himself in case of fire—knew it as surely as though I could read his thoughts."[28] One of Grant's staff, Horace Porter, later wrote, "It was as though Christian men had turned to fiends, and hell itself had usurped the place of earth."[29] A soldier in Upton's brigade remembered the night after the initial fighting with terrible clarity, later writing, "We lay in line of battle upon our arms, and shortly after dark when the firing slackened, the cries of the wounded between the lines, which were not far apart, was something terrible to hear. Some prayed, some cursed, some cried and some asked to be killed and put out of their misery."[30]

Late that night, orders flowed down from General Sedgwick directing preparations for an early morning attack by VI Corps. Upton began to prepare the brigade for the advance, but the orders were rescinded before the assault began.[31] Instead, the brigade remained in its position trading occasional shots with the enemy as intense fighting occurred on the Union left between Hancock's II Corps and those of A.P. Hill and James Longstreet. The two sides attacked and counterattacked all day before settling into the same positions they held earlier in the morning.

However, unknown to General Sedgwick, the enemy had discovered a weakness on the VI Corps' right flank. Confederate scouts observed that, for unknown reasons, there were no pickets, skirmishers, or videttes stationed in the woods on the Union right. Thus, the flank was seriously exposed to attack. At first, Confederate General Jubal Early hesitated to exploit the flank because he feared that Burnside's IX Corps might be lurking nearby and could crush any assault

This Alfred Waud sketch shows the VI Corps fighting to hold the Union right flank in the Wilderness (Library of Congress).

on the Union right. But once he discovered that was not the case, he ordered Generals Gordon and Johnston to shift their brigades to the left and try to make an attack before sunset.[32]

The two Confederate brigades moved far north of the Orange Turnpike and launched their attack about 6:30 p.m. As the butternut-clad troops screamed the rebel yell and swarmed from the rapidly darkening woods, the surprised Federal brigades of Generals Shaler and Seymour quickly gave way, running pell-mell in panic back towards the intersection of the Germanna Plank Road and the Orange Turnpike. The entire Union right was in peril. When word of the debacle reached General Sedgwick, he dispatched messengers to get help from V Corps and then sent the First Division Inspector General, Lieutenant Colonel Duffy, to Upton requesting he immediately move some of his brigade to the right flank. Duffy reached Upton around 7:00 p.m. relaying the orders from Sedgwick. Upton quickly ordered the 121st New York and 95th Pennsylvania to pull out of the line and follow Lieutenant Colonel Duffy to the right-rear at the double-quick.[33]

At the moment Upton issued his orders, many of the men in the 121st New York were digging entrenchments and had their arms stacked. Their commander, Colonel Olcott, ordered the soldiers who were still armed to move off at once while the rest went to retrieve their rifles. The resulting separation of the regiment caused much confusion made worse by the narrowness of the road and the dense underbrush.[34]

As soon as Upton issued orders to his two regiments, he sent for his horse and, when it arrived, he galloped off, following his men to the beleaguered right flank. When he arrived, he encountered a very confused situation. The enemy was pouring a deadly enfilading fire from the left into his regiments, which became stretched out as they tried to make their way through the brush.[35] Colonel Olcott faced his left companies to the front and rode to the right in an at-

In this sketch, Edward Forbes captured the moment when Union soldiers cheered Grant as the army moved towards Spotsylvania Court House (Library of Congress).

tempt to get his right companies into line. But a volley from the enemy struck him in the head, and he fell from his horse unconscious, later to be captured by the Confederates.[36]

When Upton rode up, he began to rally the two confused regiments, swatting some of his men with the flat of his sword to stop them from running and get them back into the line of battle. Once he had reorganized the men, Upton advanced them forward in a counterattack that recaptured some of the earthworks overrun by the enemy. After they had driven the Confederates back, Upton thought it best to withdraw about 300 yards to the rear where General Morris' brigade from Third Division had positioned themselves to defend against the Confederate assault. He placed his men on Morris' right, extending the Union line of defense against any other attempted flanking attack. Around 10:00 p.m., all the fighting quieted down, and Upton was ordered to move the brigade back towards the Wilderness Tavern and fortify a position near the intersection of the Germanna Plank Road and the Orange Turnpike.[37]

On the morning of May 7, Grant issued orders for a movement south, telling Meade, "Make all preparations during the day for a night march, to take position at Spotsylvania Court-House."[38] Under Grant's order, Warren would move first, passing both Burnside and Hancock, and march south to Spotsylvania Court House. Then Sedgwick's VI Corps would move via Chancellorsville to a point a few miles north of the courthouse, with Burnside right behind him, near Alrich. Finally, Hancock would pull out of his lines and move southeast to Todd's Tavern, about five miles from Spotsylvania Court House. The march was to begin after dark, around 9:00 p.m., with a goal to disengage quietly, move quickly, and surprise Lee by suddenly appearing on his exposed right flank, thus blocking the way to Richmond.

With these orders, the Army of the Potomac was seeing something new. For the first time, they would not disengage from an offensive and withdraw after having given battle to Lee's army. In doing so, Grant was telling the army that there would be no retreat, that this was going to be a campaign in the truest sense. While Meade's staff was surprised at this bold move, the reaction of the average soldier was quite different. Upon seeing Grant on horseback heading south that night, the men began to cheer, throwing their hats in the air, shouting in unison, "On to Richmond!" Horace Porter remembered that "men swung their hats, tossed up their arms, and pressed forward to within touch of their chief, clapping their hands, and speaking to him with the familiarity of comrades."[39]

Grant telegraphed Washington informing them of his intentions. He believed the fighting in the Wilderness was "decidedly in our favor," but he admitted that he had failed to exact a heavy blow on Lee. He concluded his message prophetically, writing, "My exact route to the James River I have not yet definitely marked out."[40]

As events would prove, Grant had also not marked out the cost.

8

Hell Caldron

I will carry those works. If I don't, I will not come back.
—Emory Upton to Colonel Martin T. McMahon, May 10, 1864[1]

Spotsylvania Court House

At 9:30 p.m. on the night of May 7, Upton's brigade led VI Corps onto the Orange Turnpike towards Chancellorsville, as they followed V Corps in the direction of Spotsylvania Court House.[2] Grant's reasoning for his shift by the left flank towards Spotsylvania Court House was simple and reflected the foundation for his entire campaign plan. As the general-in-chief would write in his memoirs, "My object in moving to Spottsylvania [sic] was two-fold: first, I did not want Lee to get back to Richmond in time to attempt to crush Butler before I could get there; second, I wanted to get between his army and Richmond if possible; and, if not, to draw him into the open field."[3]

Unfortunately, almost as soon as the army began to move, the plan for a rapid march to Spotsylvania that would catch Lee by surprise was unraveling. Warren's V Corps simply could not get any traction, and their march quickly bogged down, while Hancock's II Corps did no better. One soldier described the night later, saying, "The atmosphere was close and muggy, and the road narrow and dark." The men would stop, start, and then stop again, trying both patience and, especially, the strength of soldiers who had been fighting for three straight days. "The men were wearied and fretful," the same soldier later wrote. "At every halt they would fall asleep while seated on their knapsacks in the road."[4]

Worse yet, unknown to Grant or the army, Lee had anticipated Grant's move and was already racing infantry towards Spotsylvania. They arrived ahead of Union cavalry sent to seize the strategic Po River Bridge and effectively blocked the Federal advance. As the sun came up on May 8, the day grew hotter, and so did the fighting, which now developed into a full-fledged infantry battle. At first, Meade, who set up headquarters at Todd's Tavern, refused to believe the news that Confederate infantry had managed to reach Spotsylvania ahead of his army. Soon, however, it became obvious that this was the situation. Meade assumed tactical command and began directing Warren's efforts, which were not going well. As the V Corps' attacks began to stall around 1:00 p.m., Meade ordered the VI Corps to move up on Warren's left, first ordering a division up and, shortly thereafter, committing Sedgwick's entire corps to the fight. Unfortunately, Upton and the remainder of VI Corps were slow to get into position and were not able to support Warren until almost 5:00 p.m.

About 6:30 p.m., Upton formed his brigade into a column to support an attack by Warren. As he looked across the field, he and his men could see that the Confederates were well positioned on a thickly wooded hill. Commenting on the likelihood of a successful assault, one of Upton's soldiers later said that "the prospect appeared anything but cheerful."[5] The orders to attack were soon withdrawn, and Upton moved his brigade into some nearby woods to bivouac for the night.

On May 9, the brigade remained in position next to Ayres' brigade from V Corps and dug in as sporadic Confederate artillery fire harassed them throughout the day.[6] Meanwhile, Lee's entire army had arrived, and he had them go to work immediately constructing field fortifications. By nightfall, they had completed formidable entrenchments in a rough inverse "U" shape that Union soldiers called the Muleshoe. The bottom ends of the Muleshoe were almost five miles apart, and the entire Confederate line ran a total distance of over eight miles in length. They strengthened these fortifications with logs and lined them with abatis, which consisted of tree branches laid in a row, with the sharpened tops directed towards any potential attacking Union troops.

Unfortunately for Upton and the rest of VI Corps, May 9 also saw the loss of their venerable corps commander, John Sedgwick. General Sedgwick had ridden up on the line to observe the enemy when a Confederate sharpshooter shot him through the head. When informed of his death, Grant said, "His loss to this army is greater than the loss of a whole division of troops."[7] An officer in the 121st New York was very bitter about Sedgwick's death, writing his wife, "Sedgwick threw his life away. He had no business out on the skirmish line."[8] Meade immediately elevated one of Sedgwick's division commanders, General Horatio Wright, to command the corps.

Breaking the Muleshoe

Later that afternoon, Wright, accompanied by his chief of staff, Colonel Martin McMahon, rode to Meade's headquarters where he and the other corps commanders met with Meade and Grant. Meade informed Wright that they had decided that VI Corps should make an assault on Lee's lines at 4:00 p.m. the next afternoon, May 10. But Meade wanted Wright to make the assault using the column formation tactics Upton had used so successfully at Rappahannock Station. However, this time, Meade said the column should consist of between 12 to 15 regiments, and that Wright should make the attack at a weak point determined by his corps' engineers. Meade added that General Mott's division from IX Corps would cooperate with Wright's men, exploiting any gains they made in Lee's lines.[9]

Wright rode back to his own headquarters, where he selected 12 of his best regiments to make the attack. The only question now was who should organize, plan, and lead the assault. Colonel McMahon told him there was only one man suited to the task: Emory Upton. General Russell heartily agreed and told McMahon to send word to Upton that he should report to McMahon first thing the next morning.[10]

On the morning of May 10, Upton rode over to VI Corps headquarters, as ordered. He dismounted and went straight to Colonel McMahon, whom he knew well and fondly referred to as "Mack." McMahon informed him of the plan to attack Lee's fortifications, and, when he told Upton he would be in command, Upton received the news enthusiastically. McMahon then reached into his pocket, took out a list of the 12 regiments assigned to Upton, handed them to him and asked, "Upton what do you think of that for a command?" As Upton read down the list, he could see they had given him the best soldiers in the corps. "I golly, Mack," he replied, "that is a splendid command. They are the best men in the army." McMahon then said, "Upton you are to lead those men upon the enemy's works this afternoon, and if you do not carry them you are not expected to come back." Upton replied, "Mack, I will carry those works. If I don't, I will not come back."[11]

McMahon then told Upton what batteries would support him and that Mott would be ready to attack as soon as Upton's column broke through Lee's lines. The corps chief of staff then added that engineers led by Captain Ranald Mackenzie were conducting a reconnaissance to locate the best point for the assault. With their business concluded, Upton went back outside and mounted his horse for the return ride to his brigade. Just before he galloped off, he turned to McMahon. "Mack," he said, "I'll carry those works. They cannot repulse those regiments."[12] The regiments Upton referred to included his own 121st New York, 5th Maine, and 96th Pennsylvania, along with the 5th Wisconsin, 49th and 199th Pennsylvania from the 3rd Brigade, and the 43rd New York, 77th New York, 2nd Vermont, 5th Vermont, and 6th Vermont from the Second Division.[13]

As soon as Upton reached his camp, Captain Mackenzie arrived to tell him he had found the best spot in Lee's lines to make the attack. The engineer led Upton to the edge of the woods opposite the point of attack, which was at an angle in the Confederate works near the Scott house, about a half mile to the left of the Spotsylvania Road. Upton could see that they were of a "formidable character." There was a forest of abatis in front, and the top of the ramparts was "surmounted by heavy logs, underneath which were loopholes for musketry."[14] This meant that the enemy could open fire on his men without exposing themselves as the Union troops crossed the 200 yards of open ground between the woods and the entrenchments.

To the right of the Scott house at a point where the angle of the line pointed inward, there was a battery of guns with heavy traverses. These were mounds of earth running back at right angles from the main embankment designed to protect the gun crews from enfilade fire.[15] One hundred yards to the rear was a second line of entrenchments, which, while only partially complete, were already teeming with Southern infantry.[16]

Colonel Martin T. McMahon, whom Upton called "Mack" (Library of Congress).

8. Hell Caldron

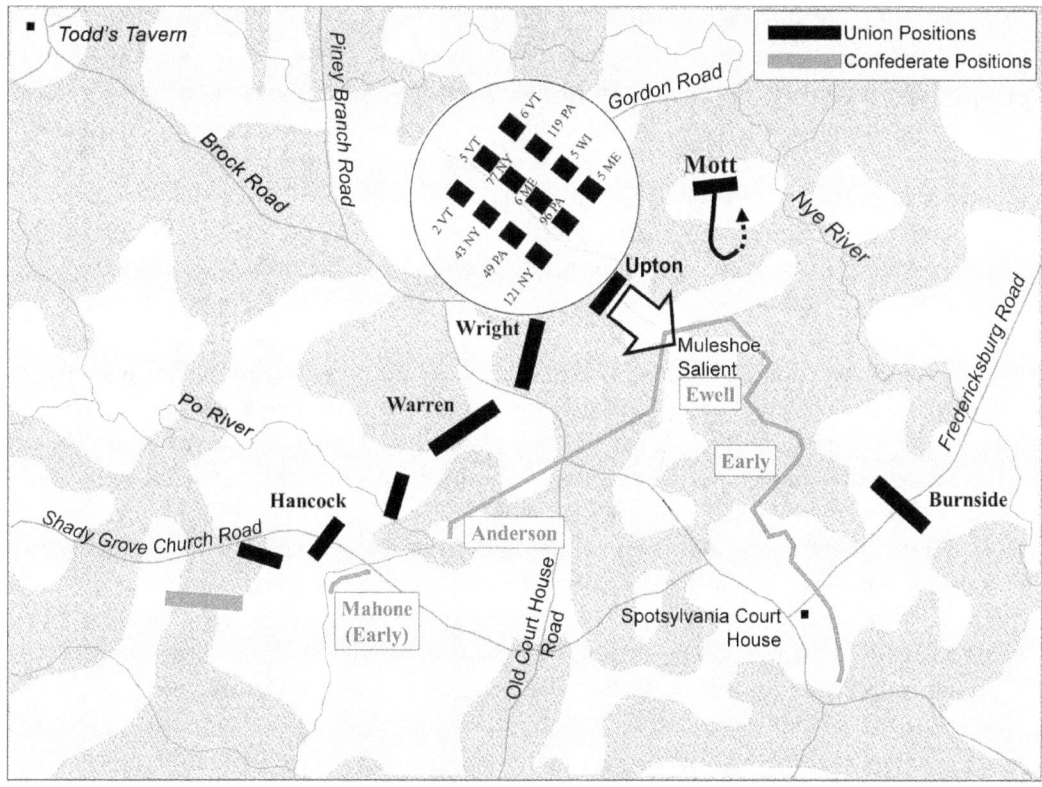

Upton's daring assault on the Muleshoe, May 10, 1864 (drawn by the author).

From the edge of the woods, a partially overgrown road led directly to the point of attack. Looking over the ground, Upton decided he would align his column to be four lines deep and three regiments wide. One line of four regiments would be on the right side of the road, and the other eight would take a position on the left side of the road. The three regiments of his own brigade, the 121st New York, 96th Pennsylvania, and 5th Maine, would line up at the head of the column and spearhead the attack. The 49th Pennsylvania, 6th Maine, and 5th Wisconsin followed them in the second line with the 43rd New York, 77th New York, and 119th Pennsylvania in the third line, and the 2nd, 5th, and 6th Vermont Regiments in the fourth line.[17]

Upton's past experiences showed him that "assaults had failed for want of minute instruction."[18] So, he had General Russell plus all 12 regiment commanders join him at the edge of the woods to view the point of attack. He carefully explained both the alignment of the column, as well as his plan for the assault. He told them the column must remain out of the enemy's view until they launched the attack. Therefore, all their men must lie down as soon as they arrived at the starting point near the edge of the woods. Furthermore, the officers must not shout any commands prior to the order to charge.[19]

Upton went on to tell them that while everyone would load their rifles and fix bayonets, only the men in the first line would cap their weapons. When a Civil War soldier "capped" his rifle, it meant that he put a copper percussion cap in the breech, allowing him to fire it instantly. Those soldiers with uncapped weapons could not fire as they charged the works. But once they were inside the enemy lines, they could quickly cap their rifles for close-range shooting.[20]

He informed the commanders of the 121st New York and 96th Pennsylvania that they would pivot their regiments to the right as soon as they broke into the trenches and attack the closest enemy artillery battery. The 5th Maine, meanwhile, would turn to open an enfilading fire on the Confederate infantry in the trenches to the left. The second line of the column was to halt as soon as they reached the works and then open fire to the front to deal with any counterattack from the second line of entrenchments. The third line would lie down behind the second and await orders, while the fourth line would advance to the edge of the woods, lie down, and wait for the command to charge. Finally, Upton told them that all officers must shout "Forward" constantly from the beginning of the attack until the column had carried the works.[21]

As the afternoon wore on, the 12 regiments made their way toward the tree line where they would assemble for the attack. The time for the assault was moved to 5:00 p.m. and, eventually, one of Russell's aides delivered a message to Upton informing him that the attack was further delayed until 6:00 p.m. The supporting artillery barrage would start at 5:50 p.m. and, once the guns stopped firing, the assault should begin.[22]

The regiments moved into position, and Upton began moving up and down the column showing both officers and men a sketch of the enemy works and briefing them on the plan of attack. Upton also added that, because speed was essential, no one was to stop to help a wounded comrade as the column moved across the open ground between them and the enemy defenses. As the sun sunk lower in the western sky, the Union artillery began to fire. It was almost time to go.[23]

Private Beckwith of the 121st New York later wrote of the moments before the attack, saying, "The day had been bright and it was warm, but the air felt damp, indicating rain. The racket and smoke made by the skirmishers and batteries, made it look hazy about us, and we had to raise our voices to be heard."[24] Upton sent his skirmishers forward, and they quickly drove their Confederate counterparts out of their rifle pits and back into the main line of trenches. As the Federal batteries blasted away, enemy guns fired back, but their counterfire was somewhat feeble.[25]

Once all preparations were complete, the lines of blue-clad soldiers rose from the grass, moving noiselessly to the edge of the woods. Upton shook hands with General Russell and his staff, mounted his horse, and rode out in front of his old regiment, the 121st New York. He gave the New Yorkers one last instruction, reminding them not to fire a shot, cheer, or yell until they were in the enemy's works. Finally, the Union artillery fell silent.[26]

The moment had arrived.

Upton shouted, "Attention," and then he called out, "Forward, double quick march!"[27] The column burst from the trees at a run towards what one soldier later referred to as "that hell caldron."[28] As soon as the first line began to sprint forward, almost all the troops seemed to forget their orders and began to yell. Despite this, the attack came as a complete surprise to the Confederates in the trenches ahead. By the time they opened fire on the attacking column, it was too late. While the abatis briefly slowed the column, the defenders only managed to fire two volleys before Upton's men swept over the parapet and into the trenches. One of the first Union officers to reach the trench jumped up onto the top log, shouting "Come on, men!" Seconds later, he was shot down, pitched forward, and disappeared.[29] Once he was in the trenches, Captain Kidder killed four Confederates with his revolver while young Private Henekir killed two before blocking a bayonet thrust, the enemy's steel going completely through his hand. Another New Yorker, George Teel, managed to fire two shots at close range, both killing Confederate officers.[30]

Alfred Waud's sketch shows Upton on horseback leading his men in the attack on the Muleshoe (Library of Congress).

The enemy did not yield at first, and this deadly hand-to-hand combat continued for several minutes. When the first of Upton's men who made it to the trenches were shot down, the soldiers who followed modified their tactics. "Others, seeing the fate of their comrades," Upton wrote after the battle, "held their pieces at arm's length and fired downward, while others, pointing their pieces vertically, hurled them down upon their enemy, pinning them to the ground." One officer from the 121st New York was bayoneted in the thigh, while a private from the 96th Pennsylvania was pinned to the parapet by an enemy bayonet.[31]

Finally, the shock of the attack and Upton's superior numbers prevailed, as the first line of his troops swept left and right as planned, with the troops on the right rapidly converging on the enemy battery. Upton rode his horse up the side of the works and jumped his horse over the trenches and galloped towards the battery with the 121st New York, constantly shouting for the men to continue forward.[32] The Union troops "ran towards the battery, passing another line of works, and the men in them passed to our rear as prisoners, or ran away after firing."[33] Upton and his men quickly overran the battery taking the cannons and capturing their gunners. They continued to the second line of trenches and, soon, there was nothing in front of them except for a few tents by the roadside.[34] Upton later wrote, "The enemy's lines were completely broken, and an opening had been made for the division which was to have supported on our left, but it did not arrive."[35] It never would.

Upton's men were now fighting almost a mile away from the main Union line, and the enemy was sure to bring up reinforcements for a counterattack. As they hung on waiting for support, Mott's division should have been making their own attack. Mott did line up his men and wait for the word to attack. But Mott's division had been shot up and driven in panic at the Wilderness, and its morale was low. They made a move forward but were hit by heavy artillery fire before they got halfway to the enemy trenches. They fell back to the woods in confusion and had scarcely reformed when an officer arrived with orders to repeat their assault. But as one officer remembered, "the whole expression" of the officer delivering the orders seemed to say, "The general commanding is doubtful of your success." "The moment the order was given," he wrote, "the messenger put spurs to his horse and rode off, lest by some misunderstanding the assault should begin before he was safe out of the range of the enemy's responsive fire."[36] As a result, the attack was not renewed, and Mott's troops scattered for the rear. In fact, brigade staff officers who were sent to retrieve the men, "found them gathered about their regimental flags, quietly preparing coffee and comparing experiences."[37]

Meanwhile, enemy reinforcements had arrived, and Upton's now beleaguered men fought viciously to hold the precious ground they had gained. Upton later reported that he "directed the officers to form their men outside the works and open fire, and then rode back over the field to bring forward the Vermonters in the fourth line, but they had already mingled in the contest and were fighting with a heroism which has ever characterized that elite brigade."[38] All the while, Upton kept his head and coolly issued orders as though his men "were on the parade grounds drilling."[39]

The weight of the enemy counterattack soon grew heavier by the minute. Private Beckwith said, "it seemed as though the firing on our front and to our right became heavier, and the whistle of balls seemed to come from all directions and was incessant."[40] As night arrived, their position became far more tenuous. Soon, Confederate batteries opened up on the men in the second line of trenches, and they fell back to the first line. As they continued firing back at the advancing enemy, Beckwith said they "could now see the flashes of the guns and knew they were coming in on us."[41] Upton asked for volunteers to make a rush on the nearest enemy battery, but no one replied. He asked for men from the 121st New York, saying, "Are there none of my old regiment here?" But there were only a few of them left there, and their ammunition was running desperately low.[42]

Upton now mounted his horse and rode back to the edge of the woods to confer with General Russell. They agreed that, if Mott was not going to move forward, Upton's position was untenable. Russell ordered him to withdraw, and Upton quickly wrote out an order to do so, sending it back to his officers still fighting in the trenches. Once they received the orders, the officers spread the word along the line to fall back quietly. As men made their way across the open field back to Union lines, they stopped here and there to assist comrades wounded during the initial assault, helping them back to the nearest field hospital.[43]

As Upton assessed the damage, he reported about 1,000 men killed, wounded, or missing.[44] The losses were especially heavy in the lead units. The 5th Maine lost over 100 men out of the 200 that went into the fight as well as 11 out of 17 officers. After the battle, he also determined that every man in the 5th Maine initially listed as missing was actually either killed or wounded.[45]

Upton estimated that the enemy had lost at least 100 men in the first line of their works with a much heavier loss in the counterattacks. Upton also reported the capture of between 1,000 and 1,200 Confederate prisoners, as well as several stands of colors. While any success gained during the assault was in great measure due to Upton's planning and leadership, he gave all due credit to the soldiers under his command. "Our officers and men accomplished all that could be expected of brave men," he wrote in his official report. "They went forward with perfect confidence, fought with unflinching courage, and retired only upon the receipt of a written order, after having expended the ammunition of their dead and wounded comrades."[46] As for Upton's much-beloved 121st New York, the next morning they found they could barely muster 100 men in a regiment that had left New York two years earlier with almost 1,000. Further, command of the regiment had fallen to a mere captain. One soldier remembered, "as we glanced along the terribly thinned ranks and upon the shattered staff and tattered colors, we were filled with sorrow for our lost comrades, and deep forebodings for the future."[47]

Immediately after the withdrawal was complete, Upton rode over to the corps headquarters and met with General Russell and Colonel McMahon. McMahon later said that Upton appeared very depressed and expressed the opinion that, had there been adequate support, he could have "swept the enemy's lines for a great distance."[48]

The Bloody Angle

May 11 found Upton's brigade idle in camp, nursing their wounds from the previous day's fighting. Unfortunately, the weather turned for the worse, adding to the men's woes. A storm arrived late in the afternoon and became quite severe around sunset. Rain poured from the heavens, and the temperature dropped, making it "raw and disagreeable." A soldier in the 95th Pennsylvania recalled that "men gathered in small groups about half-drowned fires, with their tents stretched about their shoulders." Meanwhile, some "rolled themselves up, and lay close to the simmering logs, eager to catch a few moments' sleep; many crouched about, without any shelter whatever, presenting a pitiable sight."[49]

While the rains fell that day, General Grant decided upon his next move. Given the success Upton had achieved attacking the Muleshoe with 12 regiments in a column, Grant thought doing the same thing with an entire corps might completely break Lee's line. Therefore, he issued orders for General Hancock to assault the enemy works at 4:30 a.m. the next morning with all of II Corps in a column formation. While the weather was not favorable, Grant ordered that the attack proceed regardless of the heavy rain.

The point of attack for II Corps would be just to the left of the one Upton's men had attacked on May 10, but the works were very similar. They created an obtuse angle that turned back from the ridge along which the fortifications ran. A large red oak tree stood at the apex of the angle and, from it, extended numerous traverses designed to protect the enemy infantry from enfilading fire. As for the trenches themselves, they were "of the most formidable nature" and included logs along the top to protect the defenders, who could fire under them, safe from Union bullets.[50]

Hancock moved his men into position during the night and, through rain and dense fog, attacked at the appointed time. Led by General Barlow's division and using Upton's tactics, they charged at the double quick, with rifles uncapped and bayonets fixed. Once more, the enemy was completely surprised, many not even firing a single shot at the attacking Union troops. Barlow's men quickly "crashed up, over, and into the Confederate trenches."[51] However, Lee had prepared for another such attack by stationing Gordon's infantry brigade to the rear of the main lines in the center of the Muleshoe. As II Corps was breaking through "with exulting shouts, confident, and disorganized," Gordon's men struck them hard, and the fight for what became known as the "Bloody Angle" was on. For the next 18 hours, the most brutal combat of the entire war took place amidst the torrential rain.[52]

Hancock's men fell back, clinging desperately to the ground they had just gained as Gordon made repeated counterattacks, trying to push them out of the Confederate trenches. With II Corps in trouble, Grant sent word for VI Corps to move up, attack the trenches, and take a position on Hancock's right. Once again, Upton's camp happened to be the closest to the point of attack and, around 7:00 a.m., he received orders to move his brigade forward to prepare for the assault.[53]

The brigade arrived at the rear of Hancock's corps about 9:30 a.m.[54] and, as they neared the position, numerous soldiers from II Corps streamed past them in retreat, and the wounded lined the roadside, bleeding and moaning pitifully. The brigade continued forward and cleared the woods at a patch of ground covered in thick marsh grass. Upton ordered the men to lie down as he sought out General Russell for more specific orders. As the soldiers lie there, bullets poured right over their heads from the furious fighting ahead. Private G. Norton Galloway of the 95th Pennsylvania wrote that the firing was "so keen that it split the blades of grass all about us, the minies [sic] moaning in a furious concert as they picked out victims by the score."[55]

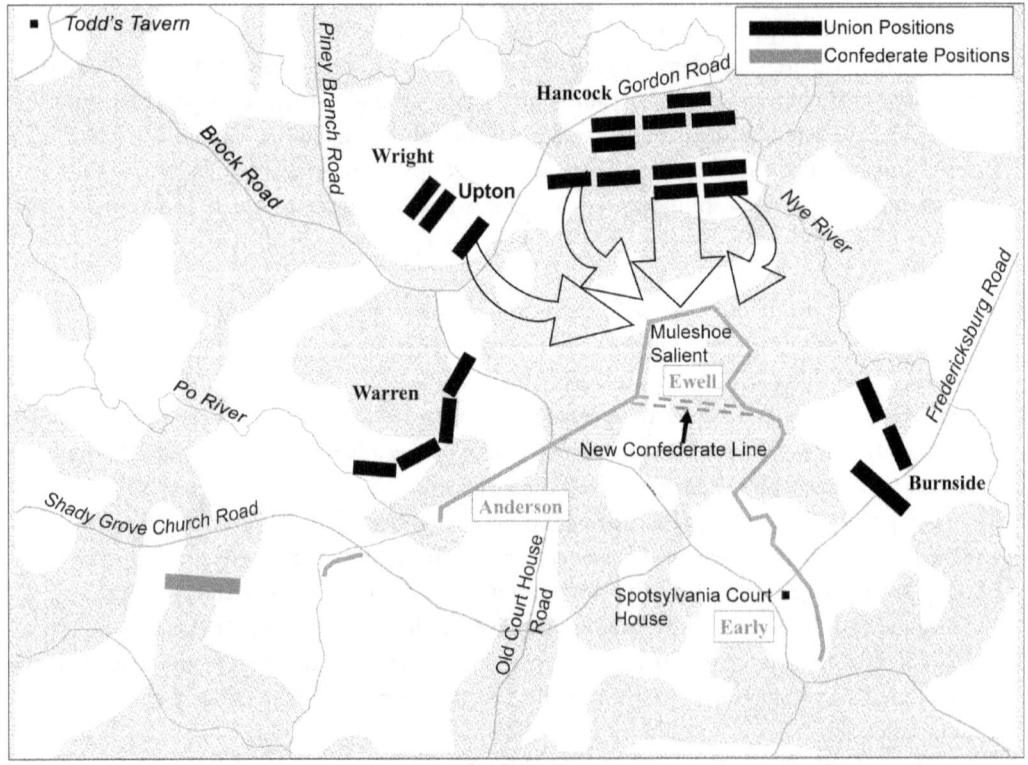

Hancock's assault at the Bloody Angle, May 12, 1864 (drawn by the author).

General Russell rode up to Upton and ordered him to move his brigade to the immediate right of II Corps at the double-quick. As the rain fell like a flood from the dark, angry sky, Upton galloped up to the 95th Pennsylvania, which was the lead regiment in the brigade, and gave the command to "rise up."[56] With that, the brigade rushed forward, shouting hurrahs as they went with Upton riding ahead and cheering them on.

The leading line of the brigade reached the works quickly, struggling through the dense tangle of abatis. Before they could mount the ramparts, the right flank of II Corps gave way. As the 95th Pennsylvania reached a point about 600 yards to the right of the Landrum house, they received a massive volley from Confederates in the second line of trenches.[57] The bullets tore through the Pennsylvanians ranks, and nearly 100 of them fell into the mud, dead or wounded.[58] The point where the brigade had arrived was at the bottom point of some V-shaped works. Upton's men held the works from the point down the left side of the V as it faced them, and the enemy held the right side. Upton could clearly see that this position must be held. Otherwise, Gordon's men would be able to sweep away the Union right flank.[59]

As the rest of his brigade arrived, Upton ordered the men to lie down and return fire. The dense smoke and the heavy rains made it difficult for his troops to make out the advancing enemy, but they poured out volley after volley in the direction of the attacking Southern infantry. Meanwhile, the Confederates would crawl forward under cover of the smoke until they were close to the brigade's line, and then "raising their usual yell," they would make a mad charge right up to the "very muzzles" of the brigade's rifles.[60]

Painting of the fighting at the Bloody Angle shows Union troops surging into Confederate entrenchments (Library of Congress).

Upton was now the only mounted officer in sight, making him an easy target. Despite this, he took his hat in hand, cheering on his men, and begging them to "hold this point." His men continued to fall and, soon, his entire staff had been either killed, wounded, or dismounted.[61]

As more enemy troops poured into the area, they choked the rear of the Confederate line, making an inviting objective for Upton's men. At that moment, a battery of the 5th U.S. Artillery rode up to Upton's line, unlimbered, and proceeded to blast the tightly grouped Confederates with double charges of canister shot. This staggered the enemy, and the battery fired again and again so fiercely that Private Galloway described the battle as now being "at white heat."[62]

The Confederates now decided to focus their counterattack on the battery. As they advanced, Upton's infantry and the Federal battery replied with an even more intense rifle and cannon fire. The enemy eventually retired having taken heavy losses, but not before every man and horse in the Federal battery was either dead or wounded.[63]

The fighting now settled into a brutal close-range battle. As the rain continued to pour down, Union and Confederate troops fought one another at distances of only six to ten feet. Men from both sides would jump atop the rampart in front of them to "quickly fire or jab out with a bayonet" at the enemy.[64] Since Upton's men were on the reverse side of the trenches, some of his men "would load and stick their guns over the head log and raising the butts of their pieces, fire down into the mass of men huddled on the opposite side."[65]

Rifle fire continued nonstop, and the wounded and dead soon lay ten-deep in the trenches. Worse, the "storm of bullets ripped through the corpses between the lines and, by the end of the fighting, most were so shredded apart that it was later impossible to count the number of dead." As the rain continued, the trenches became swamps with mud up to the men's ankles and water so deep that many of the wounded who fell in the trenches drowned before anyone could help them.[66]

As this nightmarish scene continued, the rifle fire caused the top logs of the works to be "cut and torn until they resembled hickory brooms."[67] Upton noticed that the enemy was using the large red oak tree standing at the angle of the trenches for cover. He ordered the 121st New York to pour a constant fire at the area around the tree. After several hours, the gunfire was so intense that the 22-inch diameter tree began to waver before crashing to the ground, sawed in half by bullets.[68]

Finally, about 5:30 p.m., Upton received orders to withdraw so units from II Corps could relieve his battered brigade.[69] By this time, his men had been fighting continuously for almost eight hours and were close to complete exhaustion. Each soldier had fired between 300 to 400 rounds of ammunition. As a result, many had lips encrusted with gunpowder from repeatedly biting off the ends of their cartridges. Moreover, their bodies were completely covered in mud, and many had so much mud on their hands that the butts of their rifles had to be pried from their grip.[70]

Private Beckwith later said, "This was the worst day's experience I ever had, and it thoroughly disgusted me with war."[71] Men staggered back looking for others from their regiment before stumbling into camp. "Being nearly starved," Beckwith wrote, "we got some hot coffee and cooked some pork and crackers."[72] Soon, he and the rest of Upton's brigade huddled by their fires wrapped in rubber blankets to ward off the rain, which continued to fall unabated.

After nearly 18 hours of brutal combat, Lee could see that it would be impossible to dislodge the Federals from his works. So, he ordered the hasty construction of a new line of trenches positioned 800 yards to the rear of the Muleshoe. The new fortifications connected the left and right flanks of the Confederate lines in a straight line, making them far less vulnerable than the original salient. In the early morning hours of May 13, the firing in the Muleshoe stopped, and Lee withdrew his men to their new lines. Once again, Lee's army had been viciously hammered by Meade's men, but they had not been broken.

The rain finally stopped just before dawn, and, as the sun rose, the results of the battle could be clearly seen. As Upton and others returned to the scene of the fighting, what they saw resembled something right out of the worst sort of nightmare. Horace Porter observed to his utter horror that Confederate dead "were piled upon each other in some places four layers deep, exhibiting every ghastly phase of mutilation." Even more appalling was that, below these corpses, one could see "the convulsive twitching of limbs and the writhing of bodies, indicating some poor wounded soldier was struggling to climb out of their horrid entombment."[73]

While Union soldiers struggled to identify and bury the dead, the gloomy skies broke, and sunshine poured through. However, rather than brightening the scene, the sunlight illuminated the remnants of the fighting, adding a "new horror to the scene." Upton and the other men could now see hundreds of Confederates. Many were dead while others were dying. They were piled three- and four-deep in the trenches, and most of them had been shot in the head during the close-range fighting. There were so many enemy dead that the Union soldiers detailed to the burial duty could only bury the bodies by simply filling in the trenches, which were still almost half-filled with muddy water. One Union soldier commented that this meant these poor Confederates, who dug the trenches, had "unwittingly dug their own graves." It was, he said, the most horrible sight he had ever witnessed.[74]

These sights, along with all the others he had witnessed up to now, seemed to take a terrible toll on Upton. The brutality and needless slaughter not only caused him to increasingly question the army's leadership and culture, but also his religious faith. Unknown to him, this questioning was creating the foundation for what became the driving passion of his life.

On May 13, the day after the second attack on the Muleshoe, Meade forwarded a request to Grant for Upton's promotion to Brigadier General of Volunteers for "distinguished services in the battles of the Wilderness and Spotsylvania Court-House."[75] Grant, in turn, sent a message to Secretary Stanton requesting Upton's promotion to that same rank "for gallant and distinguished services in the last eight days' battles."[76] The Secretary of War replied the next day, saying, "The brigadiers in volunteer service you name shall be appointed."[77]

Emory Upton, photographed after his promotion to brigadier general (National Archives).

The Senate confirmed Upton's promotion on May 28, and the first time he heard anything about it was in the newspapers on June 1. He was particularly proud that he had not used political connections to gain his new rank. He wrote to his sister on June 7, telling her: "I am disposed to think that it will be better in the end for me to have received my promotion at this late date. The reasons for [it] are gratifying to any soldier. It will be entered upon the records of the War Department that I was promoted for 'gallant' and distinguished services."[78]

Upton's brigade was done fighting at Spotsylvania, and eventually, they swung around behind the entire army, crossed the Nye River, and moved to Myers Hill on May 14. The Nye was a "narrow, sluggish, deep stream," and Myers Hill was a low rise of ground just north of a branch of the river. A large plantation mansion sat atop the hill with a rail fence running north to south in front of it and a large wooded area just to the north. Upton deployed the brigade in a line in front of the mansion house and along the fence. The men quickly tore down the fence to build a rough rail barricade along their line and settle down to light fires and make breakfast.[79]

The scene was quiet, and no threat appeared imminent. Since there seemed no signs of the enemy, General Meade and some of his staff rode forward of the brigade's line in front of the 5th Maine. As they looked about with their field glasses, three lines of Confederate infantry arose from concealment in some nearby woods and began a rapid advance accompanied by fire from an artillery battery.[80] As Meade's party beat a hasty retreat, Upton's men shoved what breakfast they could into their mouths and took cover behind their rail barricade. The trees where the enemy had been concealed were only about 600 yards away, and the Confederate infantry moved rapidly toward the brigade's line. The 121st New York opened a brisk fire, and the Confederates halted before moving back into the woods. Upton ordered the 96th Pennsylvania to move forward and drive the enemy from the trees. They advanced across the open ground and entered the woods. But they quickly found the Southerners outnumbered them badly, and they fell back to the brigade line.[81]

Since the 5th Maine had only managed to deploy a skirmish line when the fighting began, they fired a few volleys before breaking and running for the river. As they gave way on the left of the line, the 96th Pennsylvania and 121st New York were also compelled to fall back. As the retreat became a little disorganized, some soldiers made a panicked jump into the river, found it far too deep to wade across, and had to be rescued by their comrades. After moving in parallel to the river for a short distance, Upton rode up to the retreating soldiers and ordered them to move onto the road, where they could march to a nearby bridge. Once across, he told them to rally the colors in a field beyond the bridge. As the brigade arrived, Union artillery opened up a brisk fire on the advancing Confederates and drove them back beyond Myers Hill. That evening, under cover of darkness, the brigade advanced back to Myers Hill and reoccupied their positions.[82]

On May 20, as Grant prepared to move the Army of the Potomac once more, he also attempted to see if he could again tempt Lee into coming forward. He moved Hancock's II Corps out well ahead of the rest of the army towards Milford Station, providing a seemingly isolated, vulnerable target for Lee to strike. However, Lee would not take the bait. Instead, he noted the impending Federal shift to his right, ignored Hancock completely, and looked for the best place to position his army, so they remained between Union forces and Richmond.

In examining the military topography of the region, Lee saw the North and South Anna Rivers running in a generally easterly direction, about eight to ten miles apart, until they joined to form the Pamunkey River southeast of Hanover Junction, where the Virginia Central Railroad and the Richmond, Fredericksburg, and Potomac Railroad crossed one another. He could also see that the path of the North Anna River near the junction was only 25 miles away, about ten miles closer than the distance the Union II Corps would have to cover. If Lee started Ewell and Anderson's Corps right away, they could reach the south bank of the North Anna well ahead of Hancock and, hopefully, entrench themselves in strong positions before Union forces arrived. Therefore, at noon on May 21, Ewell's men stepped off, with Anderson's close behind.

As it turned out, Lee had once again anticipated Grant's next move, and Grant saw where Lee was headed. After allowing the weary men of the army some rest, Grant ordered Meade to move towards the North Anna at first light on May 23.[83]

Upton and his brigade were on the march again, but unknown to him and his men, even worse trials lie ahead on the road towards Richmond.

9

The Killing Ground

> Some of our corps commanders are not fit to be corporals. Lazy and indolent, they will not even ride along their lines; yet, without hesitancy, they will order us to attack the enemy, no matter what their position or numbers. Twenty thousand of our killed and wounded should to-day be in our ranks.
> —Emory Upton, June 5, 1864[1]

To the North Anna

On May 20, the same day Upton received new orders to march towards the North Anna River, he also received word that a new infantry regiment was joining his brigade, the 2nd Connecticut Heavy Artillery.[2] As the unit's number and name indicate, however, it was neither new nor was it an infantry regiment. The state of Connecticut created the 2nd Connecticut from the remaining strength of the 19th Connecticut Infantry Regiment in November 1863 and re-designated it as a heavy artillery unit.[3] Since then, the regiment had manned the large guns in the forts surrounding Washington, D.C. The 2nd Connecticut was not alone in this sudden change of assignment. There were eight heavy artillery regiments from New York alone being reassigned to fight as infantry regiments, along with others from Pennsylvania, Connecticut, Massachusetts, Maine, and Vermont.

The losses sustained thus far in the campaign combined with the end of enlistments for many veterans were quickly depleting the Army of the Potomac's ranks. Further, the men provided by the new draft were lower in quality and their desertion rates were quite high. So, Grant ordered the heavy artillery units out of their comfortable garrisons and into the field to fight as infantry. The army veterans referred to them as "bandbox" regiments because they contained well-fed soldiers with clean uniforms and virtually no combat experience.[4]

Just before these regiments departed the fortifications surrounding the capital, the Secretary of War asked General A.P. Howe to inspect the "Heavies," as they came to be known, and provide an appraisal of their fitness. Howe's report was not very encouraging. He found two units of the 2nd New York Heavy Artillery to be "insufficient" in infantry drills with discipline cited as in "great want of improvement." Howe listed another of the Heavies as having infantry drill that was "very deficient; fault is in the officer in command" with discipline described as being in a "low state; shows inefficiency in the command." The 10th New York Heavy Artillery, meanwhile, was even worse. General Howe rated every unit as being "very indifferent" in infantry drill and "indifferent" in discipline. Luckily for Upton, the 2nd Connecticut was the only regiment that Howe gave a rating as high as "fair" in both infantry drill and discipline.[5] But nonetheless, these men were fresh and fit, which gave them at least something to lend to the army's needs. They would need every ounce of that strength to just survive what lay ahead.

The 2nd Connecticut left Washington, D.C., on May 17, reached the front on the afternoon of May 20, and Upton had them in line of battle the next day. Besides the fitness and good health of these new troops, there was one other major advantage to them—their numbers. The 2nd Connecticut had over 1,800 men in its ranks, while regiments such as the 121st New York had been reduced to less than 200 men.[6] The situation was similar in all of Upton's regiments, which meant the new regiment had more than twice as many men as the entire brigade.

With the new regiment in tow, Upton marched the brigade south from Myers Hill at 10:30 p.m. on May 21, and they reached Guinea Station at 1:30 p.m. the next afternoon. They rested for four hours, and then marched again, crossing the Mattaponi River in the early evening before making camp at Lebanon Church. His men were on the road the next morning, May 23, and reached the Jericho Bridge over the North Anna at noon. Upton reported that his men were "much exhausted," but despite this, they crossed the river the next day and moved into a line opposite Lee's army next to General Griffin's division from V Corps.[7]

Lee's position across the river was very strong, as his men were becoming experts at rapidly erecting formidable field fortifications. As a result, Grant was unable to find a way to drive Lee back during fighting on May 23 and 24. So, a stalemate persisted, and Upton's men spent May 24 destroying tracks of the Central Virginia Railroad that were behind their lines. They employed a technique for this job that had become popular with Grant and Sherman's armies in the West. They would form up on the uphill side of a track, take hold and lift the track, and turn it completely over. Then, they removed the ties, stacked them, and set fire to them. Once the fire was blazing, the men tossed the rails on top of the burning ties, heating them until they were glowing and red hot. They next removed the heated rails and bent them around nearby trees or stumps, doubling them up so badly that they could never be used by the enemy again.[8]

Since Lee had stubbornly stymied Grant once more, the Union general-in-chief decided to shift to his left once again so he could continue to force Lee to move between the Army of the Potomac and Richmond. On the morning of May 26, Upton moved his brigade back over the North Anna River and then turned the men southeast toward Chesterfield Station. Once there, he rested the men for six hours before resuming the march. They trudged southeast all night and then turned south to cross the Pamunkey River around 11:00 a.m. on the morning of May 27.[9]

The brigade had traveled over 27 miles since the previous evening, and the men were completely spent. Upton ordered them to camp for the night, but they were back on the road the following morning. However, this time they only marched about two miles, pausing to rejoin the rest of the division. After a brief reconnaissance to the north toward Hanover Court House on May 29, Upton received orders to move south toward Richmond, while the bulk of the army faced Lee's men across Totopotomoy Creek. At 1:00 a.m. on June 1, as the brigade continued south, Upton received orders to move directly to the crossing at Cold Harbor as quickly as possible.[10]

Disaster at Cold Harbor

Studying the map, Grant had quickly concluded that Cold Harbor offered the best place for another major push at Lee. A reconnaissance by General Phillip Sheridan's cavalry indicated Lee had extended his lines to the right. If the Army of the Potomac could move quickly enough, they might be able to attack Lee before he could shift any more of his army towards Richmond. If successful, they could roll up Lee's flank, destroy his army, and there would be nothing between the Army of the Potomac and Richmond. Moreover, Grant realized that, as the army now approached the James River, he was running out of ground in which to keep turning to the left.

The reason for Upton's new orders to make a fast march to Cold Harbor was that Sheridan discovered Lee had already entrenched infantry and cavalry at the Cold Harbor crossing. Sheridan's cavalry under General Torbert engaged the enemy forces and, after a hard fight, drove them out. However, Sheridan's scouts told him that heavier Confederate forces were approaching, so he elected to withdraw. When Grant heard this news, the importance was apparent to him. Lee was, indeed, extending far to his right, trying to cut Grant off from the shortest route to the James River and, perhaps more importantly, the Union army's base of supply at White House.[11]

Grant immediately ordered Sheridan to return to the crossing and "to hold the place at all hazards, until reinforcements could be sent to him."[12] Sheridan replied with a dispatch to General Meade that he would hold the crossing "if at all possible."[13] Cold Harbor suddenly had become the pivotal point of the campaign.

When Upton received his orders to march to Cold Harbor, VI Corps was at the far right of the Army of the Potomac. This meant that his brigade and the rest of the corps was the farthest away from Sheridan's position at Cold Harbor. Traveling on dark, dust-choked roads, the men made slow progress. One veteran recalled, "The march was a hard one. The day was sultry, and the dust, ankle deep, raised in clouds by the column, was almost suffocating. It filled the air and hung upon the leaves of the trees like snow. Seldom had our men experienced so severe a march."[14]

Worse, the poor maps with which the army was operating slowed their movement even more. Prior to the campaign, the army's topographic engineers prepared a series of large maps compiled from every source they could find. However, despite their diligent efforts, the final product was nearly worse than useless. As a result, Upton guided his men down the dark, narrow roads using maps that one of Meade's staff referred to as "almost ludicrous."[15] The darkness, the bad roads, the distance, and the poor maps all meant that Upton and the rest of VI Corps would not make it that night. In fact, Upton's brigade did not arrive until 11:00 a.m. the next morning[16]

During the afternoon, the men of the XVIII Corps under General William "Baldy" Smith arrived at Cold Harbor following a forced march from White House. Between Wright and Smith's corps, Meade had six divisions to counter the two Confederate divisions dug in opposite the crossing. Having been criticized by Grant's staff for being too slow and cautious during the campaign, Meade apparently decided now was the moment to take aggressive action. The advantage he had in numbers made the military odds look good. But the odds were not as good as he thought.

First, the infantry from both Union corps was desperately tired from their forced marches. One of Upton's men from the 2nd Connecticut wrote that he and his comrades were "drugged, as it were, with utter fatigue." He noted that nearly a month of marching and fighting had made them "nearly dead with marching and want of sleep" and that "their stupor ... was of a kind that none can describe."[17]

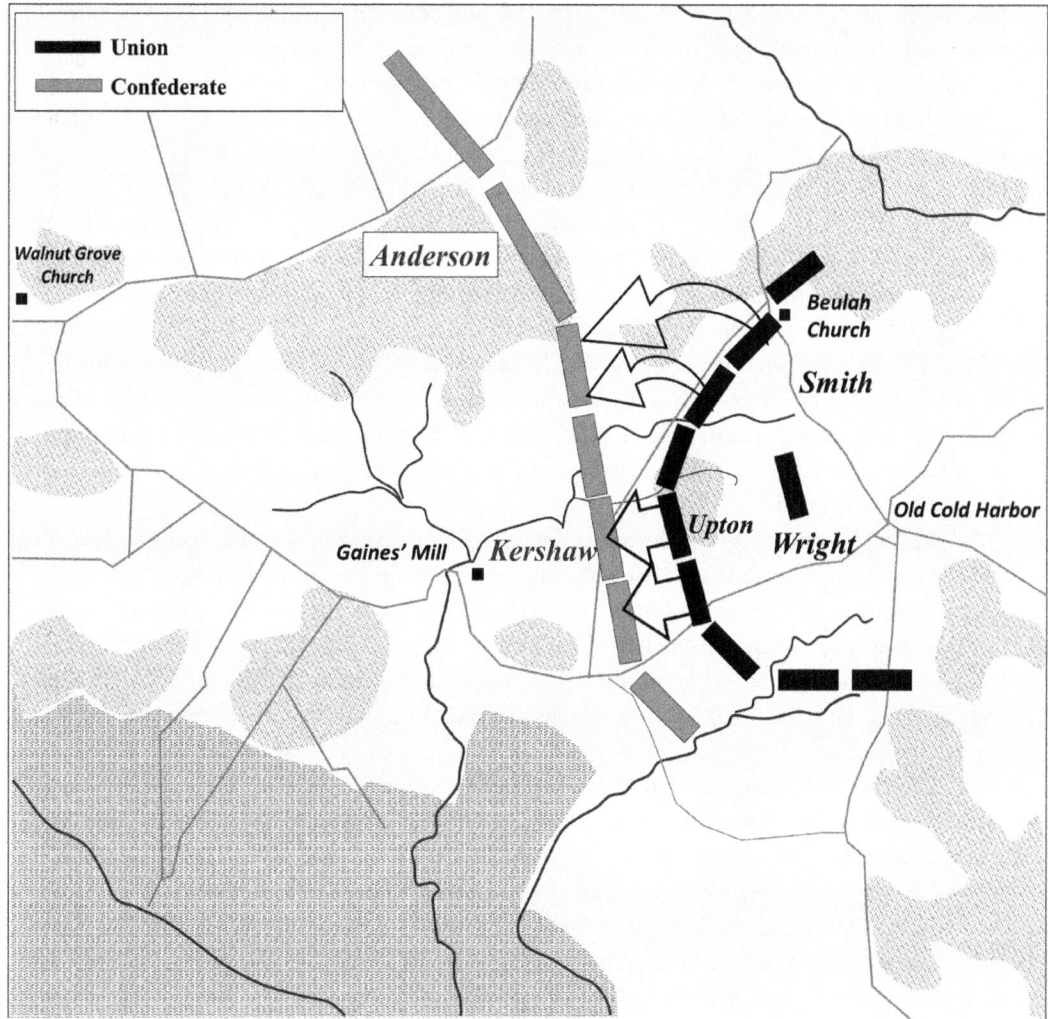

Map of the first assault at Cold Harbor, June 1, 1864 (drawn by the author).

But perhaps worse, no one knew what was in front of them. The ground around Cold Harbor was uneven and heavily forested, with deep gullies and marshes hiding among the trees. Moreover, there had only been time for a "hasty reconnaissance" of the ground in front of the Federal lines.[18] Despite this, Meade ordered an assault on the enemy positions.

Because there was no reconnaissance, Upton and the rest of VI Corps did not know that Lee's men had once again quickly built field fortifications, digging rifle pits and building breastworks with fallen timber from the woods. They also cut down thick clusters of pine tree branches and saplings, laying them down in front of their crude breastworks "to form a very effective abatis."[19]

Nevertheless, around 5:00 p.m., despite his strong reservations about the coming assault, Upton formed his brigade in line of battle just to the left of the Third Division and to the right of Second Division. He placed his men in four lines, and his orders were to maintain alignment with the Third Division as they moved forward to attack the enemy entrenchments. As the 2nd Connecticut was anxious to prove itself, Upton deployed them in column, making them the first three lines of battle for the brigade. The 95th and 96th Pennsylvania and 121st New York followed in the fourth line.[20] The attack was set to commence at 6:00 p.m.

As that time approached, Upton rode near the front of the brigade and heard Colonel Elisha Kellogg, commander of the 2nd Connecticut, address his men. Kellogg explained the plan of attack, marking out the shapes of the enemy entrenchments in the dirt for his officers and men to see. He told them how they would make the charge and instructed the officers on how to manage each of the three battalions as they crossed the open ground to their front. Finally, he reminded them of their reputation as merely being a "bandbox" regiment, telling his men, "Now we are called on to show what we can do at fighting."[21]

Men from the 121st New York prepared to move forward as the brigade's skirmishers, relieving those from Sheridan's cavalry who had been sparring with the enemy's sharpshooters since the day before. They were told that the Confederate lines were on the far edge of the plowed field to their front in a dense pine thicket. When the attack began, their assignment would be to "charge on a dead run" towards those lines and run the Confederate skirmishers back and into their rifle pits.[22]

The 2nd Connecticut now lined up at the edge of the pine woods where they had spent the afternoon, leaving knapsacks behind and preparing to move forward. As the clock finally advanced towards 6:00 p.m., Upton saw the Second Division begin to advance to his right. No one, however, was moving on the left where he was supposed to guide on Third Division. He waited only a moment before going ahead and ordering his brigade to the attack.[23] With their flags marking the center of their line, the first battalion of the 2nd Connecticut stepped off at the double quick.[24]

The 121st New York's skirmishers rose up and broke into a run, as ordered, and the enemy skirmishers abandoned their positions as soon as they saw them coming. They did not even pause at their rifle pits, retreating into the works hidden in the pine forest ahead. Meanwhile, behind the skirmishers from New York, the 2nd Connecticut pressed the main attack forward.[25]

The men from Connecticut quickly crossed the open field, entering the pine woods, where they "passed down a gentle declivity, and up a slight ascent" until they were about 70 feet from the enemy works.[26] Here, everything began to go badly.

As the brigade's first line approached the entrenchments, they ran headlong into the enemy's abatis and came to a halt. As Colonel Kellogg attempted to get the men moving through the dense entanglement of pine branches, the main Confederate line opened fire. One Connecticut soldier said that the first enemy volley was a "sheet of flame, sudden as lightning, red as blood, and so near that it seemed to singe the men's faces."[27] The 2nd Connecticut was struck "with a thousand balls that just missed the heads of the men."[28]

Kellogg ordered his men to lie down as a second volley went over their heads. He then urged his men to get back on their feet, and they resumed the attack. But suddenly, as they ran forward with a yell, a horrific enfilading fire erupted from the trees to their left. The effect was devastating. It was, as one man wrote, a barrage that "no human valor could withstand." The air in the pine woods filled with dense smoke, as well as the "shrieks and moans" of over 250 wounded and dying soldiers from the 2nd Connecticut.[29]

As he ordered the surviving members of the lead battalion to retreat, an enemy bullet struck Colonel Kellogg in the head, and he fell dead among the abatis. At that moment, the lead element of the attack fell apart. "Wild and blind with wounds, bruises, noise, smoke, and conflicting orders," one soldier later said, "the men staggered in every direction, some of them falling upon the very top of the rebel parapet, where they were completely riddled with bullets, others wandering off into the woods on the right and front ... never to be heard of again."[30]

As he always did, Upton rode with his men into the attack. However, his horse was soon shot out from under him. So, he continued to advance on foot with the second line from the 2nd Connecticut, which was about 75 yards to the rear of the first. As soon as he saw the first line cut to pieces, Upton shouted out an order for the men to lie down, take whatever cover they could find, and not return the enemy's fire. Soon, men from the first line appeared from the trees as they fell back, mixing with the second line and causing confusion. Upton quickly moved to sort the mess out and, gradually, the survivors from the first line, which included many seriously wounded men, made their way to the rear.[31]

About this time, as it became darker from a combination of the sunset and the dense smoke, Upton noticed that part of the enemy line to his right had been pierced by soldiers from the Second Division. He ordered men from the 96th Pennsylvania to follow him, and he took them to the break in the Confederate works. From there, he led them in a charge to the left, flanking the Confederate troops in the entrenchments where the 2nd Connecticut had been so badly torn up. The enemy broke after token resistance, and Upton's men secured the breastworks. While several attempts were made to drive his brigade out during the night, they continued to hold it until the Confederates finally fell back to their second line of trenches deeper in the woods.[32]

Observing the remains of the first line's attack, Colonel McMahon later described the sight as deeply sad. "I remember at one point," he wrote, "a mute and pathetic evidence of sterling valor." Because they were new to battle, the uniforms of the 2nd Connecticut were "bright and fresh." "Therefore," McMahon recalled, "its dead were easily distinguished where they lay. They marked in a dotted line an obtuse angle, covering a wide front, with its apex toward the enemy."[33]

Upton reported that the 2nd Connecticut had 53 killed, 187 wounded, and 146 missing.[34] But this latest seemingly pointless attack left him seething with anger, which he poured out in a letter to his sister. "We are now at Cold Harbor, where we have been since June 1st. On that day we had a murderous engagement. I say murderous, because we were recklessly ordered to assault the enemy's intrenchments [sic], knowing neither their strength nor position. Our loss was very heavy, and to no purpose. Our men are brave, but cannot accomplish impossibilities. My brigade lost about three hundred men. My horse was killed, but I escaped unharmed."[35]

Had Upton known what was happening at the highest command levels of the army, he would have been much angrier. At the beginning of the campaign, the atmosphere between Grant and Meade's headquarters had been somewhat confused. Grant's original plan was for him to execute the grand strategy, while George Meade directed the Army of the Potomac's tactical movements and actions. However, as soon as the army entered the Wilderness, that quickly changed.

Grant told his staff that he would send them "to the critical points of the lines"[36] where they would not only function as his eyes and ears but would also communicate his orders directly to Meade and his commanders. Clearly, this type of approach was far more than merely providing strategic direction. Within 24 hours of encountering Lee's army, Grant was sending out unambiguous tactical direction to Meade. This created both confusion and deep resentment at Meade's headquarters.

By the time the army was fighting at Spotsylvania Court House, the newspapers in the North were referring to the Army of the Potomac as being under Grant's command. While Grant's modest ego allowed him to ignore what the papers said, Meade was extremely sensitive about the implications of these reports, and he made his feelings clear in a letter to his wife written on the evening after Upton's first assault at Cold Harbor. "The papers are giving Grant all the credit of what they call successes," he wrote, "I hope they will remember this if anything goes wrong."[37]

By the time the army reached Cold Harbor, Grant and Meade's staff were in open warfare against one another. Grant's staff openly talked about Meade's "somewhat anomalous position." They told Grant that they were losing vital time in transmitting field orders through an intermediary whose position was, essentially, "a false one." Further, some stated that they believed Meade and his staff were modifying Grant's instructions or that they were "elaborated as to change their spirit."[38]

The concerns of Grant's staff about the general-in-chief's orders being delayed or altered were not without merit. Meade's staff despised both Grant and his staff officers. Further, they referred to the armies Grant had commanded in the West as nothing more than an "armed rabble."[39] The result of all this was steady corrosion in command cohesion, which was made worse by fatigue and stress. As the rest of the army moved towards Cold Harbor, that cohesion completely unraveled.

On the night of June 1, the other corps from the Army of the Potomac began moving south from Totopotomoy Creek. General Meade hoped to launch a new and much larger assault the next morning, June 2. But the other corps had an even worse time finding their way south. Again, bad maps and choking dust raised by thousands of marching soldiers slowed progress. When Meade was told that Hancock's II Corps would not arrive until 6:30 a.m., he issued new orders delaying the upcoming assault until 5:00 p.m.[40]

Concerned that Hancock's men were too tired to make an attack that afternoon, Grant advised Meade to delay the assault until the early morning hours of June 3. As a result, at 2:30 p.m., Meade sent a circular to his corps commanders informing them that the attack would be delayed until 4:00 a.m. on June 3.[41]

However, all these delays allowed Lee to shift the remainder of his army into position opposite the Army of the Potomac. As at Spotsylvania and the North Anna, he also had his soldiers erect field fortifications. Worst of all, however, no one on the Union side attempted to make a reconnaissance of Lee's lines. All that was known was that there was evidence that field fortifications had been prepared. Their nature, their orientation, and the strength of the enemy were totally unknown. So, the only thing Meade's men could see was some turned earth here and there, and that was what the army would attack. Unfortunately for the Army of the Potomac, the freshly dug earth they could see included rifle-pits and not one main line of trenches, but two and even three in some places. Lee and his men had skillfully placed their fortifications so that they followed the uneven terrain.

There also was virtually no plan for the attack beyond the starting time of 4:00 a.m. Instead, each corps was seemingly left on its own to determine how it was going to attack, with no plans for cooperation. As a result, 40,000 men would make an attack with no plan and no knowledge of what they were attacking. It was a recipe for disaster.

Luckily for Upton's brigade, the First Division of VI Corps would not participate in the attack. For the first time since crossing the Rapidan almost a month before, the brigade was ordered to simply remain in reserve and watch the assault. Despite all Upton and his men had endured up to this point, what they witnessed was beyond description.

In the early morning hours of June 3, as a damp fog clung to the ground, most of the Army of the Potomac went forward at the appointed time with colors flying. They did not advance far before a devastating volley of rifle and artillery fire greeted them. Men fell dead and wounded in groups and, in places, entire companies fell together. During the first hour, two waves went forward, and only Francis Barlow's division of Hancock's II Corps actually met with success. They managed to seize and hold a portion of Lee's far right. But despite Barlow's repeated requests, no one moved forward to exploit what his men had gained at such great cost.

The remaining four Union corps went forward, some getting further than others, until the withering fire from behind Lee's entrenchments slowed, stopped, and eventually pinned the Federals down. VI Corps, advancing to II Corps' immediate right, managed to sweep over the Confederate rifle pits, but got no farther. Faced with "frontal fire, enfilading fire from the right and from the left," they quickly came to a complete halt and "where the line stopped, it stayed, and dug in or died."[42] The best and most succinct description of the June 3 attack at Cold Harbor came from someone on the Confederate side. One of Lee's division commanders, General Evander Law, said: "It was not war; it was murder."[43]

Late in the morning, an order came down from Grant's headquarters to make another assault. This time, Upton's brigade was assigned to be part of the attack. However, as the men formed up in their makeshift trenches to go forward, General Wright and General Russell arrived on the scene. They met with Upton and some engineering officers to discuss the situation and determine if the attack ought to be made. Upton made his case that the enemy position was simply too strong to take. Given what had happened earlier in the morning, they reached the inevitable conclusion that the order to attack must be countermanded and the assault canceled.[44]

By 12:30 p.m., Grant withdrew the order, and the assault at Cold Harbor was over. The survivors hunkered down in their own rapidly growing fortifications. The magnitude of what had occurred and the ghastly cost of this command blunder would soon become apparent. Most figures for the assault indicate that approximately 7,000 Union soldiers fell, and Hancock alone reported his losses at more than 3,000 men in less than an hour of fighting.[45] No matter the exact number, it had been an unmitigated disaster. A colonel on Meade's staff wrote in his journal, "We gained nothing save a knowledge of their position and the proof of the bravery of our soldiers."[46]

If seeing the slaughter of June 3 was not bad enough, over the next few days, Upton and his soldiers had to endure the sight, sound, and smell of thousands of wounded and dying Union soldiers in the open ground between the Union lines and those of Lee's army. On June 4, Upton's men tried to retrieve as many of the wounded as they could reach without being shot dead themselves by enemy sharpshooters. The rest lay in the broiling June sun without water and without any aid while Grant and Lee exchanged notes on a truce for retrieving the wounded, an agonizing process that lasted three days. Meanwhile, Upton's men did their best to bury those dead within their lines. But those poorly interred and the thousands that lay in the open field beyond began to decompose, resulting in a "putrid ... awful stench."[47]

Once an agreement was brokered, the brigade moved out under a flag of truce to recover those wounded who had miraculously survived and bury the remaining dead. Upton's men found one wounded officer with a thigh wound infested with maggots. Some of the wounded had stayed alive by sucking their own clothing to get whatever water was left by the morning dew each day, while others had dug shallow holes with their hands and sucked on the moist clay for whatever water it might contain.[48]

On the night after the assault, Grant finally made his feelings known to his staff: "I regret this assault more than any one I have ever ordered. I regarded it as a stern necessity, and believed it would bring compensating results; but, as it has proved, no advantages have been gained sufficient to justify the heavy losses suffered."[49] With that said, as was his manner, Grant focused his energies on planning his next moves and seldom spoke of Cold Harbor again.

Grant determined that it was time for a more radical approach, and one that, perhaps, might surprise Lee. Rather than make another slight maneuver to the left, he would throw his entire army across the James River, outflank Lee, and seize Petersburg, a commercial and transportation hub whose rail lines were critical to supplying both Richmond and Lee's army. If he could take it, Grant might starve the Confederates out of their defenses around Richmond, which would allow him to finally face Lee on ground of his own choosing.

The plan involved the construction of a 1,200-foot-long pontoon bridge over the Chickahominy River and an even longer one approaching 2,000 feet in length over the James. This plan also called for the Army of the Potomac to move out undetected from Lee's front in four closely coordinated columns and cross the James before the Confederates realized what was happening. Amazingly, they succeeded, and from June 12 to 15, all 115,000 men of the Army of the Potomac made the crossing. However, the movement stalled opposite Petersburg, and both armies were forced to build trenches facing one another.

As for Upton, the fighting at Cold Harbor became a critical event in his life. It crystalized the deep resentment and anger he felt toward the army's leadership. Gone were the enthusiastic letters filled with bravado written by the young lieutenant fresh from West Point. These feelings had been slowly building since his first major action at Antietam. But now, in this campaign, the horrors he witnessed in the Wilderness, at Spotsylvania, and at Cold Harbor, fueled his fury and disgust. In a letter to his sister written on June 4, the day after the disastrous attack, he expressed his anger towards those in command. "I am disgusted with the generalship displayed. Our men have, in many instances, been foolishly and wantonly sacrificed. Assault after assault has been ordered upon the enemy's intrenchments [sic], when they knew nothing about the strength or position of the enemy. Thousands of lives might have been spared by the exercise of a little skill; but, as it is, the courage of the poor men is expected to obviate all difficulties. I must confess that, so long as I see such incompetency, there is no grade in the army to which I do not aspire."[50]

The next day, he penned another letter to his sister that was, in some ways, even more damning of the army's leadership than the previous one. "I am very sorry to say I have seen but little generalship during the campaign. Some of our corps commanders are not fit to be corporals. Lazy and indolent, they will not even ride along their lines; yet, without hesitancy, they will order us to attack the enemy, no matter what their position or numbers. Twenty thousand of our killed and wounded should to-day be in our ranks."[51]

After his brigade crossed the James River, they joined the rest of VI Corps near a plantation called Point of Rocks on June 12. While there, he received orders to have his brigade make an assault on yet another well-defended enemy position. Fortunately, the order was countermanded, but the incident caused him to write another scathing letter to his sister.

> The order was countermanded in time to prevent a deliberate murder of our troops. The line we were to assault was evacuated by the enemy on the 16th, and was occupied by our troops, who fell back from them without firing a shot. It was not till the enemy had reoccupied them in stronger force than before that it was

discovered that their possession was of great importance to us. Brilliant generalship that, which would abandon voluntarily a line of works, allow the enemy to take possession, and then drive them from it by a glorious charge! This kind of stupidity has cost us already twenty thousand men. It is time that it should be stopped.[52]

In his mind, it was becoming clear that, in the coming years, the army must reform not only its tactics but also change its very culture. If it did not, thousands more would die needlessly, and the nation might suffer even greater catastrophes.

Upton marched his brigade into the army's new lines facing the city of Petersburg. Over the next few weeks, his men would dig extensive works as a stalemate of sorts developed between the two great armies. His brigade would be shifted about up and down the line, but they saw no action as June turned into July. However, soon, he and his men would move hundreds of miles, first to Washington and then the Shenandoah Valley, to counter a new threat.

10

Winchester

> I have never been reckless, but I am sure it is a praiseworthy quality when so few of our higher commanders expose themselves as much as duty requires. It has now arrived at that point when officers must expose themselves freely if they would have their commands do their whole duty; so, whatever I may do, you must not attribute it to rashness, but to a soldier's sense of duty.
> —Emory Upton, August 9, 1864[1]

To the Valley

The Shenandoah Valley, whose name comes from a Native American word meaning "daughter of the stars," lies sandwiched between the Blue Ridge and the Appalachian Mountains. The river whose name it carries meanders serenely northward about 175 miles until it merges with the Potomac at Harpers Ferry. At the time of the Civil War, lush fields and forests filled the valley, and it was dotted with small, prosperous communities and farms.

The valley was also a critical piece of geography in the conduct of the war. From the beginning of the conflict, the valley was a potential invasion route. From a Northern perspective, it was a "back alley" into the North, and a dagger pointed at the nation's capital. Meanwhile, from a Confederate viewpoint, any Union control of the valley would threaten Richmond and allow Federal forces to cut the Tennessee and Virginia Railroad linking the two primary theaters of the war. Finally, and perhaps most importantly in this late stage of the war, the valley's farms were one of the primary sources of food for Confederate armies, especially Lee's Army of Northern Virginia.

Union efforts to maintain any hold on the valley had constantly been frustrated. While Federal forces would occupy Harpers Ferry for much of the war, they had never been able to successfully prosecute any campaign to take the remainder of the valley. In 1862, Stonewall Jackson had run rings around three different Federal armies, embarrassing them in a series of stunning defeats. After that, Lee had been able to secure the valley during his campaign into Maryland in September 1862 and use it as a route of invasion when he moved into Pennsylvania during the summer of 1863. Then, as Lee savagely struggled with Grant and Meade during the summer of 1864, he again decided to make use of the valley in a bold gamble designed to relieve Grant's stranglehold on him at Petersburg.

In mid-June, Lee ordered General Jubal Early to detach 16,000 men from the siege lines at Petersburg and take them into the Shenandoah Valley. Once there, Early's orders were to drive Union forces under General David Hunter from the valley. But in late June, Lee expanded Early's objectives, directing him to move north to threaten Washington. Lee told Jefferson Davis that Early's goal would be "to draw the attention of the enemy to his own territory. It may force Grant to attack me, or weaken his forces."[2]

In selecting Early, Lee was giving a key assignment to an officer he referred to as "my bad old man." It was a moniker that fit the irascible Early, who was known to his men as "Old Jube." Early was an aggressive, brave fighter, always cool when under fire. However, while his aggressive, offensive style was well-suited to a brigade, division, or corps commander, it could be a severe handicap as an independent army commander, especially if he had to face superior numbers. One of his subordinates and one of the finest Southern field commanders to emerge during the war, General John B. Gordon, once commented that Early tended to attack without the "courage of his convictions."[3] As a result, Early often fought boldly but blindly because he was unable to discern either his enemy's weaknesses or strengths. Gordon would later write, "He strikes in the dark, madly, wildly, and often impotently."[4]

Despite his shortcomings, Early's campaign was initially a success. He was able to slip away from Petersburg unnoticed and proceeded to drive Hunter's army back into West Virginia. From there, his army marched down the valley to the Potomac, crossed into Maryland, and turned towards Washington. While this was happening, Grant was unable to get reliable intelligence on the size or composition of the Confederate force operating in the valley, and, as a result, he did not seem overly concerned. However, once this new Southern army seemed poised to attack Washington, the pressure to act was too great. Grant had, after all, stripped the defenses of Washington of all but the lowliest of troops to support his campaign against Lee. Now, there was virtually no one left to man the fortifications surrounding the city and, if Early wanted to capture the capital, it was essentially there for the taking.

On July 6, Grant pulled the Third Division of VI Corps[5] out of the lines at Petersburg and sent them to board ships bound for Washington. He had hoped that these 5,000 men would be enough, but shortly thereafter, on July 9, he realized the entire VI Corps needed to move north.[6]

Upton received orders for his brigade that same day and marched his men to City Point on the night of July 10.[7] The first part of the brigade's journey was arduous, as the night was very dark and the ground between their position in the line and the road to City Point was where the army had obtained the logs needed for their entrenchments. As a result, tree stumps and broken fragments of trees littered the countryside. Once the brigade reached the embarkation point, all went smoothly with one small exception. Apparently, some enterprising soldiers in the 121st New York decided to "liberate" a barrel of onions, whose ownership was disputed by members of the 96th Pennsylvania, and a "rough and tumble row" took place between the men of the two regiments. Upton and the regimental officers restored order, and the brigade boarded a transport ship named the Transylvania.[8]

The ship made its way down the James before turning north to travel up the Chesapeake Bay to the Potomac. The weather was clear, and the Transylvania managed enough speed for men to enjoy a "refreshing breeze,"[9] which was a nice change from the stifling summer heat in the trenches before Petersburg.

As the first two VI Corps brigades raced northward, Early and his army were approaching Frederick, Maryland. Union General Lew Wallace, who would later gain fame as the author of Ben Hur, mobilized a motley, ragtag force of militia, cavalry, and light artillery to meet Early and headed west to Monocacy Junction, just across the Monocacy River from Frederick. Wallace was badly outnumbered, and he had little hope of even slowing the Confederates, much less stopping them. Then, late on the afternoon of July 8, the first elements of the VI Corps began to arrive, adding veteran strength to Wallace's otherwise sad, inexperienced contingent. The next morning, Early attacked Wallace's still outnumbered force in what was the Battle of Monocacy. Wallace held Early back all day and inflicted a high casualty toll on the Confederate forces. Eventually, the Union units were forced to retreat, but the time they bought turned out to be critical.

The Transylvania reached the docks at the Sixth Street Wharf in Washington on July 11 after a two-day trip. Despite the fact that the men had not eaten recently, they quickly disembarked, and Upton formed them into column. They set out up Seventh Street, and, as they marched through the capital, large crowds greeted them. "As we passed along," recalled Private Beckwith of the 121st New York, "we were greeted with clapping of hands, waving of handkerchiefs, and many remarks such as 'Bully for you,' 'Hurrah for the 6th Corps.'"[10] Upton and the men soon learned the reason for this hearty welcome—Jubal Early's army had reached the outskirts of the city.

After the Battle of Monocacy, Early paused briefly before moving forward toward Washington. On the afternoon of July 10, his army found themselves facing Fort Stevens, one of a series of works that surrounded the capital. His men were approaching exhaustion and, as he peered through his glasses at the Capitol dome, the usually aggressive Early hesitated. He waited one day to attack, but, when the moment came to begin the assault, Early discovered that the fortifications that had been almost empty the day before were now manned in force by the remainder of the VI Corps. In spite of the Federal reinforcements, the Confederate general decided to attack Fort Stevens.

As Upton and his brigade continued their march up Seventh Street toward the fort, people in the crowds lining the street cheered and supplied his troops with water and ginger beer. Private Beckwith later wrote the day was "exceedingly hot."[11] Soon, Upton led the men off the paved street, and the heat combined with the thick dust made the marching "very hard."[12]

But just after leaving the streets, the men heard the sounds of rifle fire up ahead. About that time, Upton and the brigade passed General Wright, the VI Corps commander, who was anxiously conferring with a tall gentleman dressed in a black suit and wearing a black top hat, whom they all immediately recognized as President Lincoln. Upton's men cheered when they saw the president, and he raised his hat in salute. The brigade moved up to the fort, and Upton deployed them to the left and rear of the works, which were "swarming to suffocation, with all sorts of people, invalid reserves, convalescents, clerks, citizens, marines, any and everybody who could or would be able to fire a gun."[13]

Shortly before the brigade arrived at the fort, General Bidwell's 2nd Brigade charged Early's lines, sweeping Rode's division of Ewell's corps from the field, and driving them beyond Silver Spring.[14] Early's opportunity to take the Federal capital had been lost with the arrival of VI Corps. He ordered his army to retreat west into the Shenandoah Valley, falling all the way back to encamp near Bunker Hill, Virginia.

With the immediate threat to Washington blunted, Upton's brigade and VI Corps moved forward to Harpers Ferry and then to Snicker's Gap, Virginia, just west of Leesburg on the far side of the Blue Ridge. On July 19, Upton wrote his sister, describing the beauty of the Shenandoah and telling her, "I wish you could enjoy this scenery." He added, "From our camp on the Blue Ridge the Great Valley of Virginia with its surrounding streams, its groves, its fertile fields, and elegant mansions, is spread out like a beautiful landscape. Seldom does the tourist meet with a view so enchanting. A glance of the eye comprehends the Blue Ridge, the Alleghenies, Maryland Heights, and innumerable smaller mountains dotted here and there throughout the Valley, lending additional charms to the scenery."[15]

It was a far cry from the scenes he had witnessed from May to June and must have come as a relief. But change was coming, and his peaceful reveries would soon end.

A New Army and a New Campaign

With Early's near success at Washington, Grant decided that the Shenandoah Valley must be dealt with and eliminated as both an avenue of attack and a source of supply for Lee. He traveled to Washington to confer with the president and Secretary of War Stanton. Grant proposed unifying several military departments into one, creating a new Army of the Shenandoah, and tasking its commander to drive Early out of the valley, destroying his army if at all possible, and wreaking havoc on the farms and fields that were feeding Lee's army. There was a debate as to who should lead this new army, and even George McClellan's name was mentioned in the discussions. Finally, over the objection of some, Grant named General Philip Sheridan to the new post. Initially, Sheridan was to serve merely as a field commander under the direction of General Hunter, who was the department commander. However, Hunter quickly resigned, and Sheridan assumed complete command.

Sheridan arrived at Harpers Ferry on August 6 to take command of the forces Grant had assembled near Halltown, Virginia, which was about four miles west of Harpers Ferry. Sheridan's new Army of the Shenandoah totaled nearly 30,000 men. He had three divisions of cavalry, the VI Corps, the

Major General Phillip Sheridan, commander of the new Army of the Shenandoah (Library of Congress).

XIX Corps, and the new XVIII Corps, an assemblage of units from West Virginia and Ohio led by General George Crook.

Sheridan himself was something of an oddity. At only five-feet, three inches tall, he was a tough Irishman and a West Point graduate. He had distinguished himself in the West under Grant and, like Early, was an aggressive, tough fighter. He had a personality that was magnetic and charismatic to his troops, mercurial with subordinate commanders, and, at times, almost insubordinate to superiors. He had led infantry in the West and commanded Meade's cavalry when he came east. Some considered him too cocky for independent command, but Grant liked his aggressiveness and thought him ideally suited to the job that needed to be done in the Shenandoah.

Upton also liked what he saw from his new commanding general. "A new campaign will be inaugurated to-morrow [sic] under the command of General Sheridan," he wrote his sister on August 9. "General Sheridan has the appearance of great nerve," he continued, "and hitherto has been quite successful. For one, I am better pleased with his appearance than that of any other commander under whom I have served."[16]

Grant's orders to Sheridan were very clear. He was to drive Jubal Early's army out of the valley. "Bear in mind," Grant wrote, "the object is to drive the enemy south, and to do this you want to keep him always in sight. Be guided in your course by the course he takes."[17] But more than that, Grant wanted the valley destroyed once and for all as a source of supply to Lee's army at Petersburg. "In pushing up the Shenandoah Valley," he stated, "it is desirable that nothing should be left to invite the enemy to return. Take all provisions, forage, and stock wanted for the use of your command; such as cannot be consumed, destroy."[18]

On August 10, the day after Upton had written to his sister about Sheridan, the commander of the new Federal army put his troops in motion and pointed them south, up the valley. The army moved towards Bulltown, and Sheridan hoped this would get Early's attention, causing the Confederates to fall back toward Winchester. Early did exactly as Sheridan had hoped but the Union general received some disquieting news that caused him to slow his advance. Lee had heard of the formation of Sheridan's army and knew that Early must be its target. Therefore, he began shifting a division of infantry under General Kershaw, some artillery, and Fitzhugh Lee's cavalry to Early.[19]

For the next few weeks, the two armies moved and watched each other like two boxers sizing up one another. During this period, Upton's brigade was encamped in Harpers Ferry, and he found time to write another letter to his sister. Apparently, Upton had hoped to get a furlough to visit his family, but he had to tell them that was not going to be possible now. "I would like very much to spend Saturday and Sunday, September 9th and 10th, at home," he wrote, "but do not look forward to such an event." He told his sister that the army's actions depended on Early, "who is a contrary fellow, and may give us much trouble about that time."[20] As it turned out, Upton's estimate on when things might start to happen was not exactly accurate, but Sheridan was about to set the wheels in motion to attack Old Jube.

The Battle of Third Winchester

Early had placed four divisions of his army in a large V-shaped line that began just north of the town of Winchester, Virginia and then turned to the south. In response, Sheridan had moved his army to Berryville, about ten miles to the east of Early's position, and ordered the army to begin moving toward Winchester early on the morning of September 19.

At 3:00 a.m. that morning, Upton formed his brigade and began to move them down the Berryville Pike towards Opequon Creek.[21] The brigade, which had recently been reinforced by the 65th New York Infantry, was well rested, and Upton's men carried extra ammunition plus four days' worth of rations in their haversacks.[22] At 8:00 a.m., the brigade splashed across the creek before halting about two miles down the road. Upton moved his men off the pike, which was choked with soldiers, wagons, and artillery from XIX Corps, who were following General James Wilson's cavalry towards Winchester.[23] The brigade remained there in reserve for about an hour. In the distance, they soon heard the rattle of rifle fire as the cavalry engaged and drove back the forward elements of Early's army.

Upton and his men remained in place alongside the Berryville Pike until just before noon. Then, he received orders to move his men forward so they would be in a position to provide support wherever it might be needed. As they followed the pike up the hill above Opequon

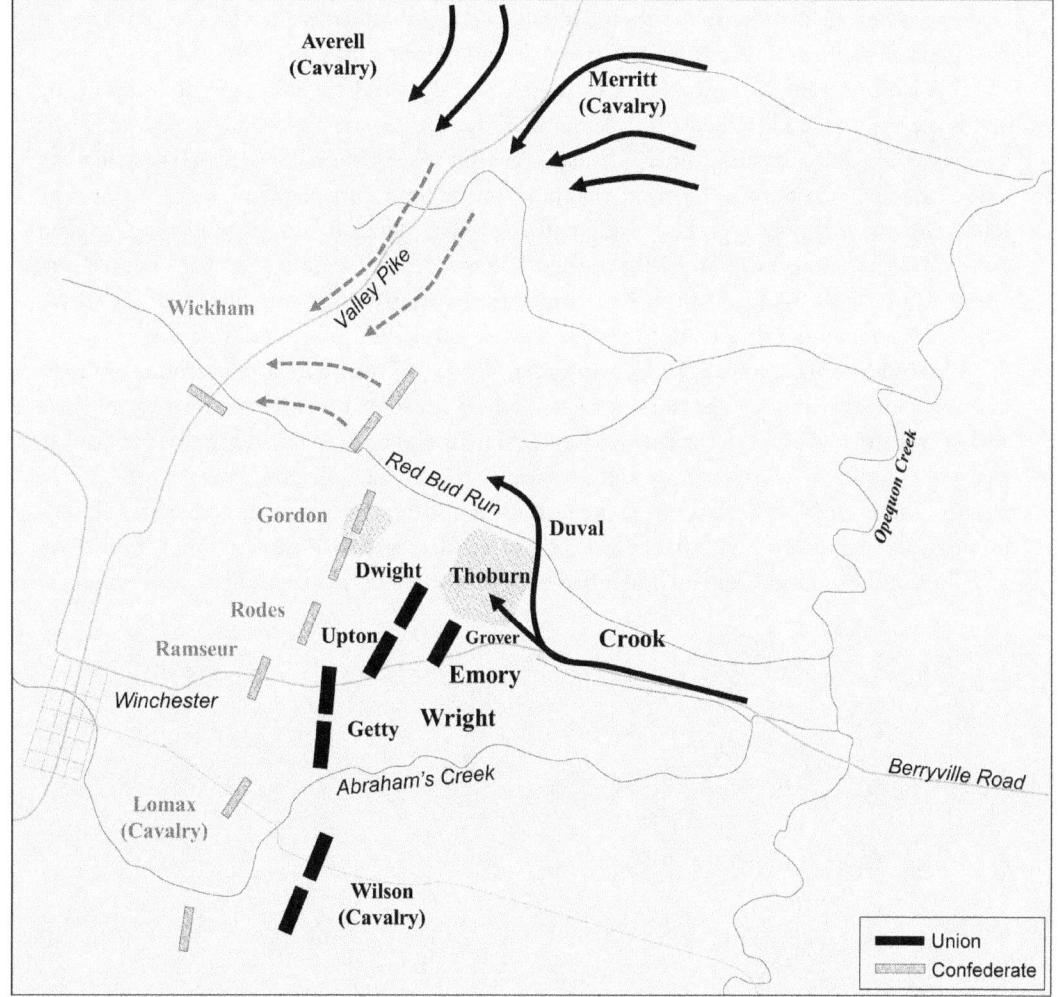

Battle of Third Winchester, September 19, 1864 (drawn by the author).

Creek, there were open fields on both sides of the road, and the uphill grade was very gradual. Soon, however, the slope became much steeper before it finally leveled out on the eastern edge of a largely wooded plateau that ran from Abraham's Creek, on the southern boundary of the battlefield, all the way north to Redbud Run. Here, Jubal Early's army waited, entirely hidden in the trees in a line of battle that ran south to north from just across the Berryville Pike to Redbud Run.[24]

As the brigade drew closer to the Confederate lines, heavy artillery and rifle fire began to reach them. Upton formed the brigade into two lines as they moved forward with the 2nd Connecticut in the lead at the center, the 121st New York to their right, and the 65th New York on the far left. As they advanced, some of the troops to the right of the pike from XIX Corps began to break and fall back, creating a gap between Upton's brigade and the remainder of XIX Corps.[25]

At this moment, Confederate infantry from Rode's division emerged from the woods to attack the XIX Corps' newly exposed left flank. Immediately seeing the danger, Upton ordered his brigade forward. The men faced to the right and advanced at the quickstep across an open field before entering a narrow belt of trees. Upton paused the brigade and ordered the men to lie down as he rode ahead into the open. He galloped up to soldiers from XIX Corps who were trying to flee the field and ordered them to get behind his brigade's line.[26]

As Upton's men lay in the cover of the trees, they could see a line of battle advancing across the open ground to their front, but at first, there was some confusion as to whether the troops were enemy or friendly forces. Upton returned to the brigade and ordered the men to fix bayonets. He then cautioned his regiment commanders not to fire until the enemy was at close range, and only when he gave the order. Finally, the Confederate infantry from Rodes' division came close enough to leave no doubt of their identity. At that moment, Upton shouted out, "Ready, aim, fire!" As a blast of rifle fire erupted from his men's weapons, dozens of the enemy fell, and the remainder were completely surprised to find Union troops on their flank.[27]

As Rodes' men began to fall back in disorder, Upton realized a critical opportunity was right in front of him. Even though he had no orders to advance further, he decided to take the initiative and exploit the confusion in the enemy's ranks.[28] He turned to his men and shouted "Forward, charge!" His soldiers quickly rose up and advanced at the double-quick from the woods.[29]

As the 121st New York reached the farthest point the Confederates had achieved, they found the ground littered with their dead and wounded, as well as those who simply took cover by falling to the ground. The remainder fled back for the woods as fast as they could run.

Alfred Waud's sketch of the fighting at Winchester (Library of Congress).

Meanwhile, the 2nd Connecticut also advanced, firing volley after volley despite a deadly return fire from the enemy.[30] They passed to the right of some woods and into an open field before halting at a spot where there was a slight depression in the ground, which provided some cover. The brigade remained there for only about three minutes before Upton had them moving forward once more. Finally, he brought them to a halt in another "hollow spot" similar to the first.[31] By now, the Confederates had withdrawn back to their original lines, and Upton had the brigade hold their position.

Upton's quick action in advancing and driving the enemy back was later credited with saving the day for Sheridan's army. Sheridan wrote that, as Rodes advanced, "the contest was uncertain," but that Upton's "gallant attack restored the line of battle."[32] Another officer from Sheridan's staff would say that Upton's attack, which resulted from his "military instincts and professional ability," had prevented a general retreat by the army.[33]

As the brigade came to a stop, Major Henry Dalton, the First Division adjutant, rode up to Upton and told him that General Russell had been killed.[34] Russell had been following the advance if the 1st and 3rd Brigades when he was struck by an enemy bullet in his chest. None of his staff noticed that he had been wounded, and the general continued to ride forward as though nothing was wrong. However, a few minutes later, a Confederate artillery shell exploded nearby, and a large fragment hit Russell in the upper left chest, going through his heart. He fell from his horse, dead before he even hit the ground.[35]

Dalton then told Upton that the VI Corps commander, General Wright, was ordering Upton to assume command of the First Division.[36] Upton immediately turned command of his brigade to Colonel Joseph Hamblin of the 65th New York and then rode off to assume command of the entire division. At only 25 years of age, Upton was now one of the youngest division commanders in the entire Union army. Moreover, he commanded three brigades and 13 regiments totaling over 5,000 men, a remarkable accomplishment for an officer who had only left West Point three years before.[37]

As one might imagine, assuming such responsibility in the midst of a major battle was terribly challenging, but Emory Upton was up to the task. His first problem as division commander was to get the division into better order. As a result of Rodes' attack, men from XIX Corps were wandering about and mixing in with regiments from his 1st and 3rd Brigades. Without resolving the confusion, there was no way the division could advance when the time came to do so. Unfortunately, there was also no time to sort out the men who did not belong to his division, especially while under enemy fire. Therefore, Upton decided to simply straighten out his line, bending the right flank back at a 30-degree angle, and order all officers to simply take command of the appropriate number of men nearest them. When this was done, Upton had the division properly dress its lines. All that was needed now was the order to renew the attack.[38]

As it turned out, he and his men did not have long to wait. Once Rodes had been driven back, Sheridan brought Crook's XVIII Corps forward and placed it to the immediate right of Upton's division. Now, the Federal line of battle had VI Corps on the left with XVIII Corps to the right and XIX Corps coming up about 150 yards to the rear. This made the line stretch all the way from below Abraham's Creek to just north of Redbud Run. About 3:00 p.m., Sheridan ordered the entire line to attack.

As the assault began, Upton moved the right flank of his division forward to a fence behind which the enemy lay in wait. His men opened up a brisk flanking fire on the Confederates there, causing them to fall back and allowing the center of Upton's division to move up to the fence. At this point, he tried to get units from the XIX Corps to move up in support of his division, but they would not come forward.[39]

Still, the pressure Upton was applying to the enemy caused them to continue to retreat. The Confederate infantry finally reformed their lines along the crest of a hill near a brick house along the Berryville Pike. Seeing that the advance of the XVIII Corps was being held up by Southern infantry dug in behind a stone wall to his right, Upton ordered the 2nd Connecticut to outflank the Confederate position, which quickly made the enemy retreat in confusion. With this enemy infantry driven away, Upton was able to make a firm connection with the left of General Crook's corps. At this point, Upton ordered the division to press the attack, and they quickly advanced over one low crest after another. The enemy's orderly retreat was now becoming a confused rout as they fell back into the outskirts of Winchester.[40]

As always, Upton rode at the head of his men, waving his hat and encouraging them to move forward. Suddenly, an enemy artillery shell burst next to his horse and a large fragment tore into the inner side of his right thigh. It lacerated his thigh muscle, tearing almost a quarter pound of his flesh away and laying bare the femoral artery. Bleeding profusely, he fell from his horse, and members of his staff rushed to his side.

Seeing Upton fall, General Sheridan also raced to the scene. Upton had been dazed by the wound and, as he regained his composure, he saw Sheridan on horseback looking down at him. The general ordered Upton to go to the rear, and then he dashed off for another part of the battlefield. Any other officer would have retired willingly under these circumstances, but not Emory Upton. As soon as General Sheridan was out of earshot, Upton called for his staff surgeon, who he directed to place a tourniquet on the wound. Once this was done and the bleeding had been stopped, Upton called for a stretcher and proceeded to have the bearers move him about the field, as he continued to direct the movements of his division. He did so for the next two hours until darkness put an end to his division's pursuit of the enemy, who had by then been driven south in panic up the Valley Turnpike.[41]

Emory Upton's photograph as a major general, probably taken in late 1864 (Library of Congress).

General James Wilson later wrote that Upton's actions at Winchester following his wounding were "heroic in the extreme, and marked him as a man of extraordinary nerve." He went on to say, "Fortitude on the part of a general upon such occasions is the greatest of military virtues."[42]

Upton lay in a field hospital for the next two days. Then, doctors determined that his wounds were too severe to allow him to return to duty for a significant period of time. As a result, he was sent home to Batavia to recover, and he would not return to duty until December 1864. However, while he was at home recuperating with his family, he learned that, upon General Wright's recommendation, he had been promoted to the rank of Major General of Volunteers for his actions at Winchester.[43]

While mending his wound at home, Upton followed the 1864 presidential election between President Lincoln and George McClellan with great interest. Like many soldiers who had served under General McClellan, he admired him as a soldier but not as a politician. McClellan's platform included a negotiated peace with the South, something that Upton referred to as "damnable."[44] Therefore, like the overwhelming majority of Union soldiers, he supported Lincoln's re-election, despite some doubts. "I am out and out for Lincoln," he wrote his sister. "He has made many gross blunders, but he is true to his purpose, and, when the South, after four years of war, finds that the North is as determined as ever to crush the rebellion, the rebellion will collapse."[45]

As it turned out, Upton's efforts at Winchester were not in vain. His actions were critical to the Federal victory there, and that led to two more major victories in the valley, with the final one coming at Cedar Creek in October. Sheridan's successful campaign in the Shenandoah and his dramatic victory at Cedar Creek were key factors that helped propel Lincoln to his re-election in November.

Not long after the election, Upton received orders to report to General George Thomas, commander of the Department of the Cumberland, in Nashville before moving on to duty under General James Wilson, a fellow former division commander in Sheridan's army.[46] Wilson had been sent by Grant to the Western Theater to reorganize the cavalry. Grant promised Wilson that he would provide him with some good officers from the Army of the Potomac to assist in making the cavalry of the Army of the Cumberland more effective. Wilson, who recognized Upton's talents and abilities, placed his name at the top of the list.[47]

After two years in the infantry, Upton would now say goodbye to that arm of the service. Before doing so, he sent a heartfelt goodbye to the men of his brigade, with whom he had served as a regiment, brigade, and division commander.

> In taking leave of the gallant brigade which I have had the honor so long to command, I cannot refrain from expressing the affection and regard I feel for those brave officers and men with whom I have been so long and pleasantly associated. I thank every one of you for the kindness and courtesy which has ever been shown me, and for the alacrity with which my orders have been obeyed. Your record is one of honor, and I shall ever with pride claim association with the Second Brigade. The distinguished part borne by you in the battles of Gaines' Mill, Rappahannock Station, Spotsylvania, Cold Harbor, Winchester, Fisher's Hill, Cedar Creek, and many others, has made for you a history second to no brigade in the army. But above this is the proud satisfaction of having voluntarily periled your lives in defense of the noblest Government on earth; by your valor helped to place its flag first among nations. Many of you cannot reap the immediate reward of your services; but the time is fast approaching when to have participated in your glorious battles will entitle you to the highest respect among men. Let your future history rival the past in valor and devotion. I leave you in brave hands, and part from you with sincere regret.[48]

Although not fully recovered from his wound and still noticeably limping, Upton bid farewell to his parents and sisters in early December and began the long journey south to Tennessee and yet another new challenge.

11

To the Cavalry

> General Upton has captured his division. When the fighting was hottest, he was right there by their side, and they know he is a brave man and a skillful general. Their hearts are with him.
> —Private E.N. Gilpin, 4th Iowa Cavalry, Diary Entry, April 1, 1865[1]

Upton arrived in Nashville in mid–December and, after briefly conferring with General Thomas, he went straight to General Wilson's headquarters. James Wilson had graduated a year ahead of Upton at West Point, and they served together in Sheridan's army. At five feet, ten inches, Wilson was taller than most men of the time, but he appeared even taller because of his erect military bearing.[2] He was blunt and often came across as somewhat overbearing to those who did not know him well. In reality, Wilson was supremely confident in himself, which was also seen in his bold manner of fighting. E.N. Gilpin, a soldier from the 3rd Iowa who would become a clerk in Upton's headquarters, noted that the two men were "alike in a way, yet very unlike—alike in this, that each has confidence in the other and in himself."[3]

Wilson noted Upton's limp as he walked into his headquarters tent and asked him if he thought he was up to command of a cavalry division. Upton replied, "that he had no doubt of his professional capacity to manage cavalry as well as either artillery or infantry."[4] His only concern was some "considerable anxiety" about how his men would see him, given that none had served under him in battle. Upton told Wilson that he also "feared that the rigid discipline he would exact and the constant instruction he would give might for a while make him unpopular." Still, he added, he "felt sure that he would remove all prejudice of that sort at the first action in which he should lead his division."[5]

Wilson proceeded to describe Upton's new command and his intentions for employing it. Like General Sheridan, Wilson believed that Union commanders had not employed the cavalry to the full extent of its capabilities. For much of the war, Federal leaders used the cavalry for reconnaissance and screening missions, only engaging them offensively on occasional raids behind enemy lines. Sheridan, however, had begun using the cavalry as an integral part of his offensive capability in the Shenandoah Valley, and Wilson now hoped to take things one step further.

Wilson's command, the Cavalry Corps of the Military Division of the Mississippi,[6] was to include more than 20,000 troopers who he hoped to equip with the best mounts and the latest in firearms, the Spencer seven-shot repeating carbine. Once trained and properly equipped, he hoped to convince General Thomas and General Grant to let him make a major strategic strike into the heart of the Deep South.

Forming the Division

Wilson told Upton that he would command the Third Division of the corps, which included two brigades. The 2nd Brigade, under the command of Colonel Israel Garrard, was currently camped outside Louisville, Kentucky. This brigade included the 5th Iowa, 1st Ohio, and 7th Ohio Cavalry Regiments. Meanwhile, the 1st Brigade, which was led by Colonel Edward Winslow, was now in Cairo, Illinois. Its men from the 3rd Iowa, 4th Iowa, and 10th Missouri Cavalry Regiments[7] were sitting on boats moored along the Ohio River, waiting for someone to decide where they should be deployed. It seems that the commander of Union forces in Memphis had ordered the troopers transferred to his command despite the fact that General Sherman and General Thomas had issued orders for the brigade to join Wilson's corps.[8]

Wilson described the 1st Brigade's situation during his initial meeting with Upton and, as soon as Upton left Wilson's office, he departed Nashville to go get his 1st Brigade, traveling by boat up the Cumberland River and then on down the Ohio River to Cairo. Once there, he visited the brigade on their boats, making sure that his entire demeanor expressed the concept that the brigade was "already his." One thing Upton had learned since he left West Point was that one needed to appear confident and be persistent if you wanted to overwhelm the army's bureaucratic processes. In this case, it "carried the day" and the authorities in Cairo released the brigade to Upton's command. His new men were immediately impressed by their young commanding officer and "everyone who met him felt the influence of his zealous spirit and shared his desire."[9] With that, the brigade sailed up the Ohio for Louisville.

On the night of December 22, 1864, Upton and the 1st Brigade unloaded from their boats in Portland, Kentucky, just west of Louisville. It was bitterly cold as the men were reunited with their mounts, who had come up the

Major General James H. Wilson, who would lead his cavalry corps on a campaign deep into Alabama and Georgia (Library of Congress).

river in barges lashed to the boats. With heavy snow falling, Upton led the brigade a few miles south where they camped for the night. The next morning, the 1st Brigade marched a short distance to rendezvous with the 2nd Brigade just outside the city in a new camp the men named Camp Upton in their commander's honor.[10]

With his entire command now in place, Upton began his part in what Wilson referred to as "the work we had in hand."[11] That work was to train and equip the largest cavalry force ever assembled in the Western Hemisphere, one capable of making a deep strategic strike into the heart of the Confederacy. In Upton's division that meant replacing outdated weapons and procuring horses. The latter was particularly true in Winslow's 1st Brigade where fewer than half the mounts were serviceable.[12]

Of course, as a commander and one new to the cavalry, both officers and enlisted men kept a close eye on Upton, trying to determine just what this eastern soldier was made of. E.N. Gilpin described their new commander as a young man who was "slightly above medium stature, keen-eyed, and carries himself as a soldier." Gilpin also noted Upton's voice as being unusually low and "rather pleasant to hear." He also observed that his general spoke "quickly when excited" and, when angry, "he is quick as a flash, and the man he is talking to thinks a revolver is going off at him." Describing Upton as being "dead earnest," Gilpin also wrote that Upton said his prayers every night, which was a "novelty." Moreover, as he had been in the artillery and infantry, Upton was a "strict disciplinarian, making the division drill, rain or shine, dismounted and with saber." But Gilpin noted that, despite this, he did "not hear any grumbling." "They are all veteran soldiers," Gilpin wrote, "he a new commander, and they are sizing him up. He has made a good impression on his division."[13] Others serving in the division recalled him as being "untiring" in his efforts to take care of his troopers, demonstrating a "zealous" spirit.[14]

Woodcutting showing the camps of Wilson's cavalry corps near Nashville (Library of Congress).

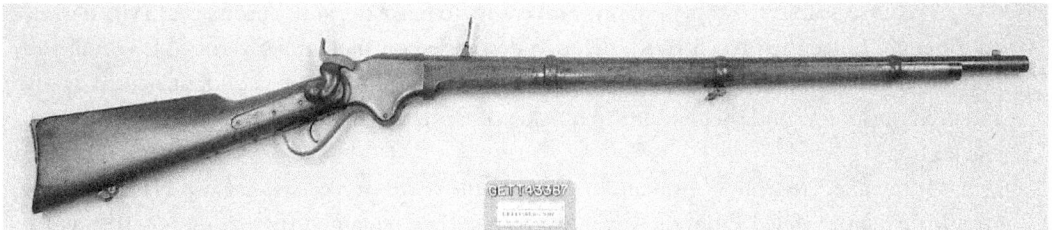

The Model 1863 Spencer Carbine used by Wilson's cavalry corps (National Park Service).

As for replacing old weapons, first the current revolvers were swapped with new six-shot versions, and only noncommissioned officers were required to carry them, which reduced the weight the enlisted cavalrymen had to carry. Next, Wilson had finally convinced the War Department that the heavy, long, and clumsy dragoon sabers had to go, replacing them with a lighter, shorter blade.[15]

The biggest change, however, was the arrival of the seven-shot carbine manufactured by the Spencer Arms Company. This revolutionary weapon had been available since 1863, but resistance to change in the War Department kept it from being widely deployed. However, when General Wilson went to the War Department as chief of the Cavalry Bureau in January 1864, he successfully negotiated a contract with Spencer for as many of the carbines as they could produce.[16]

The Spencer carbine was the ideal weapon for the cavalry. It was only 39 inches long and weighed eight pounds four ounces. Troopers would load the carbine through a tubular magazine, passing through the butt of the stock, and holding seven copper, rim-fire cartridges, which were fed forward to the breach by the action of a compressed spring inside the magazine tube. To augment rapid firing, these thin, detachable magazine tubes could be carried in a special box, making 70 rounds immediately available, which was a true asset in battle.[17] In addition, the reduced weight and flexibility of the weapon allowed many of the enlisted troopers to get rid of their revolvers since the Spencer served the purposes of both the rifle and the pistol.[18]

Most importantly, however, the use of the Spencer carbine drastically increased the firepower of the cavalrymen when fighting dismounted. Instead of only being able to fire three rounds per minute at best, troopers could get off seven aimed shots as fast as they could engage targets and then continue after a rapid reloading process. This meant that one cavalryman potentially had the capability to equal more than two infantrymen in terms of firepower, making them a force with which to be reckoned.

Unfortunately, the weather did not cooperate in allowing the men to practice with their new weapons and horses. Almost every day at Camp Upton saw snow, ice, or heavy rain, so there were few opportunities for outdoor training. As a result, most of the men spent their days trying to stay warm and dry, which was quite a challenge since all they had for quarters were what was called a "shelter tent." These were nothing more than a four-foot by six-foot piece of stiff cotton. Each trooper had one piece, and two would fasten them together on the longer side, stretch them over a ridge pole about three feet above the cold, wet ground. Normally, this was fine for light rain, but Upton's men were dealing with snow and freezing rain.[19]

Of course, soldiers always find innovative ways to make do, and Upton's cavalrymen were no different. Once their pay arrived, the men descended on the lumber yards of Louisville to procure as many boards as their combined funds would allow. They then returned to camp and used the lumber and shelter tents to quickly construct small huts in which they could even make a fire.[20]

Meanwhile, General Wilson and the rest of the corps moved south from Nashville to a grim little hamlet called Pinhook Town, Alabama. They remained there for a few days until orders arrived to move the command to Huntsville. This upset Wilson, who had been arguing with General Thomas and insisting that the cavalry should be further west. On January 1, 1865, Thomas finally relented, and Wilson began moving the 100 miles west to Eastport, Mississippi, on the banks of the Tennessee River.[21]

Once there, Wilson established a cantonment a few miles east of Eastport in Gravelly Springs, which was a small junction in the extreme northwest corner of Alabama, and sent orders to Upton on January 10, 1865, directing him to bring his division to Gravelly Springs before the end of January.[22] But the weather again proved to be an obstacle to Upton's division.

Getting the men, horses, and equipment to Gravelly Springs during a wet, cold winter required the division to move by boat, just as the 1st Brigade had done in coming from Cairo. The boats, with the horses being towed on barges, needed to move down the Ohio River to its junction with the Tennessee River and then follow the winding course of the Tennessee to Eastport. But when the orders from Wilson arrived, the Ohio River was blocked by ice. After almost three weeks of waiting for the ice to break up, Upton decided to move the division to the banks of the Ohio River just below Louisville. They arrived there on February 5 and two days later, began to embark.[23]

This proved to be a tedious process, as there were barely enough boats for the division, and all were very small. It took eight boats just to carry the men from the 4th Iowa, and more than 20 were required for each brigade. Once they began to move, progress was slow because of the remaining ice in the channel, and it took three days to reach the mouth of the Tennessee River. But after the boats turned south, the ice disappeared, and they moved quickly up the river. Upton disembarked his division a few days later at Waterloo, Alabama, just opposite Eastport, and they marched the remaining miles to their camp at Gravelly Springs.[24]

Wilson's cavalry corps was now finally all in one place. The camp where Upton's men were placed was a part of the corps cantonment, which stretched across the north bank of the Tennessee River, covering most of the ten miles between Gravelly Springs and Waterloo.

While he waited for final orders to begin a new campaign, Upton trained his men despite almost continuous rain and took special care to ensure horses and equipment were kept in top condition. With the incessant rain, the latter was a challenge for the men. "It was hard work," recalled William Scott, the adjutant of the 4th Iowa, "and so much more strictly required than before that many found it very irksome." But Upton's division was mostly made up of veterans who understood the need and, in the end, "appreciated its good results."[25]

The major feature of the training was an important change in tactics. Up to this point in the war, all of the corps' regiments had operated under the system defined in General Phillip Cooke's tactics manual. When fighting, Cooke's approach called for the cavalry to advance in a line formation with only one rank when both mounted and dismounted. Before the adoption of Cooke's tactics by the War Department, the cavalry had used General Winfield Scott's cavalry manual, which used a two-rank line of battle, and the difference between the two in terms of how you evolved from column into line formation was significant.[26]

The coming campaign was going to involve fighting in hilly, wooded terrain. Given the size of the brigades in Wilson's force, deploying in a single line while mounted would mean one brigade of 2,400 men would stretch for over a mile and a half. Because of the terrain where the corps would have to fight, this meant it would be almost impossible to get a single division, much less the entire corps, into a single line.[27]

As a result, all the brigades trained and practiced incessantly at the movements needed to form into a two-rank line while mounted. But once the troopers were dismounted, Wilson decreed that they would reform into the traditional single-line formation,[28] which required additional training and practice.

While General Wilson was justifiably pleased with how his new cavalry corps was progressing, it seems other Union generals looked at his assembled force with envy and coveted its resources. No sooner had Wilson collected his corps than requests started coming to General Thomas in Nashville, asking for parts of Wilson's cavalry. First, they took a division to support Sherman's advance into the Carolinas, and then another division for operations in middle Tennessee. Finally, on February 3, Thomas ordered Wilson to detach another full division of 5,000 men to support General Edward Canby's coming campaign against Mobile. Begrudgingly, Wilson agreed to send General Knipe's division to Canby. These transfers, combined with orders to post another division under General Hatch in northwestern Alabama, depleted Wilson's strength from seven divisions and 35,000 men to only three divisions composed of 12,500 mounted troopers plus 1,500 dismounted men. As Wilson later wrote bitterly, "Thus that magnificent body of cavalry and mounted infantry, with a full complement of horse artillery, constituting a mounted army equal to any military task that might fall to its lot, was divided and again widely scattered."[29]

Across the Tennessee

A few weeks later, on February 23, General Thomas arrived in Gravelly Springs to see Wilson and his cavalry corps. He also brought orders from General Grant. The general-in-chief, who was still facing Lee's entrenched army outside Petersburg, had proposed that Wilson use "say five thousand men to make a demonstration on Tuscaloosa and Selma" to support Canby's landings on the Alabama coast.[30]

To Wilson, such an idea was preposterous and the exact opposite of the kind of operations he wanted his corps to perform. He argued to Thomas that, rather than make a mere "demonstration," he ought to be turned loose for a major offensive into central Alabama using his entire remaining corps. Wilson told Thomas he not only would defeat any force the wily Confederate cavalry leader, Nathan Bedford Forrest, sent to stop him, but he would also "capture Tuscaloosa, Selma, Montgomery, and Columbus, and destroy the Confederacy's last depots of manufacture and supply and break up its last interior line of railway communications."[31]

Thomas was impressed by Wilson's proposal and agreed to the idea immediately. He then telegraphed Grant, requesting that the general-in-chief allow Wilson to carry out his plan.

Grant, who likely appreciated the aggressive nature of Wilson's proposed campaign, approved. Moreover, he gave Wilson all "the latitude of an independent commander."[32] This meant that Wilson and his men were no longer subordinate to either General Thomas or Sherman and that Wilson could employ his troops without interference from either.

Wilson's plan was bold and audacious. From his scouts, he knew that Forrest's command was scattered. Forrest's main body under Generals Chalmers, Buford, and Jackson, with Wirt Adams and Roddy's outlying brigades, numbered between 10,000 to 12,000 cavalrymen. Forrest's principal force was located close to the Alabama and Mississippi line, near the junction of two key rail lines, while his headquarters was at West Point, Mississippi, some 40 or 50 miles farther north and over 100 miles southwest of Gravelly Springs. Wilson calculated that, if he could confuse Forrest as to the objectives of his offensive, the deployment of Union forces would make it very difficult for the Confederate commander to react in time to stop it.[33]

To aid in confusing Forrest, Wilson planned to move his corps south on divergent routes. Upton's division would take a path through Russellville, Mount Hope, and Jasper to Saunder's

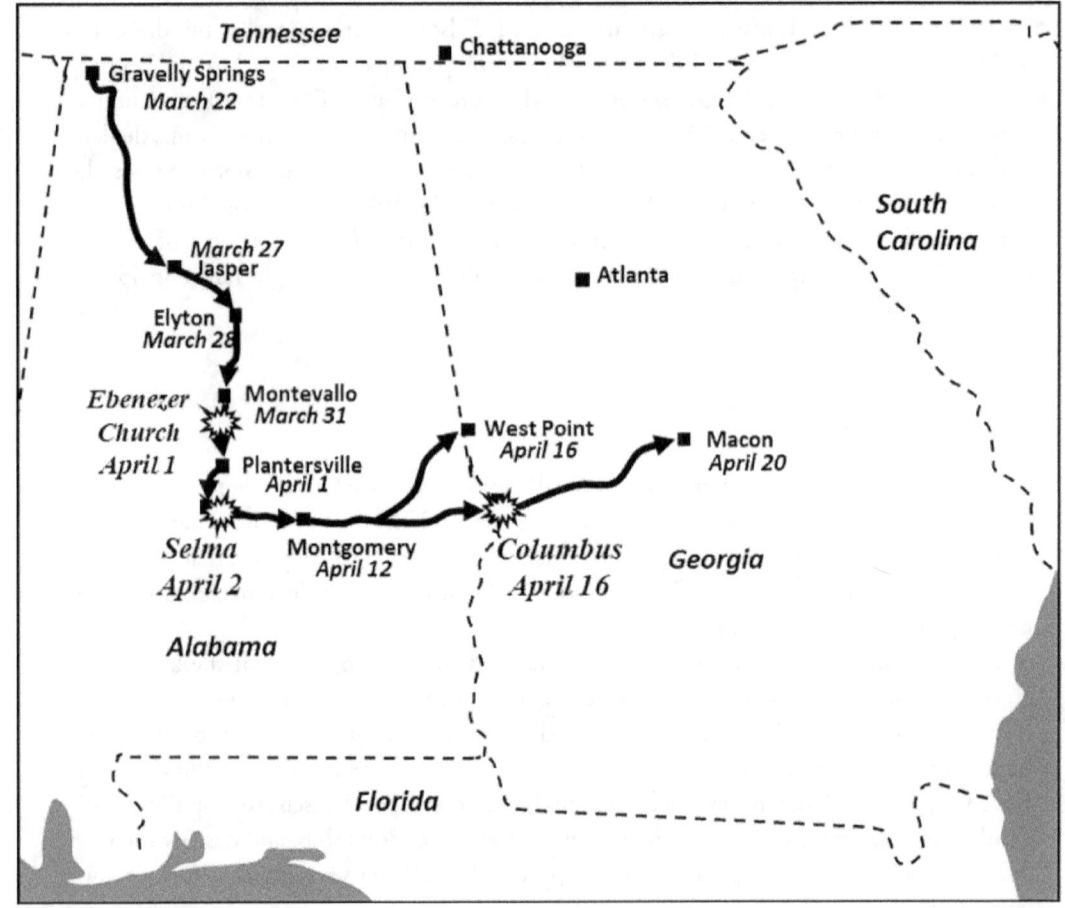

Map of Wilson's cavalry campaign into Alabama and Georgia, March 22–April 20, 1865 (drawn by the author).

Ford on the west branch of the Black Warrior River, while Long's division, followed by McCook's, would move through Cherokee Station and Frankford before turning south on the Byler Road toward Tuscaloosa to Upper Bear Creek. Once there, Long and McCook would turn east to join Upton's division at the ford on the Black Warrior. Furthermore, Wilson would impress upon each division commander that the need to move quickly was of the utmost importance.[34]

Wilson planned to begin the campaign on March 4, but once again, the weather would not cooperate. The spring rains came down in torrents, and, as a result, the Tennessee River could not be crossed. So, the corps remained in camp, waiting for the weather to break.

However, the delay allowed Upton and the other division commanders to prepare for the campaign. Wilson's orders called for 12,500 men to be mounted, with an artillery battery of four guns deployed to each division. Another 1,500 dismounted men would go along as guards for the supply wagons and act as a reserve until the column could capture enough horses to remount them. Each man in the corps would carry five days' worth of rations, one pair of extra horseshoes, and 100 rounds of ammunition. The train of 250 supply wagons, meanwhile, would carry a 45-day supply of rations, 20 of coffee, and 15 of sugar, plus ammunition. In addition, pack horses and mules would bring five days' worth of hardtack, along with ten days of additional sugar and salt. Wilson believed this, plus whatever they could forage from the countryside, would sustain his men for 60 days.[35]

By mid–March, the skies began to clear, and the river slowly receded. With this change in the weather, Wilson decided to start south on March 22. During this time, Upton worked closely with Wilson, as they laid out the details for the campaign. The two men worked well together, and one night, as Private Gilpin passed General Wilson's tent, he saw them. Gilpin noted an observation in his journal, writing, "Passing General Wilson's headquarters, he and Upton were busy with maps and papers spread out before them in the tent."[36] For his part, Wilson's estimations of Upton remained as high as ever. On March 17, he sent a message to General Grant about the coming campaign in which he said that Upton could not be "excelled in– our army or anywhere else."[37]

A little over a week before the march south would begin, Upton wrote his sister, discussing the coming campaign and his health.

> We expect to break camp tomorrow preparatory to crossing the Tennessee and entering upon the expedition to Alabama. The streams are swollen, which may delay us some days, but it is the intention to move as soon as the weather and roads will permit. The present campaign, I trust, will seal the doom of the Confederacy. I cannot see how it can be otherwise, unless great and unexpected reverses be fall [sic] our arms. In that event it will only delay the final result. Peace must soon come, and how welcome it will be to all!
>
> Hobbes was not a soldier, or he never would have advanced the idea "war is the natural condition of man." I am anxious to be on the move. Camp-life is dull and monotonous, and I always welcome the variety of campaign. Henry's wound worries me considerably, and I fear it will undermine his health. Mine has healed over, but a per verse [sic] nerve keeps it constantly in mind. I do not suffer at all from it, only there is a disagreeable sensation about the knee.[38]

Two days after he wrote his sister, Upton began moving his division out of camp to Chickasaw, Alabama, where they made their crossing of the Tennessee River on March 22. It was a blustery, cold day, unusual for the area in early spring. As the division rode east, Private Gilpin noted Upton's demeanor, writing that his commander looked "stern as fate, sitting hard in the saddle, his mouth tightly closed, his eye keen as a hawk's."[39] A few days later, as the division prepared to cross the river, Gilpin was grooming his horse, a dappled Canadian named "Charley" whom the private described as "fat and sleek, well gaited and full of fire."[40] He was just finishing up when Upton approached, admiring Gilpin's steed. "The General," Gilpin wrote, "whose sharp eyes see everything, said he liked his looks." Gilpin was almost certain that his general would like Charley for himself, so he lied to Upton, telling him that the horse was unsteady under fire. From his reaction, it was obvious that Upton saw right through the private. But respecting Gilpin's obvious love for his mount, Upton turned about, walked away, and said nothing more.[41]

As the Tennessee subsided, the regiments of the three divisions made their way across the river between March 14 and March 20, with Upton's moving last.[42] At dawn on March 22, the corps began its march into central Alabama.[43]

Upton's division was led by Winslow's 1st Brigade and the supply wagons, followed by General Andrew Alexander's 2nd Brigade. The terrain was initially hilly, covered by dense pine and oak forests with small clearings scattered about. The combination of deep, narrow valleys and muddy roads slowed progress. By nightfall, Upton's 1st Brigade had reached Throckmorton Mills, while the 2nd Brigade camped along Cane Creek, both about 25 miles from the starting point along the Tennessee.[44]

As planned, Wilson spread his forces along diverging paths, which had the desired effect on the enemy. Forrest was unaware of the corps movement until March 28 and, even then, he was at first uncertain where the Union cavalry was headed.[45] The widespread deployment of Wilson's columns also assisted the process of foraging. The entire area had been devastated by the war, and there was little in the way of food or supplies for a radius of 120 miles. So, having his men spread out allowed more opportunities to take what little there was to be had.[46]

After camping at Throckmorton Mills and Cane Creek, Upton moved his division past Russellville to Newberg, a distance of 30 miles, where they found good supplies of corn and various provisions. On March 24, the march resumed with Alexander's 2nd Brigade riding from Mount Hope, via Houston toward Clear Creek Falls, while Winslow's 1st Brigade and the supply train moved via Kinlock and Hubbard's Mill, a distance of some 16 miles.[47] The road was mountainous, and Winslow's men reached the "wild and picturesque" Sipsey Creek, where they crossed via a "high and shaky bridge" before camping at Hubbard's Mill.[48]

The next morning, the march continued with both brigades uniting as they traversed the Sipsey Valley, where, as one soldier recalled, "the hills were so bold and near each other that there could hardly be said to be a valley." This area was heavily covered in pine forest, and with only two isolated settlements in the area, there were no opportunities to forage.[49] After traveling 30 miles, Upton called the division to a halt, and they camped for the night at Clear Creek Falls.[50]

On March 26, Upton once again divided the division and sent them along different routes. Winslow marched toward Elyton via Bartonville and Hanby's Mills, while Alexander took the road that went through Jasper and Democrat. When Winslow reached the second crossing for Sipsey Creek, he found it was unfordable and moved down the Black Warrior River to Saunder's Ford, where the division united once more and camped.[51]

The next morning, Upton moved the division to the Mulberry Fork of the Black Warrior where he searched for a crossing at Burnham's Ford. This part of the river was wide and rapid with a "gorge-like bed between hills 500 or 600 feet high on either side." It was dangerous to cross at the best of times and, now, the Black Warrior was swollen by the spring rains. At first, Upton feared they might not be able to cross without the engineers erecting a pontoon bridge, which would slow the column's progress significantly. But as Wilson later wrote about this moment, Upton was "an officer who took nothing for granted." He decided he would ride into the waters personally to see if the ford was passable. It turned out to be "composed of gravel and sand lodged against a rough ledge of rock" connecting the two sides, and it could be crossed.[52]

He ordered his men into the water in loose order, hurrying them up the muddy bank on the far side. One trooper from the 1st Ohio recalled the crossing as the "roughest ford that ever was crossed by a body of mounted men."[53] The swift waters made the crossing perilous, and several men were swept away, one of whom drowned.[54] Furthermore, the pack animals could not make the crossing, given the heavy loads they carried. As a result, Upton ordered his men to build a raft for them, which was floated back and forth using ropes.[55]

That night, the division camped on the east bank of Locust Creek, with Winslow's brigade not arriving until almost 4:00 a.m. on March 28. Winslow's troopers had barely dismounted and started campfires when buglers sounded "Boots and Saddles," signaling it was time to resume the march. As the exhausted men from 1st Brigade put out their fires and remounted their horses, their misery increased as a steady, drenching rain began. An officer from the 4th Iowa later wrote, "There was never so dark a night as that. It rained heavily and constantly. It poured. The tread of the horses was an unceasing splashing in mud and water."[56]

The column moved south toward Elyton (present-day Birmingham, Alabama) and, at first, the roads were very rough. But as they approached Elyton, the ride became smoother as the Union cavalry entered "a beautiful valley, rich in provisions and forage."[57] As they approached the town, Upton's men ran into Confederate skirmishers, the first resistance they had seen since leaving the banks of the Tennessee. A Confederate cavalry regiment under General Patterson had just passed through Elyton as they raced south to block the path of Wilson's column, and they left a few men behind to trade shots with the Yankee cavalry before galloping off.[58]

Upton put his command into bivouac just west of the town at the plantation of a Mr. Hawkins.[59] The plantation was the largest seen up to this point, and it appeared that Mr. Hawkins owned most of the valley surrounding Elyton. Upton had his men take full advantage of the available provisions provided by the plantation, which included "turkeys, chickens, butter, eggs, hams in the smoke houses [sic], thousands of bushels of corn in the barns, and forage of all kinds."[60] One Ohio trooper remembered the hams they found in particular, writing, "there were great smoke-houses [sic] filled with the finest and sweetest hams that a Yankee soldier ever tasted."[61]

Young Private Gilpin and some of his comrades also located Mr. Hawkins' wine cellar and, as many soldiers before and since, they took the opportunity to "liberate" some of its contents, an act of which Upton would not likely have approved.

> Visited the wine cellar, where rows of casks and dust-covered bottles were flanked by baskets and portly demijohns. "And monks might deem their time was come again, if ancient tales say true." Rolled the barrels of peach and apple brandy from among the musty cobwebs into the light of day, and those who were fortunate enough not to have taken the pledge were seen to smack their lips even before the bungs were started! On one point my recollection is quite distinct: An ancient barrel of apple—or was it peach?—brandy, the

delightful odor of which pervaded the air as its contents flowed into our cups like syrup, was confiscated without delay, lest it might give aid or comfort to the enemy.[62]

On March 29, with many soldiers having added one of Mr. Hawkins' hams to the equipment hanging from their saddle, Upton moved the division south toward the Cahawba River. With more Confederate forces moving into the area, Wilson ordered the supply train to be left behind near Elyton, allowing the column to move faster. He feared Forrest, who now realized this was more than just a small cavalry raid, might be able to consolidate at Montevallo and put a stout defense together.[63]

When Upton and his men arrived at the Cahawba that evening, they found the river swollen like so many others in the area. However, Confederate cavalry had also blocked the only ford with a fallen tree, making a crossing impossible. Upton ordered the division to camp for the night before setting out the next morning in search of a suitable crossing. After moving a short distance downstream, General Winslow's brigade discovered a railroad bridge over the river and chased away the small enemy detachment guarding it before the Confederate guards could set it on fire. Then, employing considerable ingenuity, Winslow had his men pull up crossties to lay down as a floor over the trestle and bridge, turning a railroad bridge into a footbridge. Once complete, Upton slowly moved the division across the river, and they rode towards Montevallo.[64]

As they neared the town, the division began to run into isolated pockets of Confederate cavalry, all of which were quickly dispersed. But about 4:00 p.m., elements of two enemy brigades put up a more stubborn fight. As the lead Federal regiment, the 4th Iowa dismounted to return the enemy's fire, and their commander sent two companies riding off the left in order to flank the Confederates. A sharp skirmish ensued before the enemy retreated with the Iowans in hot pursuit. They drove the enemy cavalry into and then through Montevallo, allowing the remainder of Upton's division to occupy the town. Given that the enemy cavalry's resistance might indicate a stronger force was lurking nearby, Upton elected to wait in Montevallo for the rest of Wilson's corps to arrive before pressing on.[65]

Early the next morning, March 31, Upton assigned detachments from the division to begin destroying the many ironworks in the area around Montevallo. These facilities were the last remaining sources of raw materials for the Confederate arsenals, foundries, and navy yard that operated at Selma. Before the end of the day, Upton's men had done their job well, leaving the Central Iron Works, Red Mountain Iron Works, Cahawba Valley Mills, Bibb Iron Works, and Columbiana Works in ruins.[66]

Later in the morning, the troopers were able to take a much-needed break during which they washed clothes, groomed their horses, and took care of their equipment. However, these peaceful activities suddenly ended around 1:30 p.m. when riders galloped in from the south of town to report that elements of General Roddy's Confederate cavalry division had struck the pickets on the Selma Road. General Wilson, who had just arrived in Montevallo, was conferring with Upton when the news arrived. Wilson turned to Upton and ordered him "to sail in" and attack Roddy's command.[67]

Upton ordered Alexander's 2nd Brigade to move out at once, with Winslow and 1st Brigade right behind them. Alexander moved quickly and struck the enemy, who were posted in thick brush. Upton rode right behind the lead battalion from the 1st Ohio and, as he and his staff crested a small hill, the first Confederate volley rang out "cutting the leaves" around their heads. As the 1st Ohio charged the enemy, one trooper, a sergeant from the regiment who had been riding with Upton, dashed forward toward the enemy on his handsome gray horse "as if he had never heard the volley fired." Seeing this trooper's actions, Upton turned to a captain from the regiment and said, "Splendid soldier! Splendid soldier! Who is he?" The captain told him the sergeant's name and later wrote that, in his experience, Upton was one of those commanders who never saw bravery without "admiring" it and who never missed an opportunity to commend it.[68]

The Confederate's fell back to take a position on the crest of a nearby hill, where they quickly erected a barricade with fence rails. A creek ran along the foot of the hill, and its steep banks required an attacker to cross a small bridge directly in front of the enemy position. Upton ordered Winslow to take his brigade, pass to the front through Alexander's men, and press on with the attack. Led by the 10th Missouri, the brigade dashed forward, seizing the bridge before Roddy's men could destroy it.[69]

With the bridge secure, the Missouri troopers dismounted, crossed the creek, took positions in a thicket on the far side, and opened a brisk fire with their Spencer carbines. Now, a battery of Federal artillery arrived and opened fire on the enemy, as the 3rd Iowa took positions along the creek, mounted and ready to follow the 10th Missouri. The Missouri men began moving forward up the hill on foot, taking cover along the way. When they were within a few yards of the enemy, they rose up with a yell and rushed forward while rapidly firing their carbines. At this moment, the 3rd Iowa galloped across the bridge and charged up the hill with sabers drawn. Seeing this wave of blue coming at them, the Confederates turned and ran. The 3rd Iowa continued to pursue the enemy until they reached a creek about four miles to the south.[70]

As the 3rd Iowa pursued Roddy's cavalry, another group of Confederate troopers launched a flanking attack on Winslow's 1st Brigade. Firing on one of Upton's artillery batteries from the cover of some woods to the right of the Selma Road was causing great confusion to the artillerymen, who thought the Confederates were beaten and retreating. The 4th Iowa, which was trailing behind the guns, immediately responded, with seven companies charging the woods on foot. Rapidly firing their Spencers, they drove the enemy off, ending the fighting for the day.[71]

Ebenezer Church

On the morning of April 1, Wilson had the corps up and moving early. Knowing that Forrest was falling back down the road toward Selma, Wilson was determined to keep the initiative he had gained on the Confederate cavalryman. As for Forrest, he was still determined to stop the Union advance before it reached Selma. He sent couriers to forces under Generals Jackson and Chalmers telling them to come with all speed and join with Forrest's main body at Ebenezer Church, which lay on the main Selma road about six miles south of Maplesville.[72]

Wilson's orders for the day were for Upton to take his division a short distance south to the town of Randolph before turning east towards Old Maplesville and then follow the road from there south to Ebenezer Church. Meanwhile, Long's division would follow Forrest's path down the main Selma Road, moving parallel to Upton's division and about two miles to the west, while McCook's division moved to cover the corps' right flank and rear.[73]

As the Union column began to move south, Forrest prepared to defend the ground around Ebenezer Church. He sent out small parties of skirmishers to delay Long's progress along the main Selma road while he deployed his forces. Forrest found some high ground that overlooked both the roads coming into Ebenezer Church as well as the Alabama and Tennessee Railroad line that ran from the northeast until meeting and paralleling the road to Selma south of the church. His defensive line ran from west to east, anchored on Mulberry Creek on the right with the center just above Bogler's Creek and the left positioned in a heavily wooded area. He placed his dismounted cavalry in the woods on the left and at the center, while he threw in a battalion of unproven Alabama State Troops on the right. The entire line was protected by a barrier of fence rails and cut down pine trees. To add to the strength of the position, he placed four guns covering the main road with two more looking up the road that came from Maplesville, the one that Upton's division would move down.[74]

From the woods where Upton's division had camped for the night, there was a field about one mile wide between them and the little town of Randolph. Scouts reported a detachment of Forrest's cavalry was waiting on the far side of the field. Upton ordered General Alexander's brigade and the 1st Ohio to take the lead. Alexander sent a small battalion of the 1st Ohio forward to feel out the enemy, and Upton told his men, "Give them an April fool this morning!" The Ohioans galloped across the field, catching Forrest's men by surprise, and driving them beyond the town.[75]

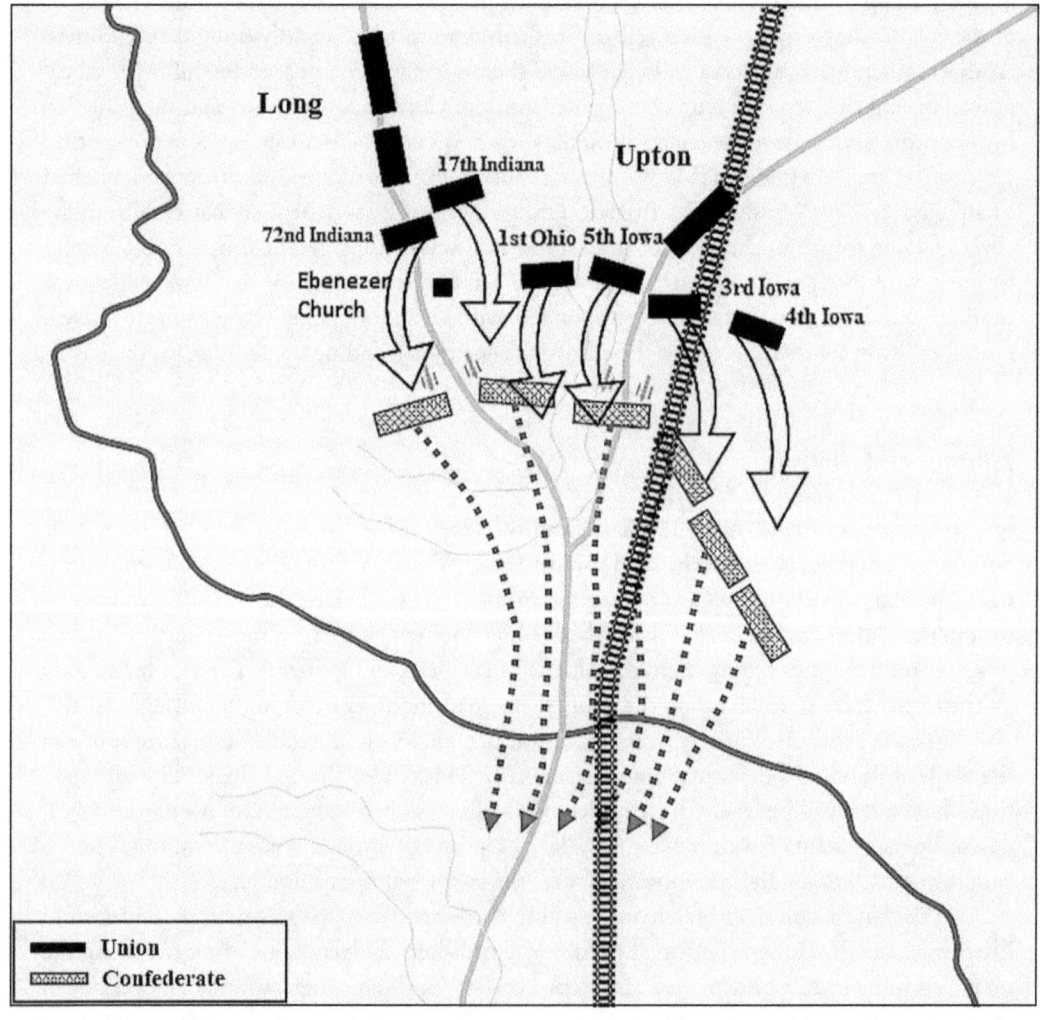

Battle of Ebenezer Church, April 1, 1865 (drawn by the author).

During the fighting, the 1st Ohio captured an enemy courier carrying dispatches from Forrest to General Jackson. Upton forwarded the documents to Wilson who discovered from them that Jackson's division was encamped at Scottsville and that McCook's brigade under General Croxton had reached Trion. The dispatches also told the Union general that Forrest had ordered Chalmers' division to cross the Cahawba River and block the road to Selma. Learning this, Wilson ordered McCook to move quickly to capture the Centerville bridge, join with Croxton, and then break up Jackson's force before rejoining the corps via the Centerville-Selma Road.[76]

With the enemy detachment driven off, Upton moved his division through Randolph and paused once he reached the road toward Ebenezer Church. When he received word that Long had his division in place on the main road to Selma, the two divisions began moving south in parallel. Forrest had focused his attention on the main road and threw out a strong force of skirmishers to slow Long's division. Every time Long's column ran into Forrest's men, he was forced to halt and order a battalion forward to drive them off. The result was a slow, leap-frog advance, and Long did not approach Ebenezer Church until almost 4:00 pm. With the road intersection only a short distance ahead, Long again ran into Forrest's skirmishers, and once more, he ordered a battalion of the 72nd Indiana to gallop off after the small group of Confederate cavalrymen.

Anticipating this action, Forrest had set a trap. As the skirmishers disappeared into a grove of trees, the 72nd Indiana crashed through the woods in pursuit expecting to finally deal with the pesky skirmishers. What they found, however, was an entire brigade of dismounted cavalry supported by four pieces of artillery. Forrest's men rose up and delivered a violent volley of rifle fire, dismounting at least 16 of the Indiana troopers. The battalion wheeled about immediately and fell back to join the division.

Long ordered the remainder of the 72nd Indiana into the fight. The regiment dismounted and formed to the left of the road. When Long gave the order to go forward, the regiment "rushed to the attack, pumping out a sheet of lead with each discharge which nothing could resist."[77] Forrest's line fell back, and Long ordered the 17th Indiana to make a mounted charge in pursuit of the enemy.

As the 17th Indiana made its charge, Upton's division was arriving on the left, with Alexander's brigade in the lead. Hearing the firing off to his right, Alexander correctly assumed that Long had engaged the enemy, and he hastened his brigade's advance. In only a few minutes, they encountered the right of Forrest's line where the untested Alabama State Troops and two of Forrest's guns had positioned themselves behind the rail barricade. Alexander ordered the 1st Ohio and 5th Iowa to move to the right, dismount, and move against the enemy's position.[78]

In less than five minutes, the two regiments galloped through a small thicket, deployed, dismounted, and formed on the crest of a hill. As the bugle "rang out the 'Forward,'"[79] the men charged the Confederate line. The Alabamans broke almost immediately, and the Federal troopers swept over the barricade.

Upton now rode forward, cleared Alexander's men out of the way, and ordered the 3rd and 4th Iowa to attack to Alexander's left. Galloping forward in column, they reached the barricade just as Alexander's men broke through. They attacked the flank of the retreating Confederates, and the fight now became a confused melee. Forrest's entire line collapsed, and his men took flight down the road toward Selma. The 3rd and 4th Iowa pursued them, capturing over 200 prisoners along the way. The fight at Ebenezer Church was over, and the battle for the key city of Selma was about to begin.[80]

12

The Final Battles

> It was in this movement that Upton displayed the extraordinary insensibility to danger which always characterized him. With his mind entirely absorbed in the various problems before him and in the measures necessary for their solution, he appeared as utterly unconscious of danger as if he were on parade.
> —Major General James H. Wilson on Emory Upton at the Battle of Selma[1]

Selma

The night of April 1 found Upton's division and the rest of Wilson's corps encamped only 19 miles north of Selma.[2] While General Wilson pondered his next move, he was confounded by the fact that he had no intelligence on the defenses surrounding Selma. He wanted to move on the city quickly, but without information about the deployment and disposition of its fortifications, any attack might be a potential disaster. However, it has been said that, sometimes, luck is a general's best weapon, and luck was about to pay a visit to James Wilson.

As Upton sat in his tent that night, General Winslow arrived, escorting a civilian. It seems an officer from the 4th Iowa encountered this man who was approaching the lines and arrested him. The officer questioned the civilian who said his name was Millington and that he was a British citizen. However, most importantly, Mr. Millington was a civil engineer who had been in the employ of the Confederate army and had assisted in the design and building of Selma's fortifications. The officer took him immediately to see General Winslow, who questioned him further. Mr. Millington proceeded to draw a sketch of Selma's defenses in the dirt, telling Winslow that he did not believe any size force of cavalry could take the city.[3]

Winslow then decided that General Upton needed to speak to Mr. Millington. When Winslow arrived at the division commander's tent, Upton had Millington brought in and also questioned him in detail. It seemed the Englishman had decided it was time to abandon the Southern cause, and he told Upton that he would be more than happy to share all he knew about the works guarding the city.[4]

Hearing this, Upton handed Millington a pencil and some paper and asked him to make a detailed sketch of Selma's defenses. The British engineer then drew a highly detailed drawing of the trace and profile of the fortifications, as well as the terrain both in front and to the rear of the works along with the locations and numbers of artillery batteries. One could not have asked for more perfect intelligence.[5]

Upton immediately took both Millington and the drawing to Wilson's headquarters tent.

As soon as Wilson looked at the sketch, he could see that overcoming Selma's defenses would be extremely difficult. The city, which sat on a terrace along the northern bank of the Alabama River, was surrounded by a line of heavy earthworks and stockades that extended in a three-mile semicircle from the riverbank below the town to a point on the river above it. Further, there were 32 guns guarding the city, all of them placed on heavy parapets surrounded by stockades five and a half feet high. The stakes that made up the stockades were six to eight inches thick and had been firmly anchored in the ground with their tops sharpened.[6]

Millington's sketch also indicated that the earthworks were continuous except for points where the defensive line crossed patches of swampy ground that the Confederates considered impassable. At those places, they constructed stockades to block any attackers approach. However, from what Millington told them, the stockades along the enemy's right flank might be almost completely undefended.[7]

Wilson wisely decided to tap Upton's unique and extensive knowledge of how to deal with fortifications. The general was well aware of Upton's experience at Rappahannock Station and Spotsylvania's Muleshoe, and Wilson knew Upton had always come up with a way to penetrate even the most formidable works. The two men spent the next hour discussing alternative ideas for subduing the defenses, a time Wilson later referred to as "anxious."[8]

The plan they finally devised called for Upton's division to approach Selma on the Range Line Road, the eastern of two parallel north-south routes that ran from Plantersville to Selma. Once in place, Upton would keep his division concealed from sight while he reconnoitered the left of the Confederate defenses where they ran through a swamp. Then, after dark, he would lead a small, hand-picked force in an assault on the enemy's right flank through the swamp where they believed the defenses might be the weakest. Once Upton's small attack group had penetrated the enemy lines, the rest of the division would follow. Meanwhile, Long's division would attack down the Summerfield Road to the west against the main entrance to the city. A single cannon shot from Upton's artillery was to signal the main attack.[9]

The men of Long and Upton's divisions were awakened before dawn on April 2 and began making careful preparations for a march they knew would bring the climactic battle of the cam-

The 3rd Iowa Cavalry Regiment, which would play a critical role in Upton's Fourth Division (State Historical Society of Iowa, Des Moines).

paign. "Arms, horses, and equipments are looked to very closely," wrote William Scott, adjutant of the 4th Iowa. "All servants, non-combatants, and led animals are sent to the rear. The column is stripped of every impediment, like a race-horse."[10]

Before the sun rose, Upton had his division mounted and formed-up in the roadway, aligned in a compact column of fours. Scott later noted, "Everything is in order. The men are very quiet. They talk less than usual, and in lower tones. Everybody expects a bloody contest."[11] Under Wilson's orders, all the supply wagons, camp followers, draft animals, and surplus equipment were left behind so that the attacking columns could move unimpeded without any delays.[12]

Long's division started out first while Upton's men waited their turn. Around 9:30 a.m., Long's division had passed, and Upton gave the order to advance. He rode at the head of his

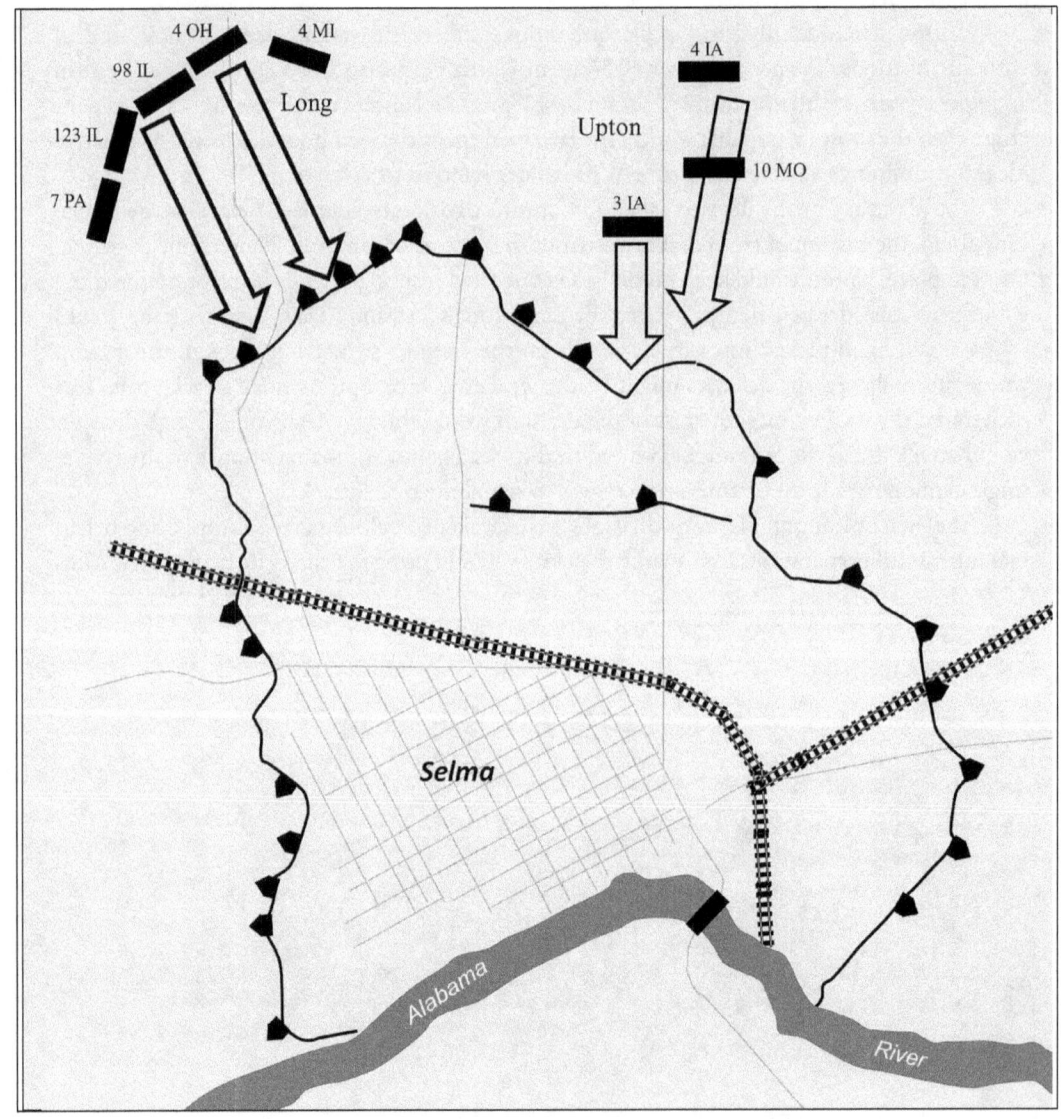

Battle of Selma, April 2, 1865 (drawn by the author).

division, and Private Gilpin recorded that Upton's face was "a little pale," and that he was "being watched by every soldier in the command."[13] The march that morning turned out to be rather pleasant, as the division rode "through a thickly settled country, dotted with houses and enclosures, and broken by corn and cotton fields."[14] Contrary to what the men had expected, their progress was not hindered by enemy skirmishers or patrols. It seemed that Forrest had elected not to oppose their advance, choosing instead to keep almost every man he had inside the city's fortifications.[15]

Around 2:00 p.m., the Federals were about six miles from Selma and the road split. Long's division continued down the westward branch, while Upton's division moved south down the eastern parallel road. Winslow's brigade led the division with the 4th Iowa at its head. The road traveled along a range of hilltops that extended to Selma's outskirts. From this vantage point, the men could see "delightfully green" fields below them, and they could clearly hear "the tinkling of bells, the lowing of cattle, and singing of larks in the fields." One of Upton's men wrote in his journal that the "indistinct murmur of life on a farm comes to my ears like music."[16] It must not have felt that war was possible amidst such pastoral beauty.

When Upton was about two miles from the city, Selma came into view from the low plateau. "Every heart is tense with suppressed emotion," wrote William Scott of the 4th Iowa. "In this scene, so beautiful in the soft sunlight of a spring afternoon, there will soon be a fearful change."[17] Here, a small group of enemy skirmishers finally appeared, and Upton ordered the Second Battalion of the 4th Iowa under Major Wilson to "drive the rebel skirmishers without stopping until they enter the fortifications."[18]

Now, at last, Upton could see the city defenses clearly and determine if Mr. Millington gave them an honest portrayal. As he peered through his field glasses, General Wilson rode up, and the two men moved forward to a small grove of trees to examine the enemy positions, which were about 600 yards ahead.[19] As it turned out, the British engineer had given them a very accurate description.

They could plainly see 24 bastions along the main defensive line, mounting from one to three guns each, standing at intervals, and connected by heavy entrenchments and redans, which were arrow-shaped embankments forming part of the fortifications. The ramparts were eight to 12 feet high and at least ten to 15 feet deep at their base.[20]

Just as Millington had drawn, the part of the works directly in front of Upton's division ran from Range Line Road to the Alabama River. This section of the city defenses was built lighter than the rest owing to the many swampy areas fronting the fortifications. A stream called Bench Creek ran roughly parallel with the enemy line, beginning in a marsh between the Summerfield and Range Line Roads. The marsh area was impassable for horses, but there were bridges on two of the roads crossing it. In the terrain between the two roads Wilson planned to use for his assault, there were several dense groves of trees that could provide advancing troops with cover. However, the ground to the west of Summerfield Road was completely open and solid, which would allow Long's men to advance quickly across it.[21]

Looking again at the fortifications, Wilson and Upton could see the earthworks were fronted by wide, deep ditches that were partially filled with water and could be easily enfiladed from the bastions. In addition, the bastions and ramparts were lined with sharpened tree trunks to slow anyone trying to mount them. Behind this line of works was another partially completed set of fortifications about midway between the front line and the outer streets of Selma. This second line was supplemented by four heavy redoubts with large guns that commanded several roads into the city. In total, there were 32 guns along Forrest's defensive line, all mounted so they could cover any approach.[22]

The two Union generals were now seen by the enemy, and the Confederates began tossing artillery shells in their direction. Upton and Wilson fell back out of range to confer. Wilson told him that he could see nothing that would alter his plans, and he told Upton to sound the signal gun at 6:00 p.m.[23]

While Wilson and Upton were viewing the enemy lines, Major Woods and his battalion of four companies from the 4th Iowa had continued to chase away enemy skirmishers. They descended off the plateau, moving along Range Line Road. A small Confederate cavalry detachment was seen aligned across the road near a grove of trees, but, as soon as they saw Woods' men coming, they turned and rode back inside the city's defenses. This was about the time the first enemy gun opened fire, and its shell sailed over the troopers' heads as it made its way toward the trees where Upton and Wilson were observing. At this, Woods ordered his men to dismount and find cover.[24]

Meanwhile, Winslow's brigade moved up to the Shackleford's house along the road about a mile from the Confederate lines. The 3rd Iowa and 10th Missouri dismounted and moved to a point opposite Long's line on the right and a few hundred yards behind Woods' men as enemy artillery fire increased. So far, it was mostly a loud nuisance, as virtually none of the rounds found a target. About 4:00 p.m., Upton rode forward to join Major Woods and his battalion. He dismounted, left his horse with a soldier, and asked a nearby sergeant to accompany him on a reconnaissance. The sergeant jumped up, brought two privates with him, and followed as Upton walked towards the swamp to their front.[25]

Once they reached the edge of the marsh, the group of four men slowly crept through the tall grass and muck, and Upton told the soldiers about the plan of attack. He asked them to look for any landmarks that might help them navigate the swamp in darkness. It was very clear that Upton hoped the plan would result in far fewer casualties. Finally, they halted at a point so close to the enemy that they could easily make out the details of the enemy works. Upton ordered the men to stay put while he went forward a little further. He crept slowly through the grass and bushes armed with nothing but his field glasses. After making a sweeping view along the entire enemy left, he went back to the men and had them return to their lines.[26]

Upton was now completely convinced his plan would work and told the troopers that a force of only 300 men from their regiment, the 4th Iowa, would move dismounted through the swamp, break into the enemy defenses and roll-up their flanks. With great enthusiasm, he said that the "whole place can be taken without losing twenty men." Upton was, once again, concerned with the idea of attacking well-manned, formidable defenses. So, he was going to great pains to develop an approach that would be successful while minimizing the losses among his men. He then mounted his horse and rode back toward Winslow's brigade.[27] However, as so often happens in war, his plan was soon overcome by unplanned events.

As Upton prepared to give his orders for the upcoming attack, he suddenly heard the loud crash of rifle fire from the direction of Long's division on the Summerfield Road. After a very short time, the sound became even louder, and he realized that Long was attacking the entrance to the city. Unknown to Upton, Chalmers' Confederate cavalry had finally arrived, and they had attacked a regiment guarding Long's rear. In response, Long decided to seize the initiative and make his assault against Selma immediately.

With about 1,100 men from the 3rd Ohio, 4th Ohio, and 4th Michigan, Long's men rushed the works on foot, blasting away with their Spencers as they moved. They charged 500 yards over the open ground in the face of withering rifle and cannon fire. Upon reaching the abatis guarding the earthworks, they quickly tore the sharpened wood obstacles down and began climbing up the slopes of the earthworks, where 7,000 defenders awaited. Within minutes, the Union troopers were over the earthen walls and in the trenches, where they engaged in brutal hand-to-hand combat.[28]

At this point, the entire Confederate defensive line began to collapse, as the defenders fled to the rear. Seeing what was happening, Upton shouted orders for his men to mount and form up in a column of fours for making an attack. The men scrambled to put their sabers and spurs back on before quickly mounting their horses. The 4th Iowa led the assault as General Winslow shouted, "Spare no horses!" Upton's men swept forward "like a hurricane," breaking through the Range Road entrance and galloping after the enemy, who now fled from even the inner defensive lines. "It is a fearful scene," wrote William Scott. "The clatter of the arms, the snorting of the horses and the thunder of their feet, the shouts of the officers, and the wild yells and cries of the men, the incessant flashing and cracking of carbines and pistols, the desperate efforts to escape or find shelter by the rebels who have lost their arms or their courage."[29]

As the Confederate defenses melted away, Forrest and his staff galloped out of the city ahead of their panicked troops, who fled so quickly that they did not have time to find or even mount their horses. Upton's men rode through the city streets in pursuit, gathering up thousands of prisoners, before riding off down the Burnsville Road into the countryside where they captured four enemy guns and many more prisoners.[30]

Night fell during the pursuit and Selma became a city of fire and destruction. As they retreated, Forrest's men set fire to a large cotton warehouse. The flames quickly spread to Confederate ammunition stores, setting off dozens of explosions. Civilians ran for shelter as the flames in the military and industrial facilities along the river leaped high into the night sky. That evening, Private Gilpin wrote in his journal that, of all his experiences, this one was "most like the horrors of war." Parts of the city were on fire with "a victorious army advancing, and a demoralized one retreating." Some soldiers, he wrote, "overpowered by weariness" wrapped themselves in blankets and lay down to rest while the city's citizens slept, "exhausted by excitement and fear." Meanwhile, the wounded from both armies were "lulled by opiates into forgetfulness of their amputated legs and arms," and the dead had gone to "their last sleep, with white faces upturned to the sky." He concluded his entry for the day by writing, "If there is a merciful God in the heavens, he must be looking down upon this scene in pity."[31]

On to Montgomery and Columbus

The next day, Wilson began organizing the occupation of Selma and seeing to the needs of its citizens. The corps was also waiting for Croxton and the supply train while they rested and completed the work of destroying the last shops, arsenal, and foundries that served the Confederate war effort.[32] However, unknown to Emory Upton, James Wilson, or even the enemy, great events were underway in Virginia.

On April 1, as Wilson's corps fought at Ebenezer Church and then prepared to move on Selma, cavalry and infantry under General Sheridan had driven Confederate forces from the key crossroads at Five Forks outside Petersburg. This meant that Union forces could now easily cut off the Southside Railroad that supplied the city and, more importantly, Lee's army. Seeing an opportunity, Grant moved immediately to seize the initiative.

Early on the morning of April 2, as Wilson's cavalry moved towards the attack on Selma, Grant launched a massive infantry assault on Lee's lines at Petersburg. Men from Upton's old brigade in the VI Corps broke through the enemy defenses near the Boydton Plank Road, forcing Lee to order a general retreat. That night, while Upton's men were beginning the destruction of Selma's factories, Jefferson Davis and the Confederate government abandoned Richmond, and, the next morning, Union forces entered the Confederate capital. So now, while Upton and the rest of the corps recuperated at Selma until April 10, Grant pursued Lee and finally caught him at Appomattox Court House, where Lee surrendered his army at last on April 9. However, it would be several weeks before this momentous news reached this deep into the South.

Wilson decided it was time to press on to Montgomery and then Columbus, Georgia. He ordered the construction of a pontoon bridge over the Alabama River, which became quite challenging due to high waters and driftwood flowing downstream. The bridge broke three times before the corps was able to push across in the early morning hours of April 10. The bridge was destroyed as soon as the last man crossed, and the column advanced eastward.[33]

Except for some challenges getting through the Big Swamp and a few minor skirmishes between Wilson's advance element and Buford's Confederate cavalry, the march to Montgomery was uneventful. In fact, after leaving the Big Swamp, the ride became pleasant, which was a great relief for men who had been riding and fighting for three weeks. Wilson recalled, "We were at last within the richest planting district of the South and found it, not only untouched by war, but abounding in forage and provisions of every sort. The roads, bordered by hedges of Cherokee roses, were redolent with spring perfumes. The march was, therefore, not only rapid, but delightful and cheering."[34]

As the column approached the former Southern capital early on the morning of April 12, everyone expected a fight was in the offing. The city was fortified by a long line of heavy earthworks, and contained large quantities of cotton and war supplies, so strong resistance seemed likely. Upton halted his division a few miles from the city, and his soldiers assumed this stop was meant to prepare for an assault on Montgomery. They carefully looked to their equipment, checking that everything was ready for battle. However, it seemed that, after another brief skirmish with Buford's men, all Confederate troops had fled and abandoned the city. So, rather than a pause to prepare for battle, the division had stopped so General Wilson could confer with civilian officials anxious to peacefully surrender the city.[35]

Once the surrender was complete, Wilson ordered preparations for a triumphal march through the city and the raising of the national colors at the state capitol building. He first sent the 4th Iowa into the city in advance to act as a provost marshal, and then halted the column, closed up the formation, and issued orders for their entrance to the city. "During this halt," he later wrote, "officers were told off to guard the public stores, to maintain order, and to prevent straggling and marauding." Furthermore, he wanted to be sure that the sight of 12,000 Union cavalrymen marching through their city made an impression on the population.[36]

The men then paraded through the city "with perfect order, every man in his place, division and brigade flags unfurled, guidons flying, sabers and spurs jingling, bands playing patriotic airs, and the bugles now and then sounding the calls."[37] There were no incidents, and many of the city's residents watched the procession in grim silence. Upton's division passed through Montgomery about 4:00 p.m. before camping four miles east of the city on the road to Columbus.[38]

While at Montgomery, Wilson saw the local newspaper reports that Lee had abandoned Petersburg and was retreating with Grant in pursuit. The reports seemed credible, but, given that the Union column was still not in communication with any friendly command authorities, Wilson could not get a confirmation of Lee's retreat, much less the fact that Lee had already surrendered. After consulting with Upton and the other division commanders, Wilson concluded that, until he received positive confirmation that the war had ended, he must continue "breaking things" from Alabama into Georgia and the Carolinas.[39]

Therefore, Upton received orders to march his division east toward the Chattahoochee River on the morning of April 14. Once there, he was to secure the bridges at either Columbus or West Point, Georgia. Upton ordered LaGrange's brigade to move via Tuskegee and Opelika to West Point.[40] While en route to the Chattahoochee, LaGrange again encountered Buford's cavalry. This time, the fight was sharper, but the Union troopers drove the enemy away easily, capturing 40 to 50 prisoners in the process.[41] LaGrange continued, reaching West Point on April 16 where he drove the small garrison out, capturing the city and seizing the bridge.[42]

Upton, meanwhile, moved his division directly towards Columbus, some 80 miles east of Montgomery. The division took the lead for the entire corps because Wilson decided that, since Long's division "had borne the brunt of the attack at Selma," Upton's division should now have the "post of honor" and lead the attack against Columbus.[43]

Columbus was a city of 12,000 people and was home to what was now some of the last remaining military factories in the Confederacy. General Alexander's brigade led the division, reaching the village of Crawford around noon on April 16. They were now only 12 miles from Columbus and ran into a small enemy cavalry detachment probably sent there to watch for the Union troopers' approach. The Southern horsemen galloped off as soon as they saw Alexander's men coming, and the Federal column continued towards Columbus.[44]

The 1st Ohio, under the command of Colonel Beroth Eggleston, led Alexander's brigade as they continued down the road to Columbus. When Eggleston's men reached Wetumpka Creek about six miles from the Chattahoochee, they found an enemy outpost guarding the bridge over the creek. The Confederates had set the bridge on fire, damaging it, and now decided to give the Ohioans a fight. But Eggleston's troopers flanked and overwhelmed them before quickly repairing the damaged bridge. Upton rode up to Eggleston, and one 1st Ohio officer, Captain J. A. O. Yeoman, recalled that is was clear Upton's "blood was up." Referring to the bridges across the Chattahoochee into Columbus, Upton asked Eggleston and Yeoman, "Can you give us the bridge across the Chattahoochee?" The two officers said that they would try.[45] They wheeled about, joined their regiment, and the 1st Ohio moved on with Alexander's brigade following close behind them. After a march of only two or three miles, they ran into and drove off the first enemy pickets from the Columbus defenses.[46]

About 2:00 p.m., Eggleston reached the hills overlooking Columbus. Like Selma, the city was heavily fortified but, unlike the Alabama city, Upton and his men had no prior knowledge of the extent or nature of the works. Upton arrived shortly after the 1st Ohio reached the outskirts of the city and began observing this new set of enemy defenses. As Upton peered through his field glasses, Eggleston pulled back his skirmishers and placed his regiment into column of fours, awaiting Upton's orders to attack.[47]

Columbus was located on the eastern banks of the Chattahoochee with the small village of Girard directly opposite on the Alabama side of the river. Girard, therefore, was the first obstacle between Upton's men and the bridges across the river. The village was scattered on both sides of Mill Creek, which snaked its way through the town before flowing into the river opposite the center of Columbus. The Union forces' objective, the bridges across the Chattahoochee were on the eastern side of the village, and there were three of them, consisting of two covered wooden wagon bridges and a railroad bridge. The two wagon bridges were about one-half mile apart, and each was around 1,000 feet long. The lower wagon bridge was near the intersection of roads from Eufaula, Sand Fort, and Crawford, and the upper wagon bridge met the roads coming in from Summerville, Opelika, and Salem. About 500 yards north of the upper bridge was the railroad bridge for the Columbus & Western railway.[48]

The terrain on the Alabama side of the Chattahoochee in and around Girard was very hilly. The hills rose 300 to 400 feet high above the river, and steep valleys and ravines separated them. South of Mill Creek, the hills formed a broken ridge that extended northwest from the Eufaula Road for several miles. North of the creek, the hills created a lower and more compact ridge that began west of the Summerville-Opelika Road and ran across the road to

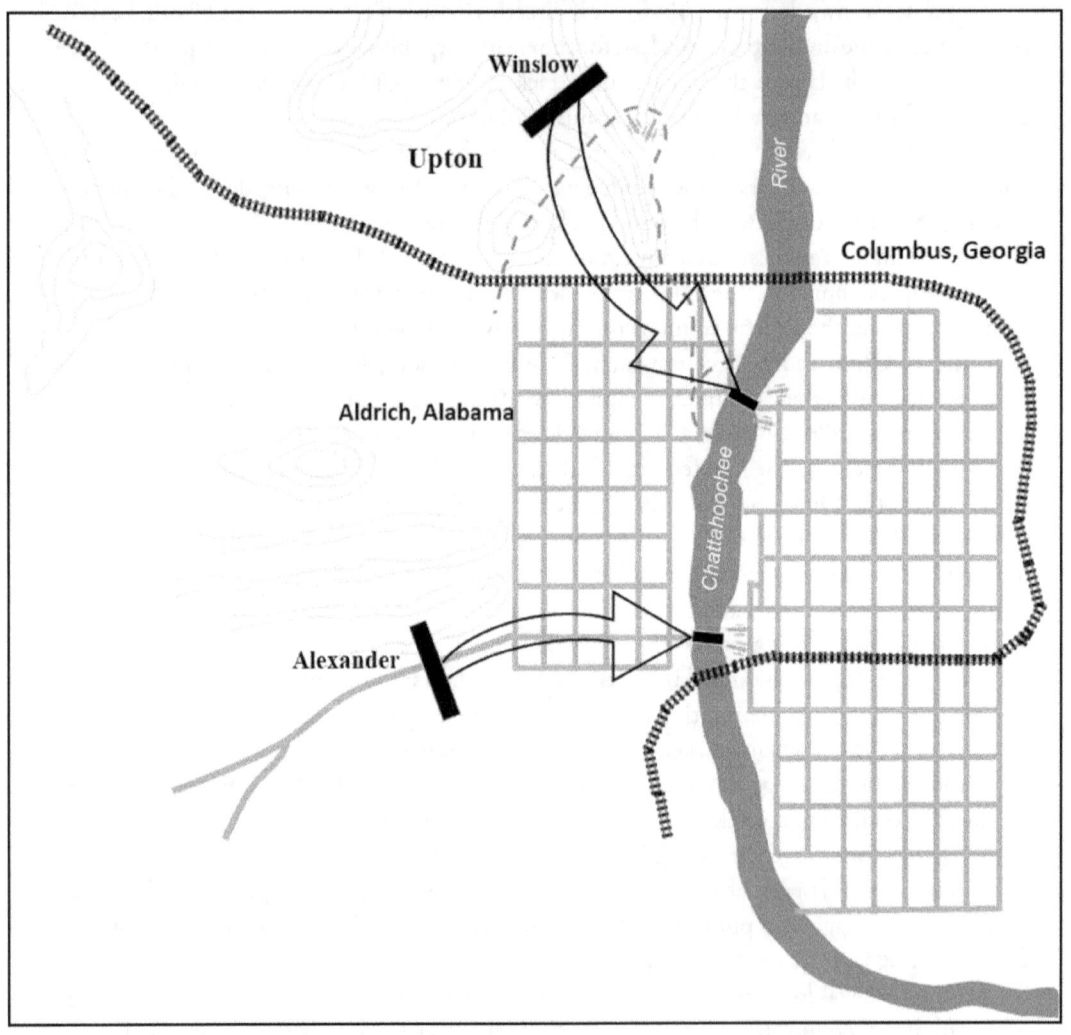

Battle of Columbus, April 16, 1865 (drawn by the author).

within 100 yards of the western bank of the Chattahoochee. In the middle of that ridge, another ridge ran south paralleling the road before eventually crossing it at the outskirts of Girard.[49]

It was on those ridges that the Confederates built their main line of outer defenses. There were forts at the western edge of the ridge with rifle pits running east until they connected with another line of the defenses that ran from the edge of the ridge nearest the river and then paralleled the southern boundary of the ridge all the way to the river banks just south of the upper wagon bridge. This outer line had two main forts, one in Girard at the far end and another at the opposite end near the river. The fort in Girard was equipped with four 12-pounder howitzers capable of sweeping the approaches to both the lower wagon bridge and the upper wagon bridge. Six 10-pound Parrott cannons placed in the nearby streets supplemented the howitzers. Meanwhile, the more northern fort was a lunette mounting one gun with two more guns nearby in the rifle pits that connected it with the fort in Girard.[50]

Additionally, Upton could make out five other outlying forts that covered the Crawford Road, the Salem Road, and any crossing of Mill Creek within a mile. One of these was a bastion like the one on the main defensive line, and the other four were very large redoubts, two square and two pentagonal, constructed for three or four guns each, and each planted on the top of a steep and thickly wooded hill. Luckily, the enemy had not been able to place any artillery at these forts.[51]

There were also three guns mounted in an earthwork on the Georgia side of the lower wagon bridge along with two brass howitzers capable of firing canister at the far end of the upper wagon bridge. These were all capable of providing devastating fire against any force trying to make it across the passageways of the two covered bridges. The enemy also placed five more guns defending the eastern side of the railroad bridge, and the entire line was defended by about 2,700 infantrymen.[52]

Upton now prepared to give orders for Alexander to have Eggleston and the 1st Ohio attack and secure the lower wagon bridge. But, after seeing the extent of the enemy's defenses, Upton decided to move part of the division in preparation for a possible second assault. He detached two companies of the 5th Iowa, sent them to swing around Girard towards the road leading north from Columbus to Summerville, and ordered them to reconnoiter the enemy lines above the upper wagon bridge. As the Iowans galloped off, Upton turned to General Winslow, whose brigade was just arriving, telling him to follow the men from the 5th Iowa and place his brigade at a point just beyond the enemy's outer defenses along the Summerville-Opelika Road. Once there, Winslow was to await further orders.[53] As Winslow rode off to join his brigade, Upton told Alexander to send in Colonel Eggleston and the 1st Ohio.

Eggleston and his staff placed themselves at the head of the 1st Ohio's six companies, which were still formed in a column of fours. Eggleston called out the command to draw sabers and nodded to the bugler, ordering him to sound the call telling the regiment to move forward at the trot. Once the entire column was moving, the bugler sounded the gallop and, only moments later, his bugle rang out the call to charge. With that, the entire column came crashing madly down the hillside into the streets of Girard toward the lower wagon bridge, now only a mile away.[54]

When the surging horsemen were only about 600 or 700 yards from their objective, Captain Yeoman realized that there were three enemy guns on the far side of the bridge pointing right down its passageway and positioned to sweep the bridge from end-to-end. He knew from hard experience that they were likely loaded with canister, which, when fired against the lead elements of the column, would cut down dozens of horses and men, blocking the roadway across the bridge. He shouted out to Eggleston suggesting the regiment dismount and attack on foot. The colonel immediately realized that Yeoman was correct about the situation, wheeled the regiment to the left into the paved streets of Girard, and ordered the men to dismount and advance on foot.[55]

As the troopers dismounted and grabbed their Spencers, Eggleston ordered sharpshooters to move forward to a position where they could shoot down the gunners on the far side before the rest of the regiment made its charge on foot across the bridge. As these riflemen took their places and opened fire on the Confederate gunners, the rest of the column formed for their advance across the bridge.[56]

Within the first few shots from Eggleston's sharpshooters, one of the gunners fell, pulling the lanyard on his cannon as he went down. The gun blasted out a canister round that set fire to the bundles of turpentine-soaked cotton the Confederates had placed to burn down the bridge. Within the flash of an eye, the entire bridge was engulfed in flames, and Eggleston ordered his men to fall back. This, as it turned out, was a good thing because any attack across the bridge would have met with disaster. It seems the Southerners had removed all the flooring planks from the center of the bridge for about 50 feet towards the far end. Had the Union troopers attacked as planned, they would have found themselves trapped, unable to go forward because the planks were gone and unable to go back because of the fires set on the bridge.[57]

When the 1st Ohio charged down the hill, Upton and his staff followed, finally halting on a little knoll about a quarter-mile from the lower wagon bridge where they could observe the attack. At first, when there was no response from Confederate gunners as the column approached the bridge, Upton thought that, perhaps, the enemy had abandoned their positions. Of course, this quickly was proven to be wishful thinking when the enemy guns opened a vigorous fire once the bridge was in flames. Within a few minutes, the Confederate gunners caught sight of Upton and his staff and directed some of their fire at them. Suddenly, shot and shell began crashing in on the knoll "fast and furious." Two of the staff's horses were killed almost immediately, and then another tore the staff bugler's horse "all to pieces." As canister shells were fired at them, more horses fell, screaming in agony. While all this was going on, Upton sat erect on his mount like "patience on a monument" calmly watching the 1st Ohio's attack until he was certain it could not succeed. Once he was satisfied no success could be gained, he ordered both his staff and the 1st Ohio to withdraw, rejoining the rest of Alexander's brigade on the hills overlooking Girard.[58]

With the lower wagon bridge destroyed, Upton decided to make plans for an assault on the upper wagon bridge. No attack from the south where he and Alexander's brigade now sat was going to be possible because any assault headed north would have to cross Mill Creek, which had very steep banks and was far too deep to ford. Therefore, only an attack from where he had sent Winslow's brigade had a chance to succeed. Upton turned to Alexander and told him to hold his position, and, about 2:30 p.m., Upton and his staff galloped off "at zealous speed" to reconnoiter the northern approaches to the upper wagon bridge.[59]

Upton divided his staff into several observing parties, each led by a different officer and ordered them to gather detailed intelligence on the enemy positions with "the utmost diligence." Two of his officers followed his orders to an extreme, actually riding right into the enemy lines. While they managed to escape, their orderlies were captured by the enemy.[60]

Meanwhile, Upton rode off with his escort to do his own scouting of the enemy lines. However, once he completed the reconnaissance, he lost some time searching for Winslow's brigade. Unfortunately, it turned out that there were two roads leading to Opelika and Summerville, and Upton chose the wrong one in his search for Winslow.[61] Around 4:00 p.m., Wilson arrived near the head of Winslow's column and, seeing Upton riding by, called out to him. However, Upton did not hear him, so Wilson sent an orderly to go catch his division commander and bring him back. It was sunset before Upton returned and, when he rode up to discuss the situation with Wilson, Upton was quite upset.[62]

He had been unable to find Winslow and told Wilson that they must delay any attack until he could find his lost brigade and get them in position. Wilson told Upton that he had passed Winslow's brigade in a nearby wooded valley and pointed in their direction. At that moment, Winslow rode up to confer with the other two generals and, as he did so, Upton began to "upbraid" Winslow severely for not obeying his instructions. Winslow politely pointed out that his 1,600 men were nearby, positioned exactly where Upton had directed and could attack almost immediately.[63]

Realizing his mistake, rather than acknowledge the misunderstanding about the Opelika roads, Upton became flustered and even more agitated. He said to Wilson, "But it is now too late. It will be dark before I can get him into position and lead the division to the attack."[64] Since the nighttime attacks at Selma had been so successful, this seems a very odd thing for a commander like Emory Upton to say. The one plausible explanation was that he had reached a point of near physical exhaustion from three weeks of campaigning. More than that, however, it was probably a sign of almost four years of intense psychological and emotional stress, stress that would haunt him for the rest of his life and eventually consume him.

Probably puzzled by this unusual emotional outburst, Wilson tried to reassure Upton by reminding him that Winslow's men were veterans and that Upton's plan was a sound one. He told Upton that it was definitely not too late to make an assault and that he should prepare to attack at 8:30 p.m. This not only seemed to calm Upton, but it also enabled him to regain some confidence and composure. He asked Wilson, "Do you mean it? It will be dark as midnight by that hour and that will be a night attack, indeed." Wilson assured Upton that it was just what he wanted and instructed him to go make all preparations. At that, Upton exclaimed enthusiastically, "By jingo, I'll do it; and I'll sweep everything before me!"[65]

Upton's plan was for a dismounted force of six companies from the 3rd Iowa to attack on foot and penetrate the outer defensive line along the Opelika-Summerville Road. As soon as these men had created a breach, two mounted companies from the 10th Missouri would charge through the gap followed closely by the men of the 4th Iowa and then sweep rapidly towards the upper wagon bridge.[66] To make sure the attack on the bridge was as swift as possible, Upton ordered that no one was to stop to take prisoners—they were to keep moving no matter what.[67]

During the time his brigade had been waiting in the woods, Winslow had studied the defensive works he was going to attack, carefully calculating the distance to the upper wagon bridge. Using intelligence gained from a local resident, Winslow was able to develop a rough idea of the main points of the enemy lines that proved to be very accurate. This would be important because the skies were turning very cloudy, which would make the night even darker.[68]

Once the plans were complete, Winslow's men made coffee, ate their dinner, and rested for an hour. Meanwhile, Upton and Wilson stood by the road behind the dismounted men from the 3rd Iowa, discussing the situation and Upton's plan. While Wilson told Upton that he had almost complete latitude in executing his plan, Upton insisted on going over every detail for Wilson's approval.[69] Perhaps this was yet another reflection of the stress that was quickly overtaking his emotional health.

As the time set for the attack approached, Colonel Noble quietly led the 300 men from the 3rd Iowa into position for the assault on the enemy's outer lines. They dismounted and crept forward without a sound until they were formed in line for the charge with their left flank resting on the Opelika-Summerville Road. They now were positioned parallel to the enemy rifle pits that lay in front of the main outer defensive lines. The 10th Missouri's 350 mounted troopers, led by Colonel Benteen, moved forward to the road in column of fours, ready to charge once the dismounted men of the 3rd Iowa penetrated the first line of defense and created a breach. They were followed by the 4th Iowa, who would trail the 10th Missouri into any gap made in the Confederate defenses.[70]

As the 3rd Iowa stealthily advanced, the whiteness of the road was virtually their only guide in the deep, impenetrable darkness. Once they finally reached the point of attack, they formed elbow-to-elbow and emerged from concealment. However, they had come so near to the enemy rifle pits while moving through the shadows that the Confederates heard their approach. Suddenly, the entire Confederate line erupted in a massive volley of rifle and artillery fire, lighting up the dark night with flames. The roar of this firing was "continuous and appalling," but, luckily for Upton's troopers, the Confederate soldiers could not clearly make out their targets in the dark. As a result, the enemy's bullets and shells sailed over the Union cavalrymen's heads.[71]

Despite the crude abatis assembled in front of the rifle pits, the lead elements of the 3rd Iowa quickly overran them and held onto the position despite an intense crossfire. As the remainder of the regiment's six companies arrived, the Confederates quickly abandoned their positions and fell back to the main outer line of defenses. In less than ten minutes, the Iowans had secured the first objective.[72]

Now, in the darkness, confusion, and roar of gunfire, Upton mistakenly believed that the 3rd Iowa had actually managed to pierce the main outer defenses, when, in fact, they had only taken the forward rifle pits. He ordered Colonel Benteen to charge the works immediately and take the upper wagon bridge. Then, as Benteen began to move his regiment forward at the trot, for reasons known only to Upton, he stopped Benteen and directed Captain Robert McGlasson to make the charge with only two lead companies rather than with the entire regiment.[73]

With nothing to guide him but the dim starlight and the flashes from the enemy's gunfire, McGlasson led his two companies forward at the gallop as his bugler sounded the charge. Incredibly, as the enemy defenders saw the Federal troopers coming at them in the night, they thought these were their own men retreating from the rifle pits. As a result, McGlasson boldly rode right through the outer defensive line as his troopers careened at full speed towards the bridge.[74]

The Union cavalry arrived at the bridge, rode across it, secured it, and captured the enemy's artillery batteries as well as its 50 defenders with ease. Now, however, the enemy counterattacked and began to close in on the men from the 10th Missouri. McGlasson had no choice but to retreat back across the bridge to the outer defensive lines.[75]

Meanwhile, having discovered the mistake regarding the fortifications and seeing McGlasson's predicament, Upton sent word for the dismounted men from the 3rd Iowa to wheel left and charge the outer defenses. At almost the same time, he ordered the 4th Iowa forward down the road to support McGlasson.[76] The 3rd Iowa rose from the rifle pits and scrambled down a steep ravine and then across a swampy stream before clawing their way through the abatis on the front slopes of the enemy works. At that moment, three battalions from the 4th Iowa arrived on the scene, and two of the battalions dismounted to join the men from the 3rd Iowa. While the third battalion remained mounted waiting an order to charge, the dismounted battalions and their comrades from the 3rd Iowa charged up and over the enemy earthworks as the defenders fled to the rear.[77]

At that moment, Upton arrived on the scene and "displayed the extraordinary insensibility to danger which always characterized him." Seemingly unconscious of the danger around him, he rode among the dismounted troopers calling out in a "high and penetrating voice, plainly heard above the rattle of carbines and the still louder roar of artillery" for his men to press the attack, shouting, "Charge 'em! Charge 'em!" As the men began to move Upton called out, "Take no prisoners! Go for the bridge!" The men responded, surging forward, leaving the confused Confederate troops behind them, and rushing down Brodnax Street toward the bridge.[78]

As the Iowans reached the Alabama side of the bridge, they quickly merged with the retreating Southern soldiers crowding onto the passageway. One trooper later wrote, "It was a covered wooden bridge, with two carriage-ways, and the whole space was now filled with the flying rebels and the advancing Iowans."[79] In the darkness and confusion, many of the Iowans passed the Confederates and reached the far side before them. The passageway across the bridge was filled with the odor of the turpentine that had been infused into cotton and stuffed throughout the bridge so it could be burned before capture. But not a single enemy soldier was able to light fire to these, and the only one who tried was clubbed down quickly by the butt of an Iowan's carbine.[80]

Winslow now ordered the remaining battalion of the 4th Iowa to attack down the road and across the bridge in a column of fours. The mounted troopers galloped through the bridge sweeping past the last of the dismounted Iowans, passing the captured guns, and charging into the streets of Columbus, completing what had now become a total rout. Soon, all the remaining Confederate troops had surrendered, and the entire battle was over in less than an hour. The city became very quiet, and the fires lit by the enemy in several buildings in Girard "cast a lurid glow upon the scene of conflict."[81]

With the city in Union hands, Upton's men began to destroy enemy war materials. They set fire to the arsenal, foundries, ammunition stockpiles, the Gunboat Jackson, and more than 60,000 bales of cotton.[82] After Upton set up his headquarters in the Battle House, General Wilson arrived to congratulate him and his division. Private Gilpin wrote in his journal that day, recording what were likely the feelings of many of Upton's men:

> This is Upton's fight. Our officers think the assault and capture of Columbus a brilliant exhibition of generalship. One thing is certain. General Upton has inspired his men with enthusiasm, and they have confidence in him. He is quick to see the point of attack, and is able on the instant to throw his force with the greatest effect. No delay, no dawdling, no mistakes; he strikes quickly and surely. He told General Wilson that he could now take his division and march through the South in any direction. He is not given to boasting, and as a military man, is sure of what he says. We are masters of the situation.[83]

Wilson moved the corps onward, capturing Macon, Georgia, on April 20. There, Confederate authorities assured him that Lee had surrendered to Grant and Johnston had capitulated to Sherman in North Carolina. Wilson said that he believed them but needed official confirmation and orders on how to proceed from General Sherman. He telegraphed an encrypted message to Sherman from Macon on April 21 and, at 6:00 p.m. that evening, Wilson received a reply informing that the stories he was hearing were true and that he should suspend all hostilities immediately.[84]

Upton next moved his division northwest to Augusta as part of the search for Jefferson Davis and then assumed to role of an occupying victor. On June 10, Upton prepared to take leave of his division and begin the life of a peacetime officer. He wrote a farewell to his men, saying, "Before severing his connection with the command, the brevet major-general commanding desires to express his high appreciation of the bravery, endurance, and soldierly qualities displayed by the officers and men of his division in the late cavalry campaign." He then listed the many triumphs the men of his command had achieved during the campaign before concluding, "You will return to your homes with the proud consciousness of having defended the flag of your country in the hour of the greatest national peril, while through your instrumentality liberty and civilization will have advanced the greatest stride recorded in history. The best wishes of your commanding general will ever attend you."[85]

Emory Upton's Civil War was over at last.

13

The Tragic Reformer

> His life was pure and upright, his bearing chivalric and commanding, his conduct modest and unassuming, and his character absolutely without blemish. History cannot furnish a brighter example of unselfish patriotism, or of ambition unsullied by an ignoble thought or an unworthy deed.
> —Major General James Harrison Wilson[1]

With the war's end, Upton's career reverted to that of a peacetime army officer. He languished in Georgia before returning to Nashville, and, eventually, he traveled to a new assignment in Colorado. He was officially mustered out of volunteer services in April 1866, and, like every other Regular Army officer who had served with volunteer forces during the war, he reverted to his previous rank as a captain in the 5th U.S. Artillery.[2] However, only two months later, he was offered a promotion to lieutenant colonel in the 25th U.S. Infantry, which he accepted, and he served with the regiment in Paducah, Kentucky, from the summer of 1866 until fall 1867 when the regiment moved to McPherson Barracks in Georgia. He served there until his assignment to West Point as the Commandant of Cadets in late June 1870.[3] His assignment to West Point should have been a time of great happiness for Upton, but he had experienced the deepest loss possible in his personal life.

Emily

From the time Upton left home for Oberlin College until the end of the war, there had been little if any time for some of life's basic joys, including courtship, romance, and marriage. So, in many ways, it is not surprising that when Emory Upton finally fell in love, it was the sort of all-consuming experience the poets write about.

During the final campaign through Alabama and Georgia, Upton became close friends with the commander of his 1st Brigade, Andrew Alexander. Alexander was married to Evalina "Evy" Martin, who came from a wealthy family that lived in a mansion called Willowbrook near Auburn, New York on the eastern shore of Lake Owasco. During the months when Upton's division was training outside Nashville, Evy traveled to Tennessee from Willowbrook to be with her husband, and Upton spent considerable time with the young couple. Evy apparently liked what she saw in Upton and told him that, whenever he might be near Willowbrook, he had an open invitation to visit her family.[4]

In mid–July 1866, when Upton was attending the review board at West Point for the first of his tactics reform proposals, he decided to take Evy up on her invitation and make a call at Willowbrook. There, he was introduced to Evy's younger sister, Emily. Described as a "fair-haired, blue-eyed maiden,"[5] Emily seems to have been a kind and gentle soul who deeply embraced her Christian faith. On Upton's first night at the Martin home, he and Emily took a long walk along the shore of Lake Owasco, which was followed by an even longer carriage ride the next day and another walk by the lake that evening.[6]

There was an obvious and immediate attraction between the two. For Upton, much of the attraction may have stemmed from the fact that it simply was the right time in his life, while for Emily, there was an attraction of sorts in Upton's badly damaged soul. She recognized from the beginning that he was someone who had lost his faith amid the carnage of the war, and she sought to redeem him. At one point over a year after the two met, Emily wrote that she "felt a constant anxiety about the salvation of his soul, and prayed earnestly day and night, that he might be brought back to God."[7]

While there was an attraction, when Upton left a few days later, there was no plan for a resumption of their budding romance. However, in January 1867, when Upton was in Washington, D.C., visiting the War Department, he happened to meet Emily, who was also visiting the capital. They made sure to see one another every day during their time in Washington, and their romance accelerated. When Upton returned to Paducah and Emily journeyed back to Willowbrook, they began a steady correspondence that led to a marriage proposal from Upton in May. She accepted his proposal but soon broke off their engagement, which did not seem to deter Upton. In August, he traveled to Willowbrook, where he made a second proposal, which Emily turned down probably because of her chronic health issues. She had long suffered from what doctors described as "neuralgia," but was likely tuberculosis. In November, Upton again returned to Willowbrook to propose. This time, Emily accepted, and the couple was married on February 19, 1868.[8]

Upton received a leave of absence from the army and, in early March, the newlyweds sailed from New York for a honeymoon in Europe. They visited France and Italy, but the trip was cut short due to Emily's health, which began to deteriorate. In August 1868, they returned to Emily's home at Willowbrook and, in October, they traveled to Key West for the winter in the hopes that the warm weather and sea air might improve her health.[9]

In February, Upton's leave of absence came to an end, and he left Emily in Key West while he joined his regiment in Memphis. By April, Emily's health had improved to the point that she traveled to New Orleans, where Upton met her en route to his regiment's new duty station at McPherson Barracks, near Atlanta. Sadly, their reunion was short-lived. Emily's health again went downhill and, in June, she was forced to return to Willowbrook where her mother could care for her. In November, Upton took leave so he could accompany Emily to Nassau where she would spend the winter, and, in December, he returned to Atlanta.[10]

However, in March 1870, Emily's condition began to decline quickly. On March 29, as Upton prepared to leave Atlanta for Nassau to be at his wife's side, he received a telegram saying that Emily was failing rapidly and that he could not possibly reach her in time. She died at 1:00 a.m. the next morning, March 30.[11] Not surprisingly, Emily's death struck Upton terribly hard. With her help, he had returned to his faith and, perhaps, begun to put away the horrors he had witnessed during the war. But now she was gone. Before her funeral service, he sat quietly beside her casket and placed his handkerchief over her heart before it was sealed.[12] It was a loss from which he would never recover.

Tactics and Army Reform

During the period from the end of the war through the time of Emily's death, despite the change to a peacetime culture in the army, Upton would never forget what he had seen and experienced during the war. Moreover, he was determined to do all in his power to make changes in the army so that the carnage he witnessed would not occur again. His first target was tactics. He studied and experimented with new approaches to deploying infantry based on the column tactics he employed so well at Rappahannock Station and Spotsylvania. His initial efforts met with success. In January 1866, he formally submitted his proposed changes, which were reviewed by a board convened at West Point in June 1866. Despite the board's recommendation for approval and the personal support of General Grant, the War Department was slow to adopt Upton's ideas. Not surprisingly, opposition arose, as it always does when major changes are proposed in any organization, especially one as insular as the 19th-century U.S. Army.[13]

The War Department ordered a second board to examine Upton's ideas in the summer of 1867. On July 15, 1867, this new board again approved Upton's proposed revisions with only minor suggested changes and referred them to the Secretary of War for adoption. On August 1, the Adjutant-General issued General Orders No. 73 incorporating the new system of infantry tactics for the army.[14] However, despite the formal adoption of Upton's tactics, opposition would continue for years, even as Upton worked to further refine and improve the army's tactical approach to warfare.

For the remainder of his career, Upton also waged a vigorous campaign to reform the culture of the army's organization and the officer corps itself. Remembering the behavior and capabilities displayed by commanders during the war, when men who had no business commanding troops in the field sent thousands to their deaths, he pressed for changes in both military education, the army's organization, and the promotion system. In February 1868, he wrote to General Sherman, the army's new general-in-chief, proposing the idea of post-graduate instruction for the officer corps. Outlining a basic curriculum, he told Sherman this schooling ought to include "a short course of study; say Tactics, Regulations, Art of War, &c, practical instruction & drill," which Upton believed "would be of incalculable benefit to the Army, as insuring uniformity of drill and discipline through-out."[15]

As for the army's organization, his ideas began with the obvious failures of the militia and volunteer state regiment system during the war. While Upton extolled the courage of those he had led in volunteer service, he rightly pointed out that, while these men loved their country, they had no passion for or belief in the ideas of military discipline and order. He wrote James Wilson in 1869 saying "that states attempt to maintain a militia organization when the freedom of election [of its officers] abolishes restraint; and makes discipline a mockery." He went on to tell his old comrade and commanding general that the experience gained in the war made "the glaring defects of the volunteer system, its cost in treasure and blood, apparent."[16]

Upton also told Wilson that he believed states should not be allowed to muster in organizations larger than a company during wartime. Most importantly, he proposed that only the War Department should be allowed to appoint field officers and that West Point should be charged with educating and commissioning "a surplus of officers, who in time of war should be appointed to the grade of field and general officers."[17]

A World Tour

Following Emily's death, a deeply depressed Upton moved to West Point, where he was assigned as the Commandant of Cadets. It was a position he had longed to fill, and he had often contemplated the happiness he and Emily would experience while strolling the grounds of the place where Upton's life had been transformed, a place he loved deeply. But now that was not to be.

As time passed, Upton's views on reforming the army's culture became ever more strident. He passed his lonely off-duty hours at the Academy working on new tactics and, as the end of his assignment as Commandant of Cadets approached, he began searching for a new position that might give him a renewed purpose. In August 1874, that search led him to suggest to General Sherman that Upton make a tour of Europe to observe their armies looking for potential military science developments that the U.S. Army might consider adopting. Sherman liked the idea so much that he expanded the concept to include an inspection of the armies of Asia, as well.[18]

It took almost a year to obtain the proper funding for the expedition and to find two officers to accompany Upton. But in June 1875, Upton received his official orders, and, in July, he and his party traveled to San Francisco before departing by ship for Yokohama on August 3.[19] The entire journey lasted 17 months and included stops in Japan, China, India, Persia, Afghanistan, Russia, Italy, France, Germany, and Great Britain.

Upton and his assistants returned to the United States in December 1876, and, after a short leave, he reported to his new assignment at the U.S. Army's Artillery School at Fortress Monroe, Virginia on March 1, 1877.[20] Once in place there, he began writing the first drafts of his report on the findings from his around-the-world journey. In December 1877, the report was forwarded to the Secretary of War and would be published in April 1878 for the general public's review as *The Armies of Asia and Europe*.[21] As planned, the report not only documented his observations, it also provided Upton's strong views on how some characteristics of the foreign armies might be applied in reforming the culture of the U.S. Army.

His recommendations were viewed as radical by many but, as he wrote his old friend Henry DuPont, the proposed changes were necessary to prevent a repeat of the "folly and immorality"[22] of the policies used during the Civil War. Among his recommendations was that the government should declare, as a matter of policy, "that every able-bodied male citizen, between certain ages, owes his country military service." Further, he recommended that the War Department divide the country into military districts that would be apportioned for the recruitment of cadres of reserve forces. In addition, he proposed that only Federal authorities perform such recruiting and that all recruiting bounties be abandoned. To support these new reserve forces, Upton proposed the construction of depots around the country that would "receive, arm, equip, and train all the recruits who volunteer, or are drafted."[23]

However, his most important ideas for reform related to the reorganization of the officer corps. Upton wrote that none of the new ideas for prosecuting the nation's wars "with economy of life and treasure" would be successful without a "radical reorganization of the army."[24] He proposed that officers be assigned to staff positions based on an evaluation process and that officers rotate between staff and line assignments. Further, he recommended that promotions based solely on regimental assignment and seniority be replaced by a merit-based system using a formal examination process.[25]

Upton also believed that changes in military education needed to be made. While he saw West Point as superior to any of the European military academies he studied, Upton recommended the establishment of a post-graduate education system. With the sole exception of the artillery school, he believed the army had nothing to compare to the war academies he observed in Europe. Therefore, he proposed the creation of "post-graduate institutions" designed specifically for the study of "strategy, grand tactics, and all the sciences connected with modern war."[26]

He also advocated that the army be capable of a rapid mobilization and expansion to a force of 150,000 men. While he acknowledged that there was more than one way to accomplish this goal, he strongly preferred the idea of prosecuting "future wars with volunteer infantry, supported by the regular artillery and cavalry"[27] with the volunteer forces led by regular officers. The source of these volunteer forces would be what Upton called the "National Volunteers." These would be battalions trained in peacetime and assigned to each of the army's 25 infantry regiments in times of war. They would train regularly at depots manned by regular officers and noncommissioned officers and would be ready for duty on short notice.[28]

While Upton's ideas found acceptance in much of the officer corps, many senior officers did not approve, especially those whose careers were based on service spent almost entirely in the staff bureaus. As is often the case, those who have prospered under an existing system oppose changes because they see those reforms as somehow invalidating their careers and success—if the system was good enough for them, it ought to be good enough for anyone. While Upton's ideas would be put forth in Congress as part of several reform bills, each bill was defeated, and his recommendations would not be realized during his lifetime.

A Tragic End

Once *The Armies of Asia and Europe* was complete, Upton began writing a new manuscript on the history of American military policy, which he titled *The Military Policy of the United States*. He wrote that the purpose of his new book would be to "bring home to Congress that all important fact; that it is entitled to the credit for all that is good, and equally responsible for all that is bad, in our military system. Until it appreciates this fact improvement will be slow and difficult."[29] As Upton worked on the book, the army notified him that he was being promoted to colonel and reassigned to the 4th U.S. Artillery, which was then stationed at The Presidio in San Francisco.[30]

However, Upton delayed his arrival in San Francisco until December 1880 due to severe health issues. He had been plagued by headaches since his arrival at West Point in 1870, and their severity and frequency had increased in the ten years since. He initially sought treatment from the West Point dentist who feared Upton might have a dangerous aneurysm. Later, another physician diagnosed the problem as resulting from a reoccurrence of malaria and recommended Upton take quinine, which provided some relief.[31]

But by the summer of 1880, the headaches became almost continuous, wearing Upton down both physically and emotionally. He consulted a doctor in Philadelphia who diagnosed his problem as being the result of a "nasal catarrh." While that term is no longer used in the medical community, it refers to severe inflammation of the mucous membrane. The doctor's treatment involved cauterizations of the nasal passages using electric probes. Upton agreed to the treatment and was in Philadelphia under the doctor's care from mid–September to early November 1880. He wrote his sister about the cautery, saying, "It is by no means severe. The actual cautery gives very little pain."[32] Unfortunately, however, the treatment brought little relief.

What Upton and his various doctors did not realize was that, in all likelihood, he was suffering from a benign tumor in the sinus cavity. Modern medical authorities say these can

Telegram to the Adjutant General informing him of Emory Upton's death (National Archives).

grow to enormous size, penetrating the sinus wall and pressing on the brain. When that happens, the tumor can cause severe depression and mental impairment, both of which were symptoms Upton experienced.[33] The combination of these with his depression over the loss of Emily and his failure to achieve his proposed military reforms was a toxic mix. When he arrived at the Presidio, he was a lonely and deeply troubled man.

On March 13, 1881, his friend and West Point classmate, Captain Henry Hasbrouck, visited Upton at the regimental headquarters. When Hasbrouck asked Upton about his headaches, Upton simply laid his head on his desk and sobbed. Hasbrouck spent most of that day and the next with Upton and later reported that his old friend was "very despondent, talked of the loss of his will-power, and of the respect of the officers of the regiment." Upton also told Hasbrouck that his tactics were a failure and of his concern that, "if his system was adopted it would involve the country in disaster in the next war." When Hasbrouck left Upton on the evening of March 14, he thought Upton was in a better mood, and his commander even spoke of a trip to Monterey the next day.[34]

What Hasbrouck and the rest of Upton's friends and comrades apparently did not see was the almost unbearable weight he was carrying in championing his proposed reforms. To Upton, it must have seemed that he owed this responsibility to change things for the better to 100,000 ghosts, many of whom were men he commanded in the field and sent to their deaths carrying out orders issued by men he had once said were not qualified to be corporals. On the night of March 13, he had written his sister, Sara, about his concerns involving the tactics revisions he had been diligently working on, but to no success. "It has seemed to me that I must give up my system and lose my military reputation," he wrote. "God only knows how it will eventually end, but I trust he will lead me to sacrifice myself, rather than to perpetuate a method which might in the future cost a single man his life."[35] He had concluded the letter by saying, "I don't feel like writing any more. Only let me feel that I have your love and sympathy. With a fervent kiss for you all, ever your affectionate brother, Emory."[36]

As the night deepened on March 14, Upton began to write a letter to the Adjutant General concerning the latest status on his development of new skirmishing tactics. "In my effort to revise the tactics so that they might apply to companies over two hundred strong," he penned, "I discovered that the double column and the deployment by numbers, when compared with the French method, was a failure. The fours, too, I was forced to admit."[37] But there, Upton stopped writing. Perhaps it was all too much to bear—the pain in his head, the inability to concentrate, the darkness in his soul. He set the letter aside and picked up a blank piece of stationery. On it, he wrote:

Presidio, San Francisco, March 14, 1881.

To the Adjutant-General U. S. A.
SIR: I hereby tender my resignation as colonel of the Fourth Artillery.

Very respectfully, your obedient servant,
E. UPTON,
Colonel Fourth Artillery.[38]

Upton then carefully placed the letter aside where his staff would find it in the morning. He rose from his desk and went to his bed, apparently pausing only long enough to pick up his service revolver. Once at his bedside, he placed the gun to his lips and pulled the trigger.

Victory

Upton's family, friends, and supporters were shocked at the news of his suicide. Most could not fathom why he would take such a drastic step. In the years immediately following his death, Upton's work on *The Military Policy of the United States* remained in the hands of his sister, Sara. She sent a copy of the manuscript to Henry DuPont and urged him to publish it. However, despite pleas from her and General Sherman, DuPont refused to have the work published. As a result, while a few copies circulated among his friends, nothing more came of either the book or the policies he recommended for the next 23 years following Upton's death.[39]

Then in 1898, the United States fought and won a brief war with Spain. As Upton had feared might someday happen, the nation did fight a war against a European power. Luckily, however, that European power was, perhaps, the weakest one on the continent. While the American victory was swift and complete, it revealed serious deficiencies in the army's organization, culture, and ability to mobilize and deploy its forces. As a result, in 1899, President McKinley appointed Elihu Root as Secretary of War and tasked him to undertake the job of reforming the army.[40]

Under Root's leadership and with the strong support of several members of Congress, four major reform bills were passed between 1901 and 1908, and many of the changes captured the spirit, if not the letter, of Upton's recommendations. As a part of his effort to gain the political support he needed for the reform bills, Root had the War Department publish Upton's *The Military Policy of the United States* in 1904. Some of the reforms instituted that reflected Upton's thinking included an expansion of the regular army's size to 100,000 men, the establishment of a system to rotate officers between line and staff assignments, and an end to the permanent assignment of officers to staff positions. In addition, while state governments still had autonomy on the activities of their National Guard units, they were required to adhere to the army's tactics and training standards, and only the army could assess these units' readiness for duty. Within a few years, additional legislation made the National Guard the country's primary reserve force.[41]

Finally, Root also reorganized the army's professional education system. He changed the School of Application at Fort Leavenworth to the Army School of the Line, making it the counterpart to the Artillery School at Fortress Monroe. Eventually, the two schools would combine to become today's' Command and Staff College at Fort Leavenworth. Root also saw to the establishment of an even higher level of professional education with the creation of the Army War College in Washington, D.C., in 1901.[42]

While his life ended tragically with his work unfinished, Emory Upton did achieve a final and lasting victory. In some ways, he can be called the architect of the modern U.S. Army. The army that resulted from the reforms he championed would perform admirably in the two world wars of the 20th century and survive the political stalemate of the Korean War and a political defeat in the Vietnam War.

One may hope that the unnecessary pain, suffering, and carnage Upton saw during the Civil War will forever be a thing of the past.

Chapter Notes

Chapter 1

1. Emory Upton to Maria Upton, February 27, 1857, Peter Michie, *The Life and Letters of Emory Upton* (New York: D. Appleton and Co., 1885), 13.
2. Michie, *The Life and Letters of Emory Upton*, 5.
3. *Ibid.*, 1–2.
4. Emory Upton to Electa Randall Upton, August 27, 1879, Michie, *The Life and Letters of Emory Upton*, 476–477.
5. Stephen Ambrose, *Upton and the Army* (Baton Rouge: Louisiana State University Press, 1993), Kindle Edition, Kindle Location 96–97.
6. Michie, *The Life and Letters of Emory Upton*, 2; Ambrose, *Upton and the Army*, Kindle Location 93.
7. Ambrose, *Upton and the Army*, Kindle Location 97–105.
8. *Ibid.*, 116–118.
9. Robert S. Fletcher, *A History of Oberlin College*, Vol. II (Oberlin, Ohio: Oberlin College Press, 1943), 536; Ambrose, *Upton and the Army*, Kindle Location 120–121.
10. Emory Upton to Maria Upton, February 3, 1858, Emory Upton Letters, Holland Land Office Museum, Batavia, New York.
11. Michie, *The Life and Letters of Emory Upton*, 3–4; Ambrose, *Upton and the Army*, Kindle Location 112–115.
12. Recollections of the Reverend Father O'Reilly, Michie, *The Life and Letters of Emory Upton*, 6.
13. *Ibid.*, 5.
14. *Ibid.*
15. *Ibid.*, 4–6.
16. *Ibid.*
17. *Ibid.*, 6.
18. Merritt Starr, "General Emory Upton—His Brothers, His Career," *Oberlin Alumni Magazine* (May 1922), 14.
19. Congressman Benjamin Pringle to Emory Upton, March 12, 1856, Michie, *The Life and Letters of Emory Upton*, 8.
20. An omnibus was a large, horse-drawn equivalent of a modern-day bus. Typically, it was long with several rows of benches and a door on the side of the vehicle for each row.
21. William Woods Averell, Edward K. Eckert and Nicholas J. Amato, eds., *Ten Years in the Saddle: The Memoir of William Woods Averell, 1851–1862* (San Rafael, California: Presidio Press, 1978), 15.
22. *Ibid.*
23. A sally port was a secure, controlled entryway to a building.
24. Averell, *Ten Years in the Saddle*, 17.
25. *Ibid.*
26. *Ibid.*
27. Michie, *The Life and Letters of Emory Upton*, 11.
28. Averell, *Ten Years in the Saddle*, 23.
29. Michie, *The Life and Letters of Emory Upton*, 26.
30. Averell, *Ten Years in the Saddle*, 18.
31. Morris Schaaf, *The Spirit of Old West Point, 1858–1862* (New York: Houghton, Mifflin and Company, 1907), 40.
32. Averell, *Ten Years in the Saddle*, 19.
33. *Ibid.*
34. *Ibid.*, 19–20.
35. *Official Register of the Officers and Cadets of the U.S. Military Academy, West Point, New York, June 1857* (Washington, D.C.: Department of War, 1857), 3–4.
36. Schaaf, *The Spirit of Old West Point*, 37.
37. *Ibid.*
38. *Ibid.*, 60.
39. *Official Register of the Officers and Cadets, 1857*, 4.
40. Averell, *Ten Years in the Saddle*, 23; *Official Register of the Officers and Cadets, 1857*, 13–14.
41. Schaaf, *The Spirit of Old West Point*, 45; *Official Register of the Officers and Cadets, 1857*, 4.
42. Ambrose, *Upton and the Army*, Kindle Location 165–169.
43. Schaaf, *The Spirit of Old West Point*, 46.
44. *Ibid.*, 63.
45. *Ibid.*
46. *Ibid.*, 63–64.
47. Averell, *Ten Years in the Saddle*, 25.
48. Schaaf, *The Spirit of Old West Point*, 64–65.
49. Averell, *Ten Years in the Saddle*, 25.
50. James L. Morrison, Jr., *The Best School: West Point 1833–1866* (Kent: Kent State University Press, 1998), Kindle Edition, Kindle Location 2449–2484.
51. Emory Upton to Maria Upton, February 25, 1857, Michie, *The Life and Letters of Emory Upton*, 12; *Official Register of the Officers and Cadets, 1857*, 17; Schaaf, *The Spirit of Old West Point*, 68.
52. *Report of the Ninth Annual Reunion of the*

Association of the Graduates of the United States Military Academy, June 13, 1878; U.S. Congress, Senate, Misc., Doc. no. 3, *Report of the Commission Appointed Under the eighth section of the act of Congress of June 21, 1860, to examine into the organization, system of discipline, and course of instruction of the United States Military Academy at West Point*, 36th Cong., 2d sess., 1860, p. 31.

53. Schaaf, *The Spirit of Old West Point*, 68.
54. Ibid., 75.
55. Emory Upton to Maria Upton, February 25, 1857, Michie, *The Life and Letters of Emory Upton*, 12.
56. Schaaf, *The Spirit of Old West Point*, 61.
57. Ibid., 62.
58. Emory Upton to Maria Upton, February 25, 1857, Michie, *The Life and Letters of Emory Upton*, 12.
59. Michie, *The Life and Letters of Emory Upton*, 21.
60. Averell, *Ten Years in the Saddle*, 26–27.
61. Ibid., 27.
62. *Official Register of the Officers and Cadets, 1857*, 14.
63. Averell, *Ten Years in the Saddle*, 28.
64. *Official Register of the Officers and Cadets, 1857*, 13.
65. Emory Upton to Maria Upton, September 7, 1857, Michie, *The Life and Letters of Emory Upton*, 13–14.
66. Emory Upton to Maria Upton, April 12, 1857, Michie, *The Life and Letters of Emory Upton*, 13.
67. Emory Upton to Maria Upton, February 13, 1858, Michie, *The Life and Letters of Emory Upton*, 14.
68. *Official Register of the Officers and Cadets, 1858*, 11; *Official Register of the Officers and Cadets, 1859*, 10; *Official Register of the Officers and Cadets, 1861*, 9.
69. Schaaf, *The Spirit of Old West Point*, 145–146.
70. Ibid.
71. Ibid., 146–147.
72. Emory Upton to Maria Upton, January 20, 1860, Michie, *The Life and Letters of Emory Upton*, 18.
73. Emory Upton to "My Dear Sister," February 5, 1860, Michie, *The Life and Letters of Emory Upton*, 22. While many of Upton's letters were specifically addressed to his sister, Maria, most are addressed to "My Dear Sister," and there is no record of which sister he was writing.
74. Emory Upton to Maria Upton, December 1, 1860, Emory Upton Letters, Holland Land Office Museum.
75. Emory Upton to "My Dear Sister," December 21, 1860, Michie, *The Life and Letters of Emory Upton*, 29–30.
76. Emory Upton to "My Dear Sister," February 2, 1861, Michie, *The Life and Letters of Emory Upton*, 31.
77. Emory Upton to "My Dear Sister," April 17, 1861, Michie, *The Life and Letters of Emory Upton*, 36.
78. Emory Upton to "My Dear Sister," April 8, 1861, Michie, *The Life and Letters of Emory Upton*, 34.
79. Ambrose, *Upton and the Army*, Kindle Location 240–255.
80. Emory Upton to "My Dear Sister," April 17, 1861, Michie, *The Life and Letters of Emory Upton*, 36.
81. Ambrose, *Upton and the Army*, Kindle Location 242–246.
82. Emory Upton to the Honorable Simon Cameron, Secretary of War, May 13, 1861, "Appointment, Commission, and Personnel File of Emory Upton," National Archives.
83. Emory Upton to Brigadier General Lorenzo Thomas, Adjutant General, June 25, 1861, "Appointment, Commission, and Personnel File of Emory Upton," National Archives.

Chapter 2

1. Emory Upton to "My Dear Sister," July 9, 1861, Michie, *The Life and Letters of Emory Upton*, 52.
2. Emory Upton to "My Dear Sister," May 8, 1861, Michie, *The Life and Letters of Emory Upton*, 44.
3. Ibid.
4. Ernest B. Furgurson, *Freedom Rising: Washington in the Civil War* (New York: Alfred E. Knopf, 2004), 80.
5. Robert Hunt Rhodes, ed., *All for the Union: The Civil War Diary and Letters of Elisha Hunt Rhodes* (New York: Vintage Books, 1985), 12.
6. Michie, *The Life and Letters of Emory Upton*, 45.
7. Furgurson, *Freedom Rising*, 116.
8. Michie, *The Life and Letters of Emory Upton*, 45.
9. Emory Upton to "My Dear Sister," May 20, 1861, Emory Upton Letters, Holland Land Office Museum.
10. Emory Upton, *Epitome of Upton's Military Policy of the United States* (Washington, D.C.: Government Printing Office, 1916), 19.
11. Ibid.
12. The typical army organization at the time of the Civil War was as follows: (1) Regiment. 800–1000 men commanded by a colonel. (2) Brigade. Made up of 2–5 regiments of approximately 2,600 or more men and commanded by a brigadier general. (3) Division. Consisted of 2–4 brigades totaling at least 8,000 men and commanded by a major general. (4) Corps. Included 2–3 divisions with 25,000 or more soldiers and commanded by a major general. (5) Army. Made up of 3 or more corps with approximately 80,000–100,000 men and commanded by a major general.
13. Frederick H. Dyer, *A Compendium of the War of the Rebellion, Part 3* (Des Moines, Iowa: Dyer Publishing Co., 1908), 1410.
14. James I. Robertson, Jr., *Soldiers Blue and Gray* (Columbia: University of South Carolina Press, 1998), 21.
15. Millet S. Thompson, *Thirteenth Regiment of New Hampshire Volunteer Infantry in the War of the Rebellion, 1861-1865: A Diary Covering Three Years and a Day* (New York: Houghton, Mifflin and Company, 1888), 35.
16. Grady McWhiney and Perry D. Jamieson, *Attack and Die: Civil War Military Tactics and the Southern Heritage* (Tuscaloosa: University of Alabama Press, 1982), 31.
17. Ulysses S. Grant, *Personal Memoirs of U.S. Grant* (Lincoln: University of Nebraska Press, 1996), 60.
18. McWhiney and Jamieson, *Attack and Die*, 31–33.

19. *Ibid.*, 150.
20. *Ibid.*, 35.
21. Emory Upton to "My Dear Sister," June 6, 1861, Emory Upton Letters, Holland Land Office Museum.
22. Emory Upton to "My Dear Sister," May 20, 1861, Michie, *The Life and Letters of Emory Upton*, 45.
23. Robertson, *Soldiers Blue and Gray*, 49.
24. *Ibid.*, 55–56.
25. L.W. Day, *Story of the One Hundred and First Ohio Infantry, A Memorial Volume* (Cleveland, Ohio: W. M. Bayne Printing Co., 1894), 39.
26. Emory Upton to "My Dear Sister," May 24, 1861, Michie, *The Life and Letters of Emory Upton*, 46.
27. Emory Upton to "My Dear Sister," June 1, 1861, Michie, *The Life and Letters of Emory Upton*, 47.
28. *The War of the Rebellion: A Compilation of the Official Records of the Union and Confederate Armies 128 vols., Series I, Vol. 2, Part 5* (Washington, D.C.: United States Government Printing Office, 1880–1901), 314. Hereafter referred to as the *Official Records*. Unless otherwise noted, all citations are to Series I.
29. Emory Upton to "My Dear Sister," June 6, 1861, Michie, *The Life and Letters of Emory Upton*, 46–48.
30. *New York Tribune*, June 25, 1861.
31. Furguson, *Freedom Rising*, 116.
32. William Howard Russell, "Recollections of the Civil War, Part IV," *North American Review*, May 1898, 620.
33. Emory Upton to "My Dear Sister," July 1, 1861, Emory Upton Letters, Holland Land Office Museum.
34. Emory Upton to "My Dear Sister," July 9, 1861, *ibid.*
35. Testimony of General Irvin McDowell to the Joint Committee on the Conduct of the War, December 26, 1861, *Report of the Joint Committee on the Conduct of the War* (Washington, D.C.: Government Printing Office, 1863), 45.
36. *Ibid.*
37. Thomas L. Livermore, *Numbers and Losses in the Civil War in America 1861–65* (New York: Houghton, Mifflin and Company, 1901), 77.
38. *Official Records, Volume 2, Part 3*, 310.
39. *Ibid.*, 310–311; Michie, *The Life and Letters of Emory Upton*, 53.
40. *Official Records, Volume 2, Part 3*, 311–312.
41. *Ibid.*, 348.
42. *Ibid.*; Emory Upton to "My Dear Sister," November 25, 1861, Michie, *The Life and Letters of Emory Upton*, 54.
43. *Ibid.*
44. *Ibid.*
45. *Official Records, Volume 2, Part 3*, 350.
46. Emory Upton to "My Dear Sister," July 22, 1861, Michie, *The Life and Letters of Emory Upton*, 53.
47. *Official Records, Volume 2, Part 3*, 351.
48. "Address by Major General William D. Belknap," *War Sketches and Incidents as Related by the Iowa Commandery, Military Order of the Loyal Legion of the United States, Volume I* (Des Moines, Iowa: Press of P.C. Kenyon, 1893). 159.

Chapter 3

1. *Official Records, Volume 11, Part 2*, 434–435.
2. Emory Upton to "My Dear Sister," October 4, 1861, Emory Upton Letters, Holland Land Office Museum.
3. Michie, *The Life and Letters of Emory Upton*, 55.
4. *Official Records, Volume 2, Part 3*, 405, 416.
5. "Artillery in the Civil War," *U.S. Army Ordnance Corps and School Staff Ride Materials-Gettysburg*, 21, http://www.goordnance.army.mil/history/staff_ride.html, accessed June 2, 2016.
6. *Ibid.*, 19.
7. *Ibid.*
8. Emory Upton to "My Dear Sister," September 30, 1861, Michie, *The Life and Letters of Emory Upton*, 57.
9. Emory Upton to "My Dear Sister," November 13, 1861, Michie, *The Life and Letters of Emory Upton*, 58.
10. Emory Upton to "My Dear Sister," November 18, 1861, Holland Land Office Museum.
11. Emory Upton to General L. Thomas, Adjutant General, War Department, November 6, 1861, National Archives, *Letters received by the Adjutant General's Office, 1860-70, during and after the Civil War period*, Roll 065, File U042.
12. *Official Records, Volume 11, Part 1*, 611.
13. *Ibid.*, 615.
14. *Ibid.*, 611.
15. *Ibid.*, 611–612, 619.
16. Alfred Davenport, *Camp and Field Life: Fifth New York Volunteer Infantry (Duryee Zouaves)* (New York: Dick and Fitzgerald, 1879), 203.
17. *Official Records, Volume 11, Part 1*, 224.
18. *Ibid.*
19. *Ibid.*, 432.
20. *Map of Battle of Gaines Mill, VA, June 27, 1862, 4:00 to 4:30 P.M.*, Civil War Trust, http://www.civilwar.org/battlefields/gainesmill/maps/gaines-mill-june-27-1862.html, accessed May 31, 2016.
21. Davenport, *Camp and Field Life*, 208.
22. *Ibid.*, 209.
23. *Ibid.*, 220.
24. *Official Records, Volume 11, Part 1*, 40.
25. George T. Stevens, *Three Years in the Sixth Corps: A Concise Narrative of Events in the Army of the Potomac from 1861 to the Close of the Rebellion, April, 1865* (New York: D. Van Nostrand, Publisher, 1870), 89.
26. *Ibid.*, 95.
27. *Ibid.*
28. *Ibid.*, 96.
29. Davenport, *Camp and Field Life*, 240.
30. *Official Records, Volume 11, Part 2*, 434–435.
31. *Ibid.*, 435.
32. *Ibid.*
33. *Ibid.*
34. Stevens, *Three Years in the Sixth Corps*, 106.
35. *Ibid.*, 106–107.
36. Rhodes, ed., *All for the Union*, 65.
37. Stevens, *Three Years in the Sixth Corps*, 109.
38. Emory Upton to President Abraham Lincoln, September 26, 1862, National Archives.

39. *Ibid.*, 124.
40. Emory Upton to President Abraham Lincoln, September 26, 1862, National Archives.

Chapter 4

1. Emory Upton to "My Dear Sister," September 27, 1862, Michie, *The Life and Letters of Emory Upton*, 63.
2. *Official Records, Volume 19, Part 1*, 176.
3. Stevens, *Three Years in the Sixth Corps*, 134.
4. *Ibid.*
5. *Ibid.*, 135.
6. *Ibid.*
7. *Ibid.*, 136.
8. *Ibid.*, 137.
9. *Official Records, Volume 19, Part 1*, 380–381.
10. Stevens, *Three Years in the Sixth Corps*, 138.
11. Daniel M. Holt, M.D., James M. Greiner, Janet L. Coryell, and James R. Smither, eds., *A Surgeon's Civil War: The Letters and Diary of Daniel M. Holt, M.D.* (Kent: Kent State University Press, 1994), 20.
12. Stevens, *Three Years in the Sixth Corps*, 138.
13. *Official Records, Volume 51, Part 2*, 618.
14. *Official Records, Volume 19, Part 2*, 610.
15. *Official Records, Volume 19, Part 1*, 140.
16. Stevens, *Three Years in the Sixth Corps*, 140–141.
17. *Ibid.*, 142.
18. Emory Upton to "My Dear Sister," September 27, 1862, Michie, *The Life and Letters of Emory Upton*, 63.
19. *Official Records, Volume 19, Part 1*, 409.
20. *Ibid.*
21. Emory Upton to "My Dear Sister," September 27, 1862, Michie, *The Life and Letters of Emory Upton*, 63.
22. *Ibid.*, 64.
23. Holt, *A Surgeon's Civil War*, 28.
24. Stevens, *Three Years in the Sixth Corps*, 153.
25. Emory Upton to "My Dear Sister," September 27, 1862, Michie, *The Life and Letters of Emory Upton*, 63.
26. *Official Records, Volume 19, Part 1*, 410.
27. *Ibid.*, 176.

Chapter 5

1. Isaac O. Best, *History of the 121st New York State Infantry* (Chicago: Jas. H. Smith, 1921), 29.
2. *Ibid.*, 1–5.
3. *Official Records, Volume 21, Part 1*, 524–525.
4. James M. McPherson, *What They Fought For: 1861–1865* (Baton Rouge: Louisiana State University Press, 1994), 27–28.
5. John Rozier, ed., *The Granite Farm Letters: The Civil War Correspondence of Edgeworth and Sallie Bird* (Athens: University of Georgia Press, 1988), 145.
6. Best, *History of the 121st New York*, 6.
7. *Ibid.*, 9.
8. *Ibid.*, 24–26.
9. *Ibid.*, 28.
10. Ambrose, *Upton and the Army*, Kindle Location 304.
11. Best, *History of the 121st New York*, 30–31.
12. Michie, *The Life and Letters of Emory Upton*, 68.
13. Best, *History of the 121st New York*, 29.
14. James M. Greiner, *Subdued by the Sword: A Line Officer in the 121st New York Volunteers* (Albany: State University of New York Press, 2003), 16.
15. Holt, *A Surgeon's Civil War*, Kindle Location 687–690.
16. Greiner, *Subdued by the Sword*, 16.
17. Best, *History of the 121st New York*, 26.
18. Michie, *The Life and Letters of Emory Upton*, 69.
19. Holt, *A Surgeon's Civil War*, Kindle Location 819–820.
20. *Ibid.*, Kindle Location 731–733.
21. Best, *History of the 121st New York*.
22. *Ibid.*, 31.
23. Greiner, *Subdued by the Sword*, 21; Best, *History of the 121st New York*, 33.
24. Greiner, *Subdued by the Sword*, 21.
25. Best, *History of the 121st New York*, 34.
26. Greiner, *Subdued by the Sword*, 79.
27. Best, *History of the 121st New York*, 36.
28. Greiner, *Subdued by the Sword*, 24.
29. *Ibid.*
30. *Ibid.*, 35.
31. Emory Upton to "My Dear Sister," December 7, 1862, Michie, *The Life and Letters of Emory Upton*, 70–71.
32. Best, *History of the 121st New York*, 34.
33. Greiner, *Subdued by the Sword*, 30.
34. *Ibid.*, 27.
35. Best, *History of the 121st New York*, 39.
36. *Ibid.*, 38.
37. Greiner, *Subdued by the Sword*, 27–28.
38. Best, *History of the 121st New York*, 41.
39. Greiner, *Subdued by the Sword*, 27.
40. Best, *History of the 121st New York*, 42; Greiner, *Subdued by the Sword*, 27.
41. Greiner, *Subdued by the Sword*, 28.
42. *Ibid.*
43. Best, *History of the 121st New York*, 46.
44. *Ibid.*, 48–49; Greiner, *Subdued by the Sword*, 30.
45. Emory Upton to Emily Upton, December 15, 1868, Throop and Martin Family Papers, Princeton University.
46. Best, *History of the 121st New York*, 50–51.
47. Greiner, *Subdued by the Sword*, 35.
48. *Ibid.*
49. *Ibid.*, 35–36.
50. *Ibid.*, 36.
51. Holt, *A Surgeon's Civil War*, Kindle Location 1105–1106. "French leave" is a term for desertion that dates back to the American revolution.
52. Best, *History of the 121st New York*, 52–53.
53. *Ibid.*, 53.
54. *Ibid.*
55. *Ibid.*, Kindle Location 1517–1518.
56. Greiner, *Subdued by the Sword*, 39.
57. Holt, *A Surgeon's Civil War*, Kindle Location 1104–1105.
58. *Ibid.*, Kindle Location 132–1337.
59. *Ibid.*
60. Best, *History of the 121st New York*, 29.
61. Greiner, *Subdued by the Sword*, 33.

62. Holt, *A Surgeon's Civil War*, Kindle Location 1422–1423.
63. Ibid.
64. Emory Upton to Dr. Bradley, medical director, 6th Corps, Nov. 15, 1862, Regimental Books, 121st New York Infantry Regiment., Record Group 94, National Archives.
65. Ibid., Kindle Location 1598.
66. Best, *History of the 121st New York*, 51.
67. Ibid.
68. Ibid.
69. Grant, *Personal Memoirs*, 657.
70. Best, *History of the 121st New York*, 54–55.
71. Greiner, *Subdued by the Sword*, 44.
72. Regimental Day Books of the 121st New York Volunteers, 5 April 1863, cited in Greiner, *Subdued by the Sword*, 46.
73. Greiner, *Subdued by the Sword*, 46.
74. Best, *History of the 121st New York*, 59–60.
75. Ibid., 60.
76. Best, *History of the 121st New York*, 67; *Official Records*, Vol XXV, Part 1, 589.
77. Best, *History of the 121st New York*, 68; *Official Records*, Vol XXV, Part 1, 589.
78. *Official Records*, Vol XXV, Part 1, 581, 589.
79. Best, *History of the 121st New York*, 68.
80. Ibid., 69.
81. Ibid.
82. Ambrose, *Upton and the Army*, Kindle Location 352–353.
83. Greiner, *Subdued by the Sword*, 49.
84. Ibid., 52.
85. Ibid., 53.
86. *Official Records*, Vol XXV, Part 1, 583.
87. Ibid., 590.
88. Ibid., 589.
89. Holt, *A Surgeon's Civil War*, Kindle Location 2122.
90. Ibid., Kindle Location 1941–1946.
91. Michie, *The Life and Letters of Emory Upton*, 75.
92. Holt, *A Surgeon's Civil War*, Kindle Location 2065.
93. Ambrose, *Upton and the Army*, Kindle Location 355–358.
94. Greiner, *Subdued by the Sword*, 58.
95. Ibid.
96. Ibid.
97. Best, *History of the 121st New York*, 76.
98. Ibid. 77.
99. Greiner, *Subdued by the Sword*, 59.
100. Ibid.
101. Ibid., 60.
102. Ibid.
103. Ibid., 61.

Chapter 6

1. *Official Records*, Volume XXIX, Part 1, 596.
2. *Official Records*, Volume XXVII, Part 3, 859.
3. *Official Records*, Volume XXVII, Part 1, 29.
4. Best, *History of the 121st New York*, 84.
5. *Official Records*, Volume XXVII, Part 1, 38.
6. Best, *History of the 121st New York*, 85.
7. Ibid.
8. Best, *History of the 121st New York*, 85.
9. Greiner, *Subdued by the Sword*, 64.
10. Ibid.
11. Best, *History of the 121st New York*, 86–87; Greiner, *Subdued by the Sword*, 64–65; Ambrose, *Upton and the Army*, Kindle Location 372–373.
12. Best, *History of the 121st New York*, 87; Greiner, *Subdued by the Sword*, 65.
13. Greiner, *Subdued by the Sword*, 65.
14. *Official Records*, Volume XXVII, Part 3, 467.
15. Emory Upton to "My Dear Sister," July 4, 1863, Michie, *The Life and Letters of Emory Upton*, 75.
16. Best, *History of the 121st New York*, 88.
17. Ibid.
18. Ibid.
19. Emory Upton to "My Dear Sister," November 6, 1863, Michie, *The Life and Letters of Emory Upton*, 80–81.
20. Emory Upton to "My Dear Sister," July 4, 1863, Michie, *The Life and Letters of Emory Upton*, 75.
21. Holt, *A Surgeon's Civil War*, Kindle Location 2548–2552.
22. Best, *History of the 121st New York*, 90.
23. *Official Records*, Volume XXVII, Part 3, 672.
24. Best, *History of the 121st New York*, 91.
25. *Official Records*, Volume XXVII, Part 3, 672.
26. Greiner, *Subdued by the Sword*, 79.
27. Holt, *A Surgeon's Civil War*, Kindle Location 2647–2653.
28. Greiner, *Subdued by the Sword*, 80.
29. Ibid., 81.
30. Ibid., 82.
31. Emory Upton to "My Dear Sister," November 6, 1863, Michie, *The Life and Letters of Emory Upton*, 79.
32. Ibid., 80.
33. G. Norton Galloway, *The Ninety-fifth Pennsylvania Volunteers ("Gosline's Pennsylvania Zouaves") in the Sixth Corps* (Philadelphia: Collins, 1884), 31.
34. Ambrose, *Upton and the Army*, Kindle Location 384–386.
35. George W. Bicknell, *History of the Fifth Maine Volunteers, Comprising Brief Descriptions of Its Marches, Engagements, and General Services from the Date of Its Muster In, June 24, 1861, to the Tome of Its Muster Out, July 27, 1864* (Portland, Maine: Hall L. Davis, 1871), 261.
36. Ibid., 262.
37. Ibid.
38. Ibid., 263.
39. Best, *History of the 121st New York*, 99; Bicknell, *Fifth Maine Volunteers*, 263.
40. Bicknell, *Fifth Maine Volunteers*, 263.
41. Emory Upton to "My Dear Sister," November 15, 1863, Michie, *The Life and Letters of Emory Upton*, 83.
42. Bicknell, *Fifth Maine Volunteers*, 264.
43. Emory Upton to "My Dear Sister," November 15, 1863, Michie, *The Life and Letters of Emory Upton*, 83–84.
44. Ibid., 84.
45. Bicknell, *Fifth Maine Volunteers*, 267.
46. Ibid.
47. Best, *History of the 121st New York*, 101.

48. Emory Upton to "My Dear Sister," November 15, 1863, Michie, *The Life and Letters of Emory Upton*, 85; Best, *History of the 121st New York*, 101.
49. Bicknell, *Fifth Maine Volunteers*, 268.
50. Ambrose, *Upton and the Army*, Kindle Location 464–469.
51. Best, *History of the 121st New York*, 102.
52. Bicknell, *Fifth Maine Volunteers*, 269–270.
53. Ibid.
54. Emory Upton to "My Dear Sister," November 15, 1863, Michie, *The Life and Letters of Emory Upton*, 85.
55. Ibid.

Chapter 7

1. Emory Upton to "My Dear Sister," June 5, 1864, Michie, *The Life and Letters of Emory Upton*, 109.
2. General William Bartlett to Major General Henry Halleck, September 21, 1863, *Letters Received by the Office of the Adjutant General, Main Series, 1861–1870* (Washington, D.C.: National Archives and Records Administration, 1970).
3. Major General Robert Schenk to President Abraham Lincoln, September 17, 1863, *Letters Received by the Office of the Adjutant General*.
4. Major General Daniel Butterfield to Secretary of War Edwin Stanton, September 18, 1863, *Letters Received by the Office of the Adjutant General*.
5. Twelve Michigan Officers to Governor Edward Morgan, April 14, 1864, *Letters Received by the Office of the Adjutant General*; Governor Edward Morgan to President Abraham Lincoln, April 19, 1864, *Letters Received by the Office of the Adjutant General*.
6. Emory Upton to "My Dear Sister," April 10, 1864, Michie, *The Life and Letters of Emory Upton*, 88.
7. Emory Upton to "My Dear Sister," April 18, 1864, Michie, *The Life and Letters of Emory Upton*, 89.
8. Emory Upton to "My Dear Sister," April 25, 1864, Michie, *The Life and Letters of Emory Upton*, 90.
9. Ibid.
10. John H. Brinton, *Personal Memoirs of John H. Brinton, Major and Surgeon U.S.A., 1861–1865* (New York: The Neale Publishing Company, 1914), 239.
11. Grant, *Personal Memoirs*, 411.
12. Emory Upton to "My Dear Sister," April 10, 1864, Michie, *The Life and Letters of Emory Upton*, 89.
13. Emory Upton to "My Dear Sister," April 18, 1864, Michie, *The Life and Letters of Emory Upton*, 89.
14. Emory Upton to "My Dear Sister," April 25, 1864, Michie, *The Life and Letters of Emory Upton*, 91.
15. Ulysses S. Grant, John Y. Simon, ed., *The Papers of Ulysses S. Grant: January 1–May 31, 1864, Vol. 10* (Carbondale: Southern Illinois University Press, 1982), 274.
16. Horace Porter, *Campaigning with Grant* (Lincoln: University of Nebraska Press, 2000), 36–37.
17. *Official Records*, Volume XXXVI, Part 2, 333–334.
18. Lemuel Abijah Abbott, *Personal Recollections and Civil War Diary 1864* (Burlington, Vermont: Free Press Printing Company, 1908), 42.
19. Stevens, *Three Years in the Sixth*, 303.
20. Frank Wilkeson, *Turned Inside Out: Recollections of a Private Soldier in the Army of the Potomac* (Lincoln: University of Nebraska Press, 1997), 46.
21. *Official Records*, Volume XXXVI, Part 2, 370.
22. *Official Records*, Volume XXXVI, Part 1, 665.
23. Ibid.
24. Ibid.
25. Bicknell, *History of the Fifth Maine*, 304.
26. *Official Records*, Volume XXXVI, Part 1, 665.
27. Wilkeson, *Turned Inside Out*, 66.
28. Ibid., 67.
29. Porter, *Campaigning with Grant*, 72–73.
30. Best, *History of the 121st New York*, 121.
31. *Official Records*, Volume XXXVI, Part 1, 666.
32. Best, *History of the 121st New York*, 117.
33. *Official Records*, Volume XXXVI, Part 1, 666.
34. Best, *History of the 121st New York*, 119.
35. *Official Records*, Volume XXXVI, Part 1, 666.
36. Best, *History of the 121st New York*, 119.
37. *Official Records*, Volume XXXVI, Part 1, 666; Ambrose, *Upton and the Army*, Kindle Location 440–443.
38. *Official Records*, Volume XXXVI, Part 2, 481.
39. Porter, *Campaigning with Grant*, 72.
40. *Official Records*, Volume XXXVI, Part 2, 526.

Chapter 8

1. Best, *History of the 121st New York*, 136.
2. *Official Records*, Volume XXXVI, Part 1, 666.
3. Grant, *The Papers of Ulysses S. Grant*, 463.
4. Warren Lee Goss, *Recollections of a Private: A Story of the Army of the Potomac* (Scituate, Massachusetts: Digital Scanning, Inc., 2002), 280–281.
5. Bicknell, *History of the Fifth Maine*, 307.
6. *Official Records*, Volume XXXVI, Part 1, 667.
7. Porter, *Campaigning with Grant*, 90.
8. Greiner, *Subdued by the Sword*, 119.
9. Best, *History of the 121st New York*, 134–135.
10. Ibid., 135.
11. Ibid., 136
12. Ibid.
13. *Official Records*, Volume XXXVI, Part 1, 667.
14. Ibid.
15. Bruce Catton, *A Stillness at Appomattox* (New York: Anchor Books/Doubleday, 1953), 113.
16. *Official Records*, Volume XXXVI, Part 1, 667.
17. Ibid.
18. Emory Upton to Adam Badeau, December 26, 1873, Library of Congress, Washington, D.C.
19. Ibid.
20. *Official Records*, Volume XXXVI, Part 1, 667; Catton, *A Stillness at Appomattox*, 113.
21. *Official Records*, Volume XXXVI, Part 1, 667.
22. Ibid., 667–668.
23. Best, *History of the 121st New York*, 128–129.
24. Ibid., 129.
25. Ibid.
26. *Official Records*, Volume XXXVI, Part 1, 668; Greiner, *Subdued by the Sword*, 122–123; Best, *History of the 121st New York*, 129.
27. Greiner, *Subdued by the Sword*, 123.

28. Galloway, *The Ninety-fifth Pennsylvania Volunteers*, 32.
29. Best, *History of the 121st New York*, 130.
30. Greiner, *Subdued by the Sword*, 123.
31. *Official Records*, Volume XXXVI, Part 1, 668.
32. Greiner, *Subdued by the Sword*, 123.
33. Best, *History of the 121st New York*, 128–129.
34. *Ibid.*
35. *Official Records*, Volume XXXVI, Part 1, 668.
36. Charles H. Banes, *History of the Philadelphia Brigade* (Philadelphia: J.P. Lippincott & Co., 1876), 243.
37. *Ibid.*, 244.
38. *Official Records*, Volume XXXVI, Part 1, 668.
39. Greiner, *Subdued by the Sword*, 124.
40. Best, *History of the 121st New York*, 131.
41. *Ibid.*
42. *Ibid.*, 132.
43. *Official Records*, Volume XXXVI, Part 1, 668; Best, *History of the 121st New York*, 132.
44. *Official Records*, Volume XXXVI, Part 1, 668.
45. Bicknell, *History of the Fifth Maine*, 315–316.
46. *Official Records*, Volume XXXVI, Part 1, 668–669.
47. Best, *History of the 121st New York*, 133.
48. *Ibid.*, 137.
49. G. Norton Galloway, "Hand-to-Hand Fighting at Spotsylvania," *Battles and Leaders of the Civil War, Vol. 4* (New York: The Century Company, 1884), 171.
50. Best, *History of the 121st New York*, 141.
51. *Ibid.*
52. *Ibid.*
53. *Official Records*, Volume XXXVI, Part 1, 669.
54. *Ibid.*
55. Galloway, "Hand-to-Hand Fighting at Spotsylvania," 171.
56. *Ibid.*
57. *Official Records*, Volume XXXVI, Part 1, 669.
58. Galloway, "Hand-to-Hand Fighting at Spotsylvania," 171.
59. Best, *History of the 121st New York*, 144; *Official Records*, Volume XXXVI, Part 1, 669.
60. Galloway, "Hand-to-Hand Fighting at Spotsylvania," 171.
61. *Ibid.*
62. *Ibid.*, 172.
63. Best, *History of the 121st New York*, 145.
64. Galloway, "Hand-to-Hand Fighting at Spotsylvania," 172.
65. Best, *History of the 121st New York*, 146.
66. Galloway, "Hand-to-Hand Fighting at Spotsylvania," 172.
67. *Ibid.*
68. Best, *History of the 121st New York*, 143. The remains of this tree can now be seen in the Smithsonian Institute's Museum of American History.
69. *Official Records*, Volume XXXVI, Part 1, 669.
70. Galloway, "Hand-to-Hand Fighting at Spotsylvania," 174.
71. Best, *History of the 121st New York*, 147.
72. *Ibid.*
73. Porter, *Campaigning with Grant*, 110.
74. Galloway, "Hand-to-Hand Fighting at Spotsylvania," 174.
75. *Official Records*, Volume XXXVI, Part 2, 698.
76. *Ibid.*, 695.
77. *Ibid.*, 746.
78. Emory Upton to "My Dear Sister," June 7, 1863, Michie, *The Life and Letters of Emory Upton*, 116.
79. Best, *History of the 121st New York*, 149–15.
80. Bicknell, *History of the Fifth Maine*, 324.
81. Best, *History of the 121st New York*, 150.
82. *Ibid.*
83. *Official Records*, Volume XXXVI, Part 1, 7.

Chapter 9

1. Emory Upton to "My Dear Sister," June 5, 1864, Michie, *The Life and Letters of Emory Upton*, 109.
2. *Official Records*, Volume XXXVI, Part 1, 670.
3. Frederick H. Dyer, *A Compendium of the War of the Rebellion Compiled and Arranged from Official Records of the Federal and Confederate Armies, Reports of the Adjutant Generals of the Several States, the Army Registers and Other Reliable Documents and Sources*, Part 1 (Des Moines, Iowa: The Dyer Publishing Company, 1908), 114.
4. Dudley Landon Vaill, *The County Regiment* (Litchfield, Connecticut: The Litchfield University Club, 1908), 35.
5. *Official Records*, Vol XXXVI, Part 2, 883–896.
6. Best, *History of the 121st New York*, 152, 121.
7. *Official Records*, Volume XXXVI, Part 1, 670.
8. Best, *History of the 121st New York*, 153.
9. *Official Records*, Volume XXXVI, Part 1, 671.
10. *Ibid.*
11. Porter, *Campaigning with Grant*, 161.
12. Grant, *Memoirs of U.S. Grant*, 495.
13. *Official Records*, Vol XXXVI, Part 3, 469.
14. Stevens, *Three Years in the Sixth Corps*, 350.
15. Theodore Lyman, *Meade's Headquarters, 1863–1865: Letters of Colonel Theodore Lyman from the Wilderness to Appomattox*, ed. George R. Agassiz (Freeport, New York: Books for Libraries Press, 1922), 136.
16. *Official Records*, Volume XXXVI, Part 1, 671.
17. Vaill, *The County Regiment*, 29.
18. William Farrar Smith, "The Eighteenth Corps at Cold Harbor," *Battles and Leaders of the Civil War, Vol. IV* (New York: The Century Company, 1888), 222–223.
19. Vaill, *The County Regiment*, 30.
20. *Official Records*, Volume XXXVI, Part 1, 671.
21. Vaill, *The County Regiment*, 30.
22. Best, *History of the 121st New York*, 153.
23. *Official Records*, Volume XXXVI, Part 1, 671.
24. Vaill, *The County Regiment*, 30.
25. Best, *History of the 121st New York*, 153; Vaill, *The County Regiment*, 30.
26. *Official Records*, Volume XXXVI, Part 1, 671.
27. Vaill, *The County Regiment*, 31.
28. *Ibid.*
29. *Ibid.*, 32.
30. *Ibid.*, 32–33.
31. *Ibid.*, 33–34.
32. Best, *History of the 121st New York*, 155.
33. Martin McMahon, "Cold Harbor," *Battles and Leaders of the Civil War, Vol. IV* (New York: The Century Company, 1884, 1888), 218–219.

34. *Official Records,* Volume XXXVI, Part 1, 671.
35. Emory Upton to "My Dear Sister," June 5, 1864, Michie, *The Life and Letters of Emory Upton,* 109.
36. Porter, *Campaigning with Grant,* 37.
37. George Gordon Meade, ed., *The Life and Letters of George Gordon Meade, Major-General United States Army* (New York: Charles Scribner and Sons, 1913), 200.
38. Porter, *Campaigning with Grant,* 114–116.
39. Lyman, *Meade's Headquarters,* 126.
40. *Official Records,* Volume XXXVI, Part 1, 481.
41. *Ibid.,* 1002.
42. Charles James Calrow, *Cold Harbor: A Study of the Operations of the Army of Northern Virginia and the Army of the Potomac from May 26th to June 13th, 1864* (unpublished typescript, completed in 1933 by a former operations officer in the U.S. First Army in World War I. Richmond National Battlefield Park), 174–175.
43. Evander M. Law, "From the Wilderness to Cold Harbor," *Battles and Leaders of the Civil War, Vol. IV* (New York: The Century Company, 1884, 1888), 141.
44. Best, *History of the 121st New York,* 163–164.
45. *Official Records,* Vol XXXVI, Part 1, 345.
46. Lyman, *Meade's Headquarters,* 148.
47. Best, *History of the 121st New York,* 158.
48. *Ibid.,* 158–159.
49. Porter, *Campaigning with Grant,* 179.
50. Emory Upton to "My Dear Sister," June 4, 1864, Michie, *The Life and Letters of Emory Upton,* 108.
51. Emory Upton to "My Dear Sister," June 5, 1864, Michie, *The Life and Letters of Emory Upton,* 109.
52. Emory Upton to "My Dear Sister," June 18, 1864, Michie, *The Life and Letters of Emory Upton,* 117.

Chapter 10

1. Emory Upton to "My Dear Sister," August 9, 1864, Michie, *The Life and Letters of Emory Upton,* 122.
2. *Official Records,* Volume XXXVII, Part 1, 769.
3. John B. Gordon, *Reminiscences of the Civil War* (New York: C. Scribner's Sons, 1903), 317.
4. *Ibid.*
5. *Official Records,* Volume XL, Part 3, 31.
6. *Ibid.,* 94.
7. *Official Records,* Volume XL, Part 1, 492.
8. Best, *History of the 121st New York,* 169–170.
9. *Ibid.,* 170.
10. *Ibid.*
11. *Ibid.,* 171.
12. *Ibid.*
13. *Ibid.*
14. *Ibid.*
15. Emory Upton to "My Dear Sister," July 19, 1864, Michie, *The Life and Letters of Emory Upton,* 121–122.
16. Emory Upton to "My Dear Sister," August 9, 1864, Michie, *The Life and Letters of Emory Upton,* 122.
17. *Official Records,* Volume XLIII, Part 1, 698.
18. *Ibid.*
19. *Official Records,* Volume XLIII, Part 1, 875–876.
20. Emory Upton to "My Dear Sister," August 24, 1864, Michie, *The Life and Letters of Emory Upton,* 122–123.
21. *Official Records,* Volume XLIII, Part 1, 173.
22. Best, *History of the 121st New York,* 179–180.
23. *Official Records,* Volume XLIII, Part 1, 173; Best, Best, *History of the 121st New York,* 180.
24. H.A. Du Pont, *The Campaign of 1864 in the Valley of Virginia and the Expedition to Lynchburg* (New York: National Americana Society, 1925), 110.
25. *Official Records,* Volume XLIII, Part 1, 173.
26. *Ibid.;* Best, *History of the 121st New York,* 180.
27. Best, *History of the 121st New York,* 181.
28. Emory Upton quoted in Du Pont, *Campaign of 1864,* 115.
29. Best, *History of the 121st New York,* 181.
30. *Ibid.*
31. Theodore F. Vaiil, *The History of the Second Connecticut Volunteer Heavy Artillery* (Winsted, Connecticut: The Winsted Printing Company, 1868), 95.
32. *Official Records,* Vol. XLIII, Part 1, 54.
33. Du Pont, *Campaign of 1864,* 115.
34. *Ibid.,* 173–174.
35. *Ibid.,* 164.
36. *Ibid.*
37. Ambrose, *Upton and the Army,* Kindle Location 613–615.
38. *Official Records,* Volume XLIII, Part 1, 162; Ambrose, *Upton and the Army,* Kindle Location 619–620.
39. *Official Records,* Volume XLIII, Part 1, 162.
40. *Ibid.,* 162–163.
41. Michie, *Life and Letters of Emory Upton,* xxiii.
42. *Ibid.,* xxiii–xiv.
43. *Ibid.,* 129; *Official Records,* Volume XLIII, Part 1, 199.
44. Emory Upton to "My Dear Sister," September 2, 1864, Michie, *The Life and Letters of Emory Upton,* 123.
45. *Ibid.*
46. *Official Records,* Volume XLIII, Part 1, 637.
47. Michie, *The Life and Letters of Emory Upton,* xxiv.
48. *Official Records,* Volume XLIII, Part 1, 701.

Chapter 11

1. E.N. Gilpin, *The Last Campaign: A Cavalryman's Journal* (Leavenworth, Kansas: Press of Ketcheson Printing Co., 1908), 636.
2. Ambrose, *Upton and the Army,* Kindle Location 648–651.
3. Gilpin, *The Last Campaign,* 625.
4. Michie, *The Life and Letters of Emory Upton,* xv.
5. *Ibid.*
6. *Official Records,* Volume XLIX, Part I, 799.
7. *Ibid.*
8. William Forse Scott, *The Story of a Cavalry Regiment: The Career of the Fourth Iowa Veteran Volunteers from Kansas to Georgia, 1861–1865* (New York: G.P. Putnam's Sons, 1893), 357.
9. *Ibid.*
10. *Ibid.*
11. James Harrison Wilson, *Under the Old Flag: Recollections of Military Operations in the War for the Union, the Spanish War, the Boxer Rebellion, Etc., Vol. II* (New York: D. Appleton and Co., 1912), 164.

12. Scott, *The Story of a Cavalry Regiment*, 369.
13. Gilpin, *The Last Campaign*, 618–619.
14. Scott, *The Story of a Cavalry Regiment*, 369.
15. *Ibid.*, 370.
16. James Pickett Jones, *Yankee Blitzkrieg: Wilson's Raid through Alabama and Georgia* (Lexington: University of Kentucky Press, 1976), Kindle Edition, Kindle Locations 95–96.
17. *Ibid.*, Kindle Locations 256–257.
18. Scott, *The Story of a Cavalry Regiment*, 369.
19. *Ibid.*, 371.
20. *Ibid.*
21. Wilson, *Under the Old Flag*, Volume II, 160–162.
22. Scott, *The Story of a Cavalry Regiment*, 369.
23. *Ibid.*, 408–409.
24. *Ibid.*
25. *Ibid.*, 426.
26. *Ibid.*, 427.
27. *Ibid.*
28. *Ibid.*, 427–428.
29. *Official Records*, Volume XLIX, Part 1, 354; Wilson, *Under the Old Flag*, Volume II, 177.
30. Wilson, *Under the Old Flag*, Volume II, 179–180.
31. *Ibid.*, 180–181.
32. *Ibid.*, 181.
33. *Ibid.*, 183; 193–194.
34. *Ibid.*, 192–193.
35. *Ibid.*, 190–191.
36. Gilpin, *The Last Campaign*, 625.
37. *Ibid.*, 623.
38. Emory Upton to "My Dear Sister," March 14, 1865, Michie, *The Life and Letters of Emory Upton*, 137–138.
39. Gilpin, *The Last Campaign*, 621–622.
40. *Ibid.*, 624.
41. *Ibid.*
42. Scott, *The Story of a Cavalry Regiment*, 425–426.
43. *Official Records*, Volume XLIX, Part 1, 356.
44. *Ibid.*, 471; Wilson, *Under the Old Flag*, Volume II, 193.
45. Wilson, *Under the Old Flag*, Volume II, 194.
46. *Official Records*, Volume XLIX, Part 1, 356.
47. *Ibid.*, 472.
48. Scott, *The Story of a Cavalry Regiment*, 428.
49. *Ibid.*
50. *Official Records*, Volume XLIX, Part 1, 472.
51. *Ibid.*
52. Wilson, *Under the Old Flag*, Volume II, 203.
53. J. A. O. Yeoman, "The Wilson Raid Through Northern Alabama and Georgia," W.I. Curry, ed., *Four Years in the Saddle: History of the First Regiment Ohio Volunteer Cavalry* (Columbus, Ohio: Champlin Printing Co., 1898), 215.
54. *Ibid.*
55. Scott, *The Story of a Cavalry Regiment*, 428.
56. *Ibid.*, 429.
57. *Official Records*, Volume XLIX, Part 1, 472.
58. *Ibid.*; Gilpin, *The Last Campaign*, 632.
59. Scott, *The Story of a Cavalry Regiment*, 429–430.
60. Gilpin, *The Last Campaign*, 632.
61. Yeoman, *Four Years in the Saddle*, 216.
62. *Ibid.*
63. Scott, *The Story of a Cavalry Regiment*, 433–434.
64. *Official Records*, Volume XLIX, Part 1, 472; Wilson, *Under the Old Flag*, Volume II, 205.
65. Scott, *The Story of a Cavalry Regiment*, 435; *Official Records*, Volume XLIX, Part 1, 472.
66. *Official Records*, Volume XLIX, Part 1, 472, 350; Wilson, *Under the Old Flag*, Volume II, 207.
67. Yeoman, *Four Years in the Saddle*, 217; *Official Records*, Volume XLIX, Part 1, 472; Wilson, *Under the Old Flag*, Volume II, 208.
68. Yeoman, *Four Years in the Saddle*, 217.
69. Scott, *The Story of a Cavalry Regiment*, 436–437.
70. *Ibid.*, 437.
71. *Ibid.*, 437–439.
72. Wilson, *Under the Old Flag*, Volume II, 213.
73. *Official Records*, Volume XLIX, Part 1, 472; Wilson, *Under the Old Flag*, Volume II, 214–215.
74. Wilson, *Under the Old Flag*, Volume II, -215; Jones, *Yankee Blitzkrieg*, Kindle Location 802–806.
75. Yeoman, "The Wilson Raid Through Northern Alabama and Georgia," W.I. Curry, ed., *Four Years in the Saddle*, 217.
76. *Official Records*, Volume XLIX, Part 1, 350–351.
77. Wilson, *Under the Old Flag*, Volume II, 216.
78. Scott, *The Story of a Cavalry Regiment*, 443.
79. Yeoman, "The Wilson Raid Through Northern Alabama and Georgia," W.I. Curry, ed., *Four Years in the Saddle*, 219.
80. Scott, *The Story of a Cavalry Regiment*, 443.

Chapter 12

1. Wilson, *Under the Old Flag*, 263.
2. *Official Records*, Volume XLIX, Part 1, 473.
3. Scott, *The Story of a Cavalry Regiment*, 434–435.
4. Wilson, *Under the Old Flag*, Volume II, 221.
5. *Ibid.*
6. *Ibid.*, 221–222.
7. *Ibid.*, 222.
8. *Ibid.*
9. Yeoman, "The Wilson Raid Through Northern Alabama and Georgia," W.I. Curry, ed., *Four Years in the Saddle*, 220; Scott, *The Story of a Cavalry Regiment*, 451; Wilson, *Under the Old Flag*, Volume II, 222.
10. Scott, *The Story of a Cavalry Regiment*, 444–445.
11. *Ibid.*, 445.
12. Wilson, *Under the Old Flag*, Volume II, 223.
13. Gilpin, *The Last Campaign*, 638.
14. Wilson, *Under the Old Flag*, Volume II, 223.
15. Scott, *The Story of a Cavalry Regiment*, 445; Wilson, *Under the Old Flag*, Volume II, 223.
16. Gilpin, *The Last Campaign*, 638.
17. Scott, *The Story of a Cavalry Regiment*, 446.
18. *Ibid.*
19. Gilpin, *The Last Campaign*, 638.

20. Scott, *The Story of a Cavalry Regiment*, 447.
21. Ibid., 447–448.
22. Ibid., 448.
23. Gilpin, *The Last Campaign*, 638–639.
24. Scott, *The Story of a Cavalry Regiment*, 449–450.
25. Ibid., 452.
26. Ibid., 452–453.
27. Ibid., 453.
28. Yeoman, "The Wilson Raid Through Northern Alabama and Georgia," W.I. Curry, ed., *Four Years in the Saddle*, 220–221; *Official Records*, Volume XLIX, Part 1, 351.
29. Scott, *The Story of a Cavalry Regiment*, 456–457.
30. Ibid., 457; Wilson, *Under the Old Flag*, Volume II, 230.
31. Gilpin, *The Last Campaign*, 640.
32. *Official Records*, Volume XLIX, Part 1, 351.
33. Ibid.
34. Wilson, *Under the Old Flag*, Volume II, 249.
35. Scott, *The Story of a Cavalry Regiment*, 473.
36. Wilson, *Under the Old Flag*, Volume II, 250.
37. Ibid., 251.
38. *Official Records*, Volume XLIX, Part 1, 473.
39. Wilson, *Under the Old Flag*, Volume II, 254.
40. *Official Records*, Volume XLIX, Part 1, 473.
41. Wilson, *Under the Old Flag*, Volume II, 254.
42. *Official Records*, Volume XLIX, Part 1, 473.
43. Wilson, *Under the Old Flag*, Volume II, 258.
44. Scott, *The Story of a Cavalry Regiment*, 488.
45. Yeoman, "The Wilson Raid Through Northern Alabama and Georgia," W.I. Curry, ed., *Four Years in the Saddle*, 223.
46. Scott, *The Story of a Cavalry Regiment*, 488.
47. Yeoman, "The Wilson Raid Through Northern Alabama and Georgia," W.I. Curry, ed., *Four Years in the Saddle*, 223.
48. Scott, *The Story of a Cavalry Regiment*, 483.
49. Ibid.
50. Ibid., 484–486.
51. Ibid.
52. Scott, *The Story of a Cavalry Regiment*, 483; *Official Records*, Volume XLIX, Part 1, 474.
53. Ibid., 490.
54. Yeoman, "The Wilson Raid Through Northern Alabama and Georgia," W.I. Curry, ed., *Four Years in the Saddle*, 223.
55. Ibid., 223–224.
56. Ibid., 224.
57. Ibid.
58. Gilpin, *The Last Campaign*, 652.
59. Scott, *The Story of a Cavalry Regiment*, 490–491.
60. Ibid., 491.
61. Ibid., 492.
62. Wilson, *Under the Old Flag*, Volume II, 259.
63. E.F. Winslow, "Memoirs of the Civil War," Edward F. Winslow Papers, University of Iowa Library.
64. Wilson, *Under the Old Flag*, Volume II, 259.
65. Ibid., 260.
66. *Official Records*, Volume XLIX, Part 1, 474; Scott, *The Story of a Cavalry Regiment*, 494.
67. Scott, *The Story of a Cavalry Regiment*, 498.
68. Ibid., 494.
69. Wilson, *Under the Old Flag*, Volume II, 261.
70. Scott, The Story of a Cavalry Regiment, 494.
71. Wilson, *Under the Old Flag*, Volume II, 261–262.
72. Scott, The Story of a Cavalry Regiment, 495; Wilson, *Under the Old Flag*, Volume II, 262.
73. Scott, The Story of a Cavalry Regiment, 495; Wilson, *Under the Old Flag*, Volume II, 262.
74. Wilson, *Under the Old Flag*, Volume II, 262; *Official Records*, Volume XLIX, Part 1, 474.
75. Wilson, *Under the Old Flag*, Volume II, 262–263; Scott, *The Story of a Cavalry Regiment*, 496.
76. Scott, *The Story of a Cavalry Regiment*, 496.
77. Ibid., 497.
78. Wilson, *Under the Old Flag*, Volume II, 263; Scott, *The Story of a Cavalry Regiment*, 498.
79. Scott, *The Story of a Cavalry Regiment*, 498.
80. Ibid., 498–499.
81. Ibid., 499–500.
82. Gilpin, *The Last Campaign*, 654.
83. Ibid.
84. Wilson, *Under the Old Flag*, Volume II, 283.
85. *Official Records*, Volume XLIX, Part 1, 478.

Chapter 13

1. Wilson, *Under the Old Flag*, xxvii.
2. Michie, *The Life and Letters of Emory Upton*, 194.
3. David J. Fitzpatrick, *Emory Upton: Misunderstood Reformer* (Norman: University of Oklahoma Press, 2017), Kindle Edition, 95; Michie, *The Life and Letters of Emory Upton*, 245.
4. Michie, *The Life and Letters of Emory Upton*, 219.
5. Ibid., 220–221.
6. Fitzpatrick, *Emory Upton: Misunderstood Reformer*, Kindle Edition, 97.
7. Emily Martin Upton, November 29, 1867, Emily Martin Upton Diary.
8. Michie, *The Life and Letters of Emory Upton*, 229.
9. Ibid., 229–233.
10. Ibid., 233–234.
11. Ibid., 235.
12. Fitzpatrick, *Emory Upton: Misunderstood Reformer*, Kindle Edition, 111.
13. Michie, *The Life and Letters of Emory Upton*, 192–197.
14. Ibid., 205.
15. Emory Upton to William T. Sherman, February 5, 1868, William T. Sherman Papers, Library of Congress, Washington, D.C.
16. Emory Upton to James Wilson, October 27, 1869, James H. Wilson Papers, Library of Congress, Washington, D.C.
17. Ibid.
18. Emory Upton to W. T. Sherman, September 3, 1874, Letters Received by Headquarters of the Army, 1800–1899, RG 108, National Archives.
19. Michie, *The Life and Letters of Emory Upton*, 309.
20. Ibid., 389.

21. Fitzpatrick, *Emory Upton: Misunderstood Reformer*, Kindle Edition, 183–184.
22. Emory Upton to Henry du Pont, January 13, 1878, Henry A. du Pont Papers, Winterthur Manuscripts, Hagley Museum and Library.
23. Emory Upton, *The Armies of Asia And Europe: Embracing Official Reports on the Armies of Japan, China, India, Persia, Italy, Russia, Austria, and Germany, Accompanied by Letters Descriptive of a Journey from Japan to the Caucasus* (New York: D. Appleton and Company, 1878), 323–324.
24. *Ibid.*, 324.
25. *Ibid.*, 327–367.
26. *Ibid.*, 362–363.
27. *Ibid.*, 323.
28. *Ibid.*, 367–369.
29. Emory Upton to James Garfield, October 14 and November 16, 1878, as cited in Fitzpatrick, *Emory Upton: Misunderstood Reformer*, Kindle Edition, 210–211.
30. Michie, *The Life and Letters of Emory Upton*, 468.
31. Fitzpatrick, *Emory Upton: Misunderstood Reformer*, Kindle Edition, 232–233.
32. Emory Upton to "My Dear Sister," September 22, 1880, Michie, *The Life and Letters of Emory Upton*, 484.
33. Fitzpatrick, *Emory Upton: Misunderstood Reformer*, Kindle Edition, 242.
34. Michie, *The Life and Letters of Emory Upton*, 492.
35. Emory Upton to Sara Upton, March 13, 1881. Michie, *The Life and Letters of Emory Upton*, 494.
36. *Ibid.*, 495.
37. *Ibid.*
38. *Ibid.*
39. Fitzpatrick, *Emory Upton: Misunderstood Reformer*, Kindle Edition, 242–243.
40. *Ibid.*, 243.
41. *Ibid.*, 243–244.
42. *Ibid.*, 244.

Bibliography

Abbott, Lemuel Abijah. *Personal Recollections and Civil War Diary 1864*. Free Press Printing Company, Burlington, VT, 1908.

Adams, John R. *History of the Fifth Regiment Maine Volunteers Comprising Brief Descriptions of Its Marches, Engagements, and General Services from the Date of Its Muster In, June 24, 1861, to the Time of Its Muster Out, July 27, 1864*. Hall L. Davis, Portland, ME, 1871.

Ambrose, Stephen. *Upton and the Army*. Louisiana State University Press, Baton Rouge, 1993.

Appointment, Commission, and Personnel File of Emory Upton. War Department, Washington, D.C., 1861.

"Artillery in the Civil War." *U.S. Army Ordnance Corps and School Staff Ride Materials-Gettysburg*, http://www.goordnance.army.mil/history/staff_ride.html, accessed June 2, 2016.

Averell, William Woods. *Ten Years in the Saddle: The Memoir of William Woods Averell, 1851–1862*. Edward K. Eckert and Nicholas J. Amato, eds. Presidio Press, San Rafael, CA, 1978.

Banes, Charles H. *History of the Philadelphia Brigade: Sixty-Ninth, Seventy-First, Seventy-Second, and ne Hundred and Sixth Pennsylvania Volunteers*. J.B. Lippincott & Co., Philadelphia, 1876.

Barry, Rickard. "Emory Upton, Military Genius." *The New York Times*, June 16, 1918.

Belknap, William D. "Address by Major General William D. Belknap." *War Sketches and Incidents as Related by the Iowa Commandery, Military Order of the Loyal Legion of the United States, Volume I*. Press of P.C. Kenyon, Des Moines, IA, 1893.

Best, Isaac O. *History of the 121st New York State Infantry*. Jas. H. Smith, Chicago, 1921.

Bicknell, George W. *History of the Fifth Maine Volunteers, Comprising Brief Descriptions of Its Marches, Engagements, and General Services from the Date of Its Muster In, June 24, 1861, to the Tome of Its Muster Out, July 27, 1864*. Hall L. Davis, Portland, ME, 1871.

Brinton, John H. *Personal Memoirs of John H. Brinton, Major and Surgeon U. S. V., 1861–1865*. The Neale Publishing Company, New York, 1914.

Calrow, Charles James. *Cold Harbor: A Study of the Operations of the Army of Northern Virginia and the Army of the Potomac from May 26th to June 13th, 1864*. Unpublished typescript, completed in 1933 by a former operations officer in the U.S. First Army in World War I. Richmond National Battlefield Park.

Carter, William Harding. "Army Reformers." *The North American Review*, Vol. 208, No. 755, October 1918.

Cassidy, Robert M. "Prophets or Praetorians? The Uptonian Paradox and the Powell Corollary." *Parameters, U.S. Army War College Quarterly, August 2003, Vol. XXXIII, No. 3*. U.S. Army War College, Carlisle, PA, 2003.

Catton, Bruce. *A Stillness at Appomattox*. Anchor Books/Doubleday, New York, 1953.

The Centennial of the United States Military Academy at West Point, New York, 1802–1902, Volume I, Addresses and Histories. Government Printing Office, Washington, D.C., 1904.

Davenport, Alfred. *Camp and Field Life: Fifth New York Volunteer Infantry (Duryee Zouaves)*. Dick and Fitzgerald, New York, 1879.

Day, L.W. *Story of the One Hundred and First Ohio Infantry, A Memorial Volume*. W. M. Bayne Printing Co., Cleveland, OH, 1894.

Du Pont, Henry A. *The Campaign of 1864 in the Valley of Virginia and the Expedition to Lynchburg*. National Americana Society, New York, 1925.

_____. Henry A. du Pont Papers, Winterthur Manuscripts, Hagley Museum and Library.

Dyer, Frederick H. *A Compendium of the War of the Rebellion Compiled and Arranged from Official Records of the Federal and Confederate Armies, Reports of the Adjutant Generals of the Several States, the Army Registers and Other Reliable Documents and Sources*. Dyer Publishing Co., Des Moines, IA, 1908.

Emory Upton Letters, Holland Land Office Museum, Batavia, New York.

Fitzpatrick, David J. *Emory Upton: Misunderstood Reformer*. University of Oklahoma Press, Norman, 2017.

Fletcher, Robert S. *A History of Oberlin College, Vol II*. Oberlin College Press, Oberlin, OH, 1943.

Furgurson, Ernest B. *Freedom Rising: Washington in the Civil War*. Alfred E. Knopf, New York, 2004.

Galloway, G Norton. "Hand-to-Hand Fighting at Spotsylvania." *Battles and Leaders of the Civil War, Vol 4*. The Century Company, New York, 1884.

_____. *The Ninety-fifth Pennsylvania Volunteers ("Gosline's Pennsylvania Zouaves") in the Sixth Corps*. Collins, Philadelphia, 1884.

Gilpin, E.N. *The Last Campaign: A Cavalryman's Journal*. Press of Ketcheson Printing Co., Leavenworth, KS, 1908.

Gordon, John B. *Reminiscences of the Civil War*. C. Scribner's Sons, New York, 1903.

Goss, Warren Lee. *Recollections of a Private: A Story of the Army of the Potomac*. Digital Scanning, Inc., Scituate, MA, 2002.

Grant, Ulysses S. *The Papers of Ulysses S. Grant: January 1–May 31, 1864, Vol. 10,* John Y. Simon, ed. Southern Illinois University Press, Carbondale, 1982.

_____. *Personal Memoirs of U.S. Grant*. University of Nebraska Press, Lincoln, 1996.

Greiner, James M. *Subdued by the Sword: A Line Officer in the 121st New York Volunteers*. State University of New York Press, Albany, 2003.

Holt, Daniel M., M.D. *A Surgeon's Civil War: The Letters and Diary of Daniel M. Holt, M.D.,* James M. Greiner, Janet L. Coryell, and James R. Smither, eds. Kent State University Press, Kent, OH, 1994.

Humphreys, A.A. *The Virginia Campaign of '64 and '65*. Charles Scribner's Sons, New York, 1883.

Jones, James Pickett. *Yankee Blitzkrieg: Wilson's Raid through Alabama and Georgia*. University of Kentucky Press, Lexington, 1976.

Law, Evander M. "From the Wilderness to Cold Harbor." *Battles and Leaders of the Civil War, Vol. IV*. The Century Company, New York, 1888.

Letters Received by Commission Branch, 1874–1894. National Archives, Washington, D.C.

Letters received by the Adjutant General's Office, 1860–70, during and after the Civil War period, National Archives, Washington, D.C.

"The Life of Gen. Emory Upto. *Science*, Vol. 6, No. 144, November 6, 1995. The Science Company, New York, 1885.

Livermore, Thomas L. *Numbers and Losses in the Civil War in America 1861–65*. Houghton, Mifflin and Company, New York, 1901.

Lyman, Theodore. *Meade's Headquarters, 1863–1865: Letters of Colonel Theodore Lyman from the Wilderness to Appomattox,* ed. George R. Agassiz. Books for Libraries Press, Freeport, NY, 1922.

Map of Battle of Gaines Mill, VA, June 27, 1862, 4:00 to 4:30 P.M., Civil War Trust, http://www.civilwar.org/battlefields/gainesmill/maps/gaines-mill-june-27-1862.html, accessed May 31, 2016.

McMahon, Martin. "Cold Harbor." *Battles and Leaders of the Civil War, Vol. IV*. The Century Company, New York, 1888.

McPherson, James M. *What They Fought For: 1861–1865*. Louisiana State University Press, Baton Rouge, 1994.

McWhiney, Grady, and Perry D. Jamieson. *Attack and Die: Civil War Military Tactics and the Southern Heritage*. University of Alabama Press, Tuscaloosa, 1982.

Meade, George Gordon ed. *The Life and Letters of George Gordon Meade, Major-General United States Army*. Charles Scribner and Sons, New York, 1913.

Michie, Peter. *The Life and Letters of Emory Upton*. D. Appleton and Co., New York, 1885.

Montgomery, Frank A. *Reminiscences of a Mississippian in Peace and War*. The Robert Clarke Company Press, Cincinnati, OH, 1901.

Morrison, James L., Jr. *The Best School: West Point 1833–1866*. Kent State University Press, Kent, OH, 1998.

New York Tribune, June 26, 1861.

Official Army Register, 1865. Adjutant General's Office, Washington, D.C., 1865.

Official Register of the Officers and Cadets of the U. S. Military Academy, West Point, New York, June 1857. Department of War, Washington, D.C., 1857.

Official Register of the Officers and Cadets of the U. S. Military Academy, West Point, New York, June 1857. Department of War, Washington, D.C., 1859.

Official Register of the Officers and Cadets of the U. S. Military Academy, West Point, New York, June 1861. Department of War, Washington, D.C., 1861.

Porter, Horace. *Campaigning with Grant*. University of Nebraska Press, Lincoln, 2000.

Rankin, R.C. *History of the Seventh Ohio Volunteer Cavalry*. J.C. Newcomb, Printer, Ripley, OH, 1881.

Regimental Books, 121st New York Infantry Regiment., Record Group 94, National Archives, Washington, D.C.

Report of the Commission Appointed Under the eighth section of the act of Congress of June 21, 1860, to examine into the organization, system of discipline, and course of instruction of the United States Military Academy at West Point, 36th Cong., 2d sess., 1860.

Report of the Ninth Annual Reunion of the Association of the Graduates of the United States Military Academy, June 13, 1878; U.S. Congress, Senate, Misc., Doc. no. 3.

Rhodes, Robert Hunt, ed. *All for the Union: The Civil War Diary and Letters of Elisha Hunt Rhodes*. Vintage Books, New York, 1985.

Robertson, James I., Jr. *Soldiers Blue and Gray*. University of South Carolina Press, Columbia, 1998.

Rozier, John, ed. *The Granite Farm Letters: The Civil War Correspondence of Edgeworth and Sallie Bird*. University of Georgia Press, Athens, 1988.

Russell, William Howard. "Recollections of the Civil War, Part IV." *The North American Review* 166, No. 498, May 1898.

Schaaf, Morris. *The Spirit of Old West Point, 1858–1862*. Houghton, Mifflin and Company, New York, 1907.

Scott, William Forse. *The Story of a Cavalry Regiment: The Career of the Fourth Iowa Veteran Volunteers from Kansas to Georgia, 1861–1865*. G.P. Putnam's Sons, New York, 1893.

Sherman, William T. Papers. Library of Congress, Washington, D.C.

Smith, William Farrar. "The Eighteenth Corps at Cold Harbor." *Battles and Leaders of the Civil War, Vol. IV*. The Century Company, New York, 1888.

Starr, Merritt. "General Emory Upton—His Brothers, His Career." *Oberlin Alumni Magazine,* May 1922.

Stevens, George T. *Three Years in the Sixth Corps: A Concise Narrative of Events in the Army of the Potomac from 1861 to the Close of the Rebellion, April, 1865*. D. Van Nostrand, Publisher, New York, 1870.

Testimony of General Irvin McDowell to the Joint Committee on the Conduct of the War, December 26, 1861. *Report of the Joint Committee on the Conduct of the War*. Government Printing Office, Washington, D.C., 1863.

Thompson, Millet S. *Thirteenth Regiment of New Hampshire Volunteer Infantry in the War of the Rebellion, 1861–1865: A Diary Covering Three Years and a Day*. Houghton, Mifflin and Company, New York, 1888.

Throop and Martin Family Papers, Princeton University.

Upton, Emily Martin. Emily Martin Upton Diary.

Upton, Emory. *The Armies of Asia And Europe: Embracing Official Reports on the Armies of Japan, China, India, Persia, Italy, Russia, Austria, and Germany, Accompanied by Letters Descriptive of a Journey from Japan to the Caucasus.* D. Appleton and Company, New York, 1878.

_____. *Epitome of Upton's Military Policy of the United States.* Government Printing Office, Washington, D.C., 1916.

_____. *A New System of Infantry Tactics, Double and Single Rank.* D. Appleton & Co., New York, 1868.

Vaail, Theodore F. *The History of the Second Connecticut Volunteer Heavy Artillery.* The Winsted Printing Company, Winsted, CT, 1868.

Vaill, Dudley Landon. *The County Regiment.* The Litchfield University Club, Litchfield, CT, 1908.

The War of the Rebellion: A Compilation of the Official Records of the Union and Confederate Armies 128 vols. United States Government Printing Office, Washington, D.C., 1880–1901.

Wilkeson, Frank. *Turned Inside Out: Recollections of a Private Soldier in the Army of the Potomac.* University of Nebraska Press, Lincoln, 1997.

Wilson, James Harrison. *Under the Old Flag: Recollections of Military Operations in the War for the Union, the Spanish War, the Boxer Rebellion, Etc. Vol. II.* D. Appleton and Co., New York, 1912.

Winslow, E.F. "Memoirs of the Civil War." Edward F. Winslow Papers, University of Iowa Library.

Yeoman, J. A. O. "The Wilson Raid Through Northern Alabama and Georgia." W.I. Curry, ed., *Four Years in the Saddle: History of the First Regiment Ohio Volunteer Cavalry.* Champlin Printing Co., Columbus, OH, 1898.

Index

I Corps (Army of the Potomac) 67, 76
II Corps (Army of the Potomac) 57, 69, 77, 87, 101, 102, 105, 108, 115–118, 120–121, 128–129
III Corps (Army of the Potomac) 46, 76
V Corps (Army of the Potomac) 40, 46, 61, 77, 101–104, 106, 108–109, 123
VI Corps (Army of the Potomac) 46, 58, 61, 67, 69, 73, 75–77, 80, 83–85, 88–89, 96, 101–103, 105, 107–109, 116, 124–125, 128–130, 133–135, 139, 162
IX Corps (Army of the Potomac) 101–102, 105, 109
XI Corps (Army of the Potomac) 34, 38, 40–41, 44, 46, 47–48, 51, 53, 56, 58, 77, 85
XVIII Corps (Army of the Shenandoah) 124, 136, 139–140
XIX Corps (Army of the Shenandoah) 136, 137–140
1st Ohio Cavalry Regiment 143, 151–152, 154; at Columbus 163, 165–166; at Ebenezer Church 155
2nd Connecticut Heavy Artillery Regiment 122–124, 138–140; at Cold Harbor 125–127; Origins 122
2nd U.S. Artillery Regiment 34, 48
3rd Iowa Cavalry Regiment 142–143, 153, 157; at Columbus 167–169; at Selma 160
4th Iowa Cavalry Regiment 142–143, 146, 151–153, 156, 162; at Columbus 167–169; at Ebenezer Church 155; at Selma 158–161
5th Maine Infantry Regiment 85, 104; at Rappahannock Station 93–94; at Spotsylvania Court House 110–112, 114, 120
5th Iowa Cavalry Regiment 143, 155; at Columbus 165
7th Ohio Cavalry Regiment 143
10th Missouri Cavalry Regiment 143, 153; at Columbus 167–168; at Selma 160
12th New York Infantry Regiment 24–28
95th Pennsylvania Infantry Regiment 85, 90, 104, 106; at Spotsylvania Court House 115, 117
96th Pennsylvania Infantry Regiment 78–80, 85, 126–127, 133; at Spotsylvania Court House 110–113, 120
121st New York Infantry Regiment 53–54, 60–86, 89, 93–94, 106, 109–115, 118, 120, 123, 126, 133–134, 138; arrival in Maryland 61; Belle Plain Landing camp 65–66; desertion 71–72; discipline issues 70–72; Fredericksburg, Battle of 67–70; Gettysburg Campaign ; health of soldiers 72; Mud March 72–74; Rappahannock Station, Battle of 93–94; recruiting 60; Salem Church, Battle of *see* Salem Church, Battle of; Spotsylvania Court House, Battle of 110–115, 118, 120; training 64

Alexander, Andrew 150, 152, 154–155, 165
Antietam, Battle of 55–59
artillery: ammunition, types of 39, 42; battery size 34; caisson and limber 34, 36; Napoleon cannon 34–35, 42, 58

Bartlett, Joseph 45, 85, 87–89, 96
Beauregard, Pierre 29–32
Beckwith, Charles 71, 87, 112, 114, 118, 134
Best, Isaac O. 60, 64, 66–67, 72, 74
Buford, John 85
Burnside, Ambrose 66, 69, 74, 107
Butterfield, Daniel 24, 85, 96

Campbell, Douglas 62–64
Cavalry Corps, Department of the Mississippi 142–170; tactics 146–147; weapons 145
Chancellorsville, Battle of 76–77
Cold Harbor, Battle of: fate of the wounded after 129–130; June 1 fighting 124–127; June 3 battle 128–129; Upton's opinions on leadership at 130–131
Columbus, Battle of 163–169
Crampton's Gap, Battle of 53–56
Crook, George 136, 139–140

Davis, Jefferson 13, 18, 40, 133, 162, 170

Early, Jubal 105, 132–138
Ebenezer Church, Battle of 153–155
Eggleston, Beroth 163, 165–166
Emancipation Proclamation, soldiers' opinion of 71
Ewell, Richard 40, 102–103, 121

Forrest, Nathan Bedford 147–148, 150, 152–155
Fort Stevens, Battle of 134
Franchot, Richard 60–61, 64
Franklin, William 38–40, 45, 53, 56
Frederick, Maryland 51–52, 133
Fredericksburg, Battle of 65–70

Galloway, G. Norton 116, 118
Garrard, Israel 143
Gettysburg Campaign 83–89; Lee's plan 83; pursuit of Lee 87–89; Upton's march to Gettysburg 85–87
Gilpin, E.N. 142, 144, 149–151, 159, 161, 169
Gordon, John B. 106, 116–117, 133
Grant, Ulysses S. 26, 74, 97–102, 105–109, 115–116, 119–124, 127–130, 132–133, 135–136, 141–142, 147–149, 162–163, 169, 173
Gravelly Springs 146–148

195

Index

Halleck, Henry 85, 96
Hancock, Winfield Scott 101–102, 105, 107–108, 115–116, 120–121, 128–129
Hardee, William 13, 17, 26–27
Harrison's Landing 43, 46
Harpers Ferry 19, 51–54, 56, 85, 132, 134–136
Hill, A.P. 40, 83, 105
Hill, D.H. 40, 44, 46
Holt, Daniel 53, 58, 63–64, 71–73, 80
Hooker, Joseph 57, 74–77, 83–85, 96

Infantry: tactics 26–27; weapons 28

Kellogg, Elisha 126
Kidder, John 64–72, 75, 79–82, 90, 112

Lee, Robert E. 40–41, 46–49, 51–59, 61, 69, 74, 76–77, 81, 83–85, 87–89, 91–92, 99–108, 116, 118–121, 123–124, 128–130, 132–133, 135–136, 162–163, 169; assumes command of Army of Northern Virginia 40; during Overland Campaign 99–108, 116, 118–121, 123–124, 128–130; plan for Gettysburg Campaign 83; plan for Maryland Campaign 48–49
Lincoln, Abraham 21, 24, 29–30, 36–37, 47–48, 51, 59–60, 71, 74, 85, 88, 92, 96–97, 134, 141

Mackenzie, Ranald 110
Manassas, Battle of First 29–33; McDowell's plan 30; Union retreat 32; Upton at 29–32
Manassas, Battle of Second 48, 83
Maryland Campaign 48–59; Antietam, *see* Antietam, Battle of; Crampton's Gap, Battle of; Harpers Ferry 51–54, 56; Lee's plan *see* Lee, Robert E., plan for Maryland Campaign; Special Order 191 51–52; Upton's movements 49–51, 53, 57–58
McClellan, George B. 36–40, 43, 46–48, 51–53, 56–57, 59, 141
McDowell, Irvin 29–30, 32–33
McMahon, Martin 108–110, 115, 127,
Meade, George 85, 87–89, 92, 96, 99, 102–103, 107–109, 119–121, 124–125, 127–128, 132
Middleburg and Salem raids 89–90
Monocacy, Battle of 13–134
Mosby, John 89–90
Mud March 72–74

Oberlin College 7–9, 19, 24, 171
Olcott, Egbert 81, 89, 106

Peninsula Campaign 38–47
Pope, John 47–48, 51
Porter, Horace 105, 107, 119

Rappahannock Station, Battle of 91–95
Russell, David 92–93, 109, 111–112, 114–117, 129, 139
Russell, William 29

Salem Church, Battle of 76–80
Schaaf, Morris 15–16
Schenk, Robert 31–32, 96
Scott, Winfield 25–27, 29–30, 36
Sedgwick, John 75–77, 85, 97, 105–109
Selma, Battle of 156–161
Seven Days Battles 39–47; Gaines' Mill 40–43; Glendale 44–46; Malvern Hill 46–47; Seven Pines 40

Shenandoah Valley 30, 51, 83–84, 89, 131–132, 134–136, 141–142; 1864 campaign 135–141
Sheridan Phillip 101, 123–124, 126, 135–136, 139–142, 161
Sherman, William T. 31–33, 123, 143, 147–148, 169, 173–174, 178
Slocum, Henry W. 34, 41, 44–45, 53, 57, 59, 61
Smith, William "Baldy" 124
Spencer Carbine, Model 1863 142, 145, 153, 161, 166
Spotsylvania Court House, Battle of 108–121; attack on the Bloody Angle 115–119; Muleshoe, description of 109; Upton's assault on the Muleshoe 109–115
Stanton, Edwin 81, 96, 119, 135
Stevens, George 46, 58, 102

Thomas, George 141–143, 146–148
Thomas, Lorenzo 24
Tyler, Daniel 28–33

Upton, Daniel 6–8
Upton, Electa 6–7
Upton, Emily 172–173, 174, 177
Upton, Emory: as 121st New York commander 60–82, 83–84; army culture/organization reforms 173–175; assault at Spotsylvania 108–121; as cavalry commander 142–170; at Cold Harbor 124–127, 129–131; commissioning 21–22; death of 175–177; early family life of 6–7; incident with Southern West Point cadets 19; marriage of 172; at Oberlin College 8–9; opinions of army leadership 33, 59, 119, 130–131; postwar military service of 171, 173–177; promotion campaign for 96–97; promotions of 22, 48, 61, 119–120, 141; at Rappahannock Station 92–95; religious faith 7, 18–19, 72, 119, 172; at Salem Church 76–80; tactic innovations 93–95, 109–112; tactical system by 173; tactics reform 173–174; at Third Winchester 137–141; views on secession of Southern states 19–21; on volunteer service 25, 27, 173, 175; as West Point cadet 10–22; world tour 174–175; wounding of 32, 34, 140–141
Upton, Henry 8–9, 75, 80–81
Upton, James 7–8
Upton, John 7–8
Upton, Maria 8, 17–20

Valentine, Stephen 63–64, 73

Wallace, Lew 133–134
White Oak Church 70, 74, 80
Wilderness, Battle of the 100–107; Confederate attack on VI Corps right flank 105; decision to move to Spotsylvania Court House 107–108; march to the Rapidan 101–102; wildfires 104–105
Wilson, James Harrison 137, 141–153, 155–163, 167–169
Winchester, Battle of Third 136–141
Winslow, Edward 143, 150, 152–153, 156, 161, 165, 167, 169
Wright, Horatio 109, 124, 129, 134, 139

Yeoman, J.A.O. 163, 165–166

www.ingramcontent.com/pod-product-compliance
Lightning Source LLC
Chambersburg PA
CBHW060344010526
44117CB00017B/2957